THE POSITIVE STATE

Robert A. Solo

PROFESSOR OF ECONOMICS
MICHIGAN STATE UNIVERSITY

Published by

H50 SOUTH-WESTERN PUBLISHING CO.

CINCINNATI   WEST CHICAGO, ILL.   DALLAS   PELHAM MANOR, N.Y.   PALO ALTO, CALIF.

PREFACE

A peculiar crisis, this. We remain afloat in calm seas, and the currents that carry us are relatively benign. Our crises is, not of a sinking ship, but of one with its rudder gone, and its maps turned, useless. The two decades after World War II was a time of good and easy sailing, of unprecedented prosperity, extraordinary growth, and the compassionate amelioration of inequities and insecurities with at least the illusion that all this was of the helmsman and mapmakers' doing. As the 1960s came to a close, the mechanism of control was visibly failing, and we found ourselves in a region of time where the well-drawn maps could no longer guide us. Everywhere throughout the world, the helmsmen who had seemed like giants shrank to the stature of pygmies. And throughout the world there was the same twofold response. First alienation without ideological alternative, silent and sullen, indifferent and resigned or angry without issue, distrusting the system, its leadership, its elites, its doctrines, forming perhaps a discipleship ready for prophets and saviours, accumulating the psychic potential for radical change. The other response to the same uncertainty has been the resurgence of old orthodoxies, a fervent reembrace of ancient verities and resurrected theories seeking safe haven there.

Thus the vast population of an area that sweeps from Iran and the Near East through Pakistan and the lower rim of Asia to the great Indonesian archipelago, turns from its westernizing, industrializing, back to the imagined glories of ancient Islam. China abandons Mao Tse Tung's tattered image of a new socialist man, to return to the mandarinate and the pragmatism of Sun Yat Sen. In the Soviet Union, the vistas that Khrushchev opened, are dimmed down and closed off; we hear of a grass roots resurgence of Stalinism there; while from exile Solzenetzin cries out for a return to autocracy and theocracy. From the secular socialism and humanist communism of its founders, Israel returns to the freewheeling, greed driven market replete with rabbinic pieties and bible-based imperialism. The new Pope closes, one by one, the doors opened by John XXIII, drawing the Church back to its old place of dogma, authority, and ritual. Political leaders follow the crowds to baptismal founts, all Christians born again. Back to the womb, but each to his own. In our own arena of public choice and academic discourse, dominating the formation of our national policy, we seek to regain the golden age of laisser faire.

The miseries of those good old days, the catastrophic failures of an earlier time of political impotence are softened and lost in the haze of memory. Both political parties race to the right. Hayek is resurrected. To multi-millions avid to receive the word, Milton Friedman proclaims the "freedom to choose." Back to rugged individualism, with hard nosed patriots carrying a big and bigger stick—less spending, more armaments, more to warfare, less to welfare. Lift the burden of taxation from the businessman's back, make the corporation free. Deregulate. Trust competition to do it all. Amend the Constitution to require balanced budgets. Eliminate property taxes by constitutional fiat. Dismantle big government, tear down the ship of state. No more of the gross manipulation by government bureaucrats, return our individual and collective destiny to the deft and sure fingers of the invisible hand. You have heard it all, and perhaps you have believed it.

This book takes the opposite position. Accepting the bankruptcy of the Keynsian paradigm and the inadequacies of the Welfare State, in response to the question, "where do we go from here?," it rejects Friedman's capitalism as it would Lenin's socialism, as a pernicious mythology, a path to disaster and one that pain and turmoil will eventually force us to abandon. It accepts the coexistence of individual self-seeking and the autonomous powers of corporate organizations; and insists that collective will, collective purpose, and the instrumentalities and processes of collective choice—in sum, the state—in relationships that are at once conflictual and symbiotic must play not a lesser but a greater role in dealing with phenomena more complex and problems more crucial than ever before. It is for us not to debilitate not to eliminate but to strengthen and prepare those processes and instruments of collective choice and action for tasks that must be done and responsibilities that must be borne.

For the economist, the state has been a blank space, a giant *X,* or *deus ex machina,* actor or doctor of last resort, to be condemned or proclaimed, everything but understood. By whatever criterion we may choose to judge it, the state may be (has been) good, bad, honest, corrupt, efficient, inefficient, regressive, progressive, competent, incompetent. A complex of organizations, instruments, institutions, the state is what we make it.

Part 1 of this book attempts to understand and to explain what it is that creates, forms, and transforms the character of the state in the roles it plays *via* a *vis* the economy and society; where it comes from, how it has fared, where it has failed, and where it is going. Where is it going? Here we will stress those forces and those problems that press collective choice and the instrumentalities of collective action towards the organization and management of complex systems and beyond the death trap of national sovereignties, in other words, into the realm of the global and the positive.

What goals then, and what policies, for a positive state? We can specify problems. Can we also suggest solutions? How to reverse the slowdown and absolute decline in productivity? How to reindustrialize? How to eliminate trade deficits and find a workable basis for international trade? How to harness the force of science to human and social need? How to vitalize the political system? How to obtain another lease on urban life? How to make the corporation answerable for its policies? How to survive or how to escape the nuclear trap? Part 2 proposes some answers, partial answers of course, offered as options intended not to settle these fundamental questions but to plunge them into discourse.

This book is dedicated with deep affection to my daughter, Tova Maria Solo, who is the apple of my eye.

Robert A. Solo

CONTENTS

PART ONE
The Emergence of the Positive State

Chapter

PART TWO
Options for the Positive State

Chapter

THE EMERGENCE OF THE POSITIVE STATE

CONCEPTUAL FRAMEWORK

The Domains of Experience

Given our present level of awareness, we can specify the dimensions of experience in primal terms of earth, flesh, mind, and society; incommensurables, none to be coupled, each demanding a form of understanding, a language, a science particular to itself; thus the domains of:

1. the lifeless, inanimate, inorganic, indestructible, physical universe: domain of physics.

2. organism that lives, reproduces, grows, dies: domain of biology.

3. the knowing, remembering, forgetting, dreaming, believing, desiring, imagining systems of the psyche: domain of the individual mind.

4. the organization that associates, integrates individuals in discourse, in learning, in value-generation and evaluation, and in the functional activities of groups: domain of society and of the social sciences.

Thus the inorganic, the organic, the psychic, the social—fundamentally different, absolutely incommensurable, and yet not separate or separable: but overlapping, interdependent, interlinked.

Organic life arcs out from and returns to the inorganic. The organic feeds upon, and exists within the frame of the inorganic. From dust to dust.

The mind, universe of images, image-maker, locus of volition and learning, place of memory, is activated within and requires a pulpy blood-fed organ called the brain. And the mind, with all its fantastic and immaterial store, vanishes when the body dies. The psychic requires the organic as the organic requires the inorganic. The organic, in turn, is penetrated by, permeated with, the powers of the psychic.

Society inculcates values and imprints guiding images upon the mind. Society represses and society directs the drives of the psyche. Society and its systems form the mind. And yet only through the image making creativity of the mind can society change and take new forms.

Our concern is the individual and the collective—which is to say with the psychic, locus of individual choice and behavior; and the social, locus of collective choice and collaborative activity; and their interlinkage and overlap.

The Systems of Society

There are the *functional systems* of society associating and integrating the efforts of individuals to produce some desired product, to serve some valued purpose as the goal of collaborative activity; for example, in the manufacture and distribution of goods and services, in waging war, in the protection, care, and acculturation of children, or in the performance of religious rite and ritual. There are four basic forms of functional organization: market systems, political systems, institutional systems (like pure science or the Catholic church), and familial systems (the tribe, the household). Elsewhere I have developed the rationale of these functional systems.[1] Suffice it is to say that any actual functional organization will be a variant and a hybrid of these.

Traversing and transcending functional organizations are: *cognitive systems* that develop, preserve, perpetuate, propagate, test, and disseminate information and related problem-solving techniques; and *cultural systems* that generate, transform, establish, preserve, perpetuate, and propogate values and that critique, challenge and replace values, and otherwise bear upon and organize evaluation.

Thus, we may conceive of any society as a complex of functional, cognitive, and cultural systems. The functional systems are vectored to a specifiable purpose or purposes. The cultural and cognitive systems cut across all functional systems but are integrated into each, since all functional organizations act upon information and require problem-solving; and, certainly in the choice of ends and means, all functional systems practice evaluation, and hence require, reflect, and are constrained by values.

The Sytems of the Psyche

But where do individuals and their volitions fit into this schemata? How can we relate the complex systems of the individual psyche to the social systems wherein every individual is enmeshed?

---

[1]Especially, Robert A. Solo, *Economic Organizations and Social Systems* (Indianoplis: The Bobbs-Merrill Co., Inc., 1967).

From Freud we can at least deduce the existence of relationships integrating a surface of consciousness and reason with (1) memories and figments accumulated in the storehouse of the unconscious, and (2) the unplumbed, depthless sea of the subconscious, turbulent with primal energies, and (3) a constituent element that censures, shames, and guides in the name of inculcated, ancient fears, beliefs, and a heritage of tradition, habit, and imbued constraints. The work of Jean Piaget suggests that consciousness and reason operate always within a frame of "cognitive" structures, that fix boundaries upon and determine the form of observation, the character of problem solving, and the capacity to assimilate information and to understand statement, with fundamental learning taking place through the formation and transformation of such structures.

The individual and society, the psychic and the social, mind on the one hand, cognitive, cultural, functional systems on the other—the link between them is ideology.

Ideology

The arguments and theories to be developed here will turn in good part on the notion of *ideology*. Because this is a term loosely and variously used, it must from the outset be carefully defined. "Ideology" will mean *a set of ideas as to what is and ought to be with respect to a field of choice and action*—an image of the real coupled with an idea of purpose. It has no necessary relationship to the good, the moral, the ideal. Sometimes the "ought to be" is equated to "best for me," or "more for mine." The thief planning a break-in, the politician buying votes, the OPECer raising the price of petroleum are, in each case, operating by reference to an idea of *what is* (the layout for the thief, the corruptibility of a set of voters for the crooked politician, the oil supply-demand relationship for the cartelite), and of *what ought to be* (more for me, more for us). Hence their choice and activity, pernicious in the eyes of others, reflects and expresses ideology. Their ideologies to be sure are not universally accepted; it is that nonacceptance (an ideological difference) which differentiates the thief from one who does not steal, the crooked from an honest politician, the competitor from the cartelite.

Thus understood, ideology, simple or complex, humble or high-flown, is a commonplace of human behavior. There can be no coherent and purposeful choice that is other than a function of ideology. Neither individual nor group can choose coherently or act with a clear purpose and a conception of consequence without ideology. Not that all action requires ideology. One also moves blindly, acts intuitively, imitatively, obediently. Behavior can as well be the consequence of drift, of impulse, of habit, of instinct, of convention. It is to say that purposeful behavior and coherent choice require an idea of what is and of what ought to be. How can it be otherwise?

Nor in the domain of mind is there ever a single, all-encompassing ideology, any more than there is a single, all-encompassing field of choice and action. Instead, there will be numerous ideological configurations, correspondingly as there are different fields of choice and action, different and distinct ideas of what is and ought to be for me and mine, for us and them, for you and yours, with respect to home, to family, to friends, and with respect to neighbors, and to strangers, and with respect to God, religion, ritual, the Church and to the churches, and with respect to the school, teachers, parents, professors, learning, and with respect to the company, clients, associates, creditors, competitors, as well as to the grand arena of political choice and policy.

Ideologies are not the same as the cognitive-cultural structures of the psyche. Those structures determine (or fix limits upon) the spectrum of potential ideologies. Cognitive-cultural structure is the cup. Ideology is what the cup contains. It could contain another, but not any other ideology. Ideology is a value-knowledge construct, residue of teaching, indoctrination and experience. It is the image-forming nexus of the observed, communicated, accepted, desired, believed.

1. Ideology is the overlap and the interlink between the psychic and the social system. It is the individual's eye upon society. It is society's harness upon the individual.

2. It is through ideology that the individual finds purpose and *identity*. A shared ideology is the basis of a shared identity and of a common purpose. Shared ideological commitment brings collective energies into focus. Shared ideology constitutes the blueprint for collective choice and institutional formation.

3. A group (any, every group) is a community of ideological commitment, where the shared ideology specifies a place and role for the individual who therein finds an identity.

4. All groups are ideological formations and their coherence, cohesiveness, character, durability and force depend upon an ideological underpinning.

5. The nation is such a group, and the state has developed as its instrument.

6. The breakdown of ideology produces individual disorientation, alienation, bankruptcy of group or collective policy, a dissolution of the capacity for coherent collective choice, the loss of identity, a release of the capacity for commitment, hence, possibly an explosion of decontrolled energies.

7. The process of ideological breakdown, transformation, replacement is the pivot of social change.

8. More fundamental, universal and revolutionary change comes about through the breakdown and transformation of those cognitive-cultural structures of the psyche that contain and determine the spectrum of potential ideologies.

What follows will develop upon these propositions.

Like Janus, the god who looks at once ahead and behind, ideology faces in two directions. It faces outward from the psychic system, for it is through ideology that the individual comprehends and evaluates, supports or opposes, participates within and acts upon the functional activities and institutional formations for the social complex. And ideology turns inward upon the psychic system, for it is through the inculcation of ideologies that social organization impacts upon the psyche, forms, disciplines, socializes, organizes, controls, directs the energies of all those who compose it. The idologies that shape behavior and that constitute the individual's image of the world come from somewhere, They are not invented by those who are controlled by them; they are inculcated, indoctrinated, taught, and learned as a function of the cultural system. But if it is through ideology that society shapes the individual, it is only the individual who can recreate ideology and, in that way, reshape society.

Persons born on April 7, 1960, blue-eyed children, bald men, curly-haired women, people under six feet in height, these are *categories,* sets of individuals with some characteristic in common, but they are not social groups. Alcoholics are a category, but Alcoholics Anonymous is a group. Fat people are a category, but Weight Watchers is a group. Why so? Because and inasmuch as weight watchers or alcoholics anonymous, committed to collaborative action share a goal, and an idea of things as they are; and in the frame of that idea devise strategies to achieve that goal—because, in other words, they share an ideology in terms of which, in relations to which they identify themselves. Redheads are a category, but Blacks are a group. Why so? Because, and only because, Blacks share, and inasmuch as they share an idea of what is and what ought to be in that universe of black-white relationships wherein they find a place. Groups simply and specifically are those who share an ideology in which they themselves find an identity and have a place.

All groups without exception are communities of ideological commitment. It is, however, only approximately true that those who constitute a group share a single ideology. Each individual's idea of what is and ought to be with respect to a given field of choice and action is always in some sense and to some degree particular and unique. Rather than a single ideology shared by all, the group is composed of ideologies clustered tightly or clustered loosely around a norm; out of their variations and differences, subgroups, parties, factions are formed. And a number of different ideological commitments will link the psyche of any individual with a number of different groups, and give to that individual not one, but a set of identities.

So it is for every group, hence for all collective existences, whether transitory as the day, like legionnaires on parade, or continuing through millenia, like the great religions. The coherence, cohesion, and durability of any collective existence depends always on the force and character of an ideological commitment.

The collective existence, the community of ideological commitment, can exist without functional organization. It need not have any instruments for *collective* action. Devotees of a religious sect, spread over the earth, isolated from each other, without the means of collective choice and action, are a group, a collective existence. Nevertheless, it is only when they have established a church for common worship and for the collective performance of the sacred ritual, that they, *qua* group, become integrated into the operation of a functional system.

The group which in due course we will be concerned with is the *nation,* with the state, a functional complex, as its instrument of choice and action.

Ideological Failure and Social Change

More than interface between mind and society, ideology is the intersect and link between idea and experience, between action and its objective, and between expectations and consequences. As a blueprint for social policy, as a guideline for individual choice, ideology becomes hypothesis under test. It is a preconception thrust into the cauldron of experience. Hence ideology is the nexus of social learning—social learning occurs through the failure, breakdown, transformation, or replacement of a prevailing and guiding ideology.

Every ideological blueprint must fail. If it does not fail today, it will fail tomorrow. It will fail because the idea of the field of choice and action is insufficient, inadequate, or in error, or because the purpose upon which it vectors palls; and all this must come to pass because of the psychic needs that an ideology serves, and the field of choice and action in which ideology operates both, inevitably, change with time.

The failure of an ideology begins a painful process—of disorientation, alienation, frustration; of the chaotic explosion of energies without outlet; of the emptiness that invades a being without commitment. Ideological failure spells institutional erosion, group disintegration, identity crisis; the failure and disintegration of an ideology precipitates polarization and confrontation between those who would hold on to the untenable and those who reach for rainbows across the horizon, between those who rush forward and those who scramble back, a time of gurus, demagogues, con artists, dropouts, and prophets, in the groping for a different vision, for another idea that will not fail, that will be true, that will invite commitment and recreate cohesion. Then again polarization and confrontation between those who adhere to this or that emergent alternative—until a new, operational, acceptable, ideological blueprint for collective choice and action prevails—if one ever does.

Transformation of the Cognitive-Cultural Understructure

The acceptability of ideological alternatives, their capacity for taking root, and the form that, in practice, they assume, depend on deeper cognitive-cultural structures of the mind. Those structures, under psychic impulsion and the dialectic of fundamental learning also can change.

In the past 1,500 years of Western history, perhaps there have been three such fundamental transformations in the cognitive-cultural understructure. In what follows, we will account for change in the character of the state, and the counterpoise between individual and collective being, over the past several centuries by reference to those critical transformations of the deeper structures of the psyche. It will be seen that the theories of the state produced through generations of Western discourse have been only one figure in a larger landscape of thought, with their meaning properly to be understood and evaluated only in relation to the whole landscape of which they are a part. For always, in appraising statement and theory, we are dealing at once with a way of seeing and with an object seen; with cognitive-cultural structure and analytic process on the one hand and the character of an external reality on the other—and both are transitory and fleeting.

The first of the great mutations of the psychic understructure of concern to us here is to be associated with the Renaissance; occurring in the Italian cities, as early as the Thirteenth Century and made manifest in Northern Europe in the Fifteenth and Sixteenth Centuries.

The Renaissance thought broke away from an Age of Authority; authority of church, authority of faith, authority of timeless revelations, authority of ancient seers, authority of the traditions, allegiances, fealties, obligations, status. The Renaissance ushered in the *World of Man,* where no longer the force of authority but the unbridled self-interest and free-roaming reason of the individual formed a fundamentally new cognitive-cultural understructure.

At the close of this new age, when the explosive force of unbounded egoism and unleashed self-seeking burst upon the crumbling institutions of feudalism and the fading constraints of traditional authority, Thomas Hobbes wrote the first great treatise on the state.

LANDSCAPES OF THOUGHT

The Monarchical State of the World of Man

Thomas Hobbes was born in 1588. He died in 1679 at the ripe age of 91. He knew the disorder and heroic fury of the Renaissance, with its supreme and unconstrained individualism. He knew as well the ushering in of the society of liberty and order in the Classical Age, with ancient independencies and privileges crushed under the juggernaut of the national sovereign. Throughout Europe autonomous feudalities had been and were being gathered into the fold of a national power. The barons became courtiers, high servants in the household of a monarch.

Genius will not be seen, it will not be located and found, Lucien Goldmann has argued, in the supremely particular, the unique, the idiosyncratic mind. On the contrary, that accolade goes to those who express, who first express, the commonplaces of an age. In that sense certainly Hobbes deserves to be called a genius. On that ground Michael Oakshott's judgment of Hobbes' *The Leviathan,* as "the greatest, perhaps the sole masterpiece of political philosophy written in the English language"[1] is just. And, for the same reason, because it expresses the commonplace thought and wornout credos of another time, it is for me a total bore, archaic, and without surprises.

Hobbes' work has not to do with the state as such. His concern is to demonstrate that the vesting of a sovereign with absolute power is required as a constraint upon an atomistic society of autonomous individuals each engaged in the ruthless, cease-

---

[1]Michael Oakshott (ed.) *The Leviathan,* (New York: Sadlier-Oxford, 1946).

less but reasoned pursuit of self-interest; the supposition of such a society is the base of his work and the frame of his theory.

Beyond Hobbes this presupposition illumines the critical cognitive structure that underlies the discourse, shapes the institutions, and marks the character of the Classical Age. The idea of social reality as, and as no more than a universe of self-contained beings, acting in unremitting but reasoned aggression in pursuit of self-interest, becomes the universal landscape of thought. It is a familiar landscape surely; we have hardly left it yet. It remains the format of ideological liberalism and of neoclassical economics today. Given this cognitive structure, every social, political, and economic event is to be explained as the consequence of individual aggression and interaction, operating through a universal calculus of self-interest within the context of given institutions and circumstances, with the social institutions created and circumstances reshaped out of ceaseless and dynamic force of reason seeking the fuller realization of self-interest through time. History finds its rationale as the time-path of self-seeking, more fully realizing its interests in the light of reason.

Thus for Hobbes, history begins with the unleashed proclivities for self-seeking, unbridled, and socially unconstrained. Each then is a hunter. All are prey. Life must be nasty, brutish, and short. None can escape the calculus of survival, and time is trapped in a ceaseless cycle of man destroying and man destroyed *unless* there are rules to contain and constrain the greed and ambition natural to any (hence to every) man! Unless all under reason submit, or are submitted to such rule, none can know tranquillity, security, peace; there can be no meaningful liberty or true autonomy in enjoying the bounties of one's own labor, nor the safe and private space for a reasoned and foresightful creation of ordered life. Therefore self-interest enlightened by reason dictates the ultimate value and universal need for a rule-maker with an unconstrained power to constrain. The power of rule and of ruler must be beyond the reach of any conspiracy of self-interest; it must be sovereign. Absolute and unchallengeable in a claim upon the whole domain, the sovereign can have no self-interest but in the prosperity and tranquillity of that which is his own. Hobbes formulates thus a political ideology—an idea of that which was and of that which ought to be—that finds its highest value in a space, tranquil and secure, for the exercise of private volitions, called "liberty." His history of the state is in no way concerned with the actual chronological formation of political entities; nor does his theory account for the particular solidarities, and their boundaries. He does not wonder or explain why England was England, France was France, Spain was Spain. The chain of observed events were incidents, mere accidents in the realization through time of the immanent rationale of sovereign power.

A century earlier Machiavelli had dreamed of and schemed for an absolute sovereign power lodged in the hands of the Prince who would break the independent baronies, subdue the cities, and bring the brigands and mercenaries to heel, forming Italy into a single nation with a single law with secure boundaries and internal order, free from external threat and internal turbulence and terror, open to social and commercial intercourse, assuring the tranquil private space of liberty. And Machiavelli devised his immortal strategies to obtain for poor Italy what would for centuries prove unattainable. Hobbes on the other hand was offering no blueprint for change. His, on the contrary, was an apologia for an established power, a rationalization of the absolute monarchy, and a defense of it against the interest and still unarticulated outlook of a new class, neither peasant nor aristocrat, but men of the city and the town (burghers, bourgeoisie), clerks, lawyers, physicians, brokers, bankers, traders, craftsmen, commercial farmers, ministers, printers, publishers, journalists, merchants, the initiators and organizers and operators of enterprise; in sum the mobile, variegated, and proliferating breed who worked, saved, and invested, and made their way through disciplined effort, wit, and skill in the emerging economy of property and trade. In disarming and subduing autonomous feudalities, in forming a national domain secure from the marauding armies of the stranger without, and ordered under law within, the absolute monarch had served their interests; indeed was essential to their interests in his time. But once these things had been obtained, then the adventuring and bullion-hungry ambitions of kings and the expenses of their courts became a needless burden upon this class; and the location of the sovereign power in a cultural system different from theirs was a threat to its values. Reason was ready to take another step in perfecting the World of Man. The decisive and underlying cognitive-value structure would not change. Still conceiving a universe of self-seekers, still valuing liberty, but now taking as given a secure national domain for the exercise of individualized choice and for private commerce, another idea of the state would be formed; another ideology would come to prevail.

Liberalism and the State

The new ideology vectored upon and emphasized Liberty as the highest human value. Utopia was the "Sweet Land of Liberty." And liberty meant quite simply, individual rather than collective choice. Activity in the sweet land of liberty is organized through the autonomous will of individuals in the control of their property. Activity in the monstrous other-land of unliberty is organized, directed, or controlled through the political apparatus and the power of the state.

Society was seen as a flat and endless grid, a vast checkerboard of private spaces, carefully delineated sovereign spaces, each for the individual in the exercise of liberty. That private and sovereign space wherein the individual acted in liberty was the beginning and end all of society; there was and could be nothing else. Each in his liberty in the pursuit of his satisfaction, acting from the firm base of property, entered into transactions, engaged in trade and in social or commercial intercourse only if, and only when there was for him a positive advantage in so doing; only if and when he was made better off thereby. Hence all transactions undertaken in liberty must be to the mutual betterment and general advantage of those who so engaged.

Granted the state was necessary. Rules there must be, and those who broke the rules must be chastised. The conflicting claims of persons and of ownership must be settled. Contracts must be enforced. Security must be provided, and property protected. The sovereign power of the state was necessary but dangerous, a continuous threat to liberty. Hence that power must be constrained. The ruler must be ruled; ruled first by a transcendental and inviolable law, natural, constitutional, that guaranteed the space of individual liberty, privacy, and property from collective intervention and control; second by a system of representation through election to insure that the state was answerable to the electorate, that there should be no governance except with the consent of the governed; third, by the "eternal vigilence" of those devotees of liberty, who would draw the line of the permissible, and then be forever alert to mobilize their forces against any transgression of that line by the state.

To draw that line of the permissible was a task for the economist. The economics which took form in the Eighteenth Century, was a "scientific" expression of this ideology of liberalism. It had its beginning as an argument against intervention and "meddling" by the state, and developed as an apologia for the free market as the perfect instrument for the organization of economic activity and for the allocation of resources. Conversely it proposed as a fundamental principle of policy, the total exclusion of the political authority from the affairs of Man; hence laisser faire, limiting the sovereign power to the provision of security and support for the parameters of private choice.

Through the years, liberal (now neoclassical) economics has drawn this line of the permissible across the social topography: in recent decades that line has been drawn and redrawn in perpetual retreat, always as an *ex post* rationalization of events, justified not because of what the state is, but because of what the market is not, not because of what the state can do but because of what the market cannot do, because market externalities distort choice, or because of some intractable, natural power of monopoly, or because the costs of market transactions are too great in relation to the product sold or the service transacted, or because free riders cannot be excluded, and so on. What this economics has had to say about the state is and has always been simply "This far, no further." Such is the liberal nontheory of the state.

Synthetic Man

Michel Foucault, analyzing across-the-board changes in the character of the sciences and philosophy, has documented in depth a transformation, occurring at the end of the Eighteenth and during the early decades of the Nineteenth Centuries in the cognitive-cultural structure (which he calls an *episteme*) that underlay European and American thought.[2] One facet of this transformation, we would characterize as follows:

1. Social reality ceased to be understood as a universe of self-contained autonomous beings each engaged in the rational pursuit of a private interest with a social event the consequences of the competitive interaction or mutual accord of such rational self-seekers. Nor was history anymore to be explained as the path of reason realizing itself.

2. Instead phenomena and event were conceived as the function of deep forces, social and psychic, that transcended private volition. Group, class, the

---

[2]Michel Foucault, *The Order of Things* (New York: Pantheon Books, 1970).

mass, mob, race, people, nation replaced the autonomous reasoning self-seeker as the locus of action. The grid gives way to evolutionary or revolutionary force upstreaming from a past without beginning.

3. Nevertheless, imageries from the World of Man, remained. These transcendental forces that swept away the domain of private volition, and the group or mass responses that replaced individual self-seeking, were endowed with something of the rationale of the reasoning self-seeker. They become in the eyes of the age, Synthetic Man. The World of Man has become the World of Synthetic Man.

This transformation in the way of seeing is to be associated with change in the reality that was seen. It is to be associated with, and may have been rooted in certain historical experiences. Thus the French Revolution anticipated as the culmination of the path of reason realizing itself in the perfection of a World of Man, produced a bloody terror, and ended in the regime of the first of those synthetic superbeings, the modern dictator. But of greatest importance to this cognitive-cultural transformation, was the experience of the industrial revolution, which swallowed the hosts of private manipulations and individual enterprises that once had been the instrument of the will and purpose of a multitude of individual self-seekers, into huge corporate aggregations, and these vast evermore encompassing corporate aggregations in turn were tight-bound into a globe-encompassing web of gold and iron that lifted them up and flung them down, boomed and busted, pouring out wealth and laying on years of idleness and desperate poverty—as the whiplash of forces beyond the volition or comprehension of any man. Industrialization based itself on a working mass, none with property to provide that vital space of liberty; the volitions of the working mass was empty even of the knowledge of what they did or for what their labors were intended. Instead the knowledge of technology was now embodied in machines, with men as the servitors of these. No more a private space for the sovereign will and independent volition, the terrain of corporate aggregations swarmed with a thousand diverse ambitions, driven by the energies of the dumb, disciplined, proletarian mass, and in toto held afloat or allowed to sink, blind in the sea of market demand, swept by the raging technological "gales of creative destruction." And yet those corporate aggregations were conceived in the ego-centered image of rational and self-seeking man; immortal persons in the eyes of the law; in the eyes of the economist, the omnipresent firm, forever expressing the volition and reasoned self-seeking of an individual entrepreneur, just like the one who once ran his own shoe repair shop or owned and operated the corner grocery store. Synthetic Man. So also at this time, the state is subsumed in the genus, Synthetic Man.

The Hegelian State

All of the three most formidable minds of the Nineteenth Century to give a central place to the State in their systems of thought, Georg Frederich Hegel, Karl Marx, and Max Weber, were Prussian born, with ideas shaped by an experience of the Prussian State. In Great Britain, in France, in the United States, the state had provided the security and law within whose frame capitalism took form and industrialization came about first through individual initiatives and then through the autonomous operation of corporate aggregations. In Prussia capitalism and industrialization came by a different path.

Prussia was poor, rural, and technologically backward; but the Prussian State, controlled by an aristocratic military elite, was powerful, disciplined, efficient. The Prussian State established the first system of universal education and the first system of social security. It installed a powerful science capability, and linked that capability to the development of science-based industries. It organized the formal training of the spectrum of industrial technologists, and it established industrial capitalism in Germany. And the Prussian State, in a strategy of diplomacy and war pursued through generations, linked together the elements of a German nation. This Prussian State, powerfully creative force that it was, was also the bulwark of political reaction.

Georg Wilhelm Friedrich Hegel (1770–1831) was perhaps the most influential philospher of the Nineteenth Century. For Hegel the state was the embodied Idea, the realized meaning of the collectivity, the manifest spirit of a nation or a people. The competition of nations and the conflicts of states were, hence, a struggle between the central Idea of each of the peoples, between the particular message and meaning that a nation brings into the world. In this struggle, the stronger, the more complete, the higher Idea surmounts, replaces, encompasses the lesser and weaker. Thereby the prevailing level of Idea or Spirit is lifted to a higher, more universal plain.

Thus Hegel endows the state with the mind of a reasoning, prodigious, sovereign individual, albeit one without body or brain. And the Hegelian dialectic of history proceeds as a disputation between learned philosophers. One philosopher puts forward his truth (thesis). The second philosopher refutes the position of the first with another opposing truth (antithesis). The third philosopher understands and reconciles the two seemingly opposing truths into a new and higher truth (synthesis). The fourth philosopher refutes this new position with an opposing truth (antithesis), on and on, thesis, antithesis, synthesis, argument, counterargument, resolution, carrying the discourse to an ever higher, more universal level of contention.

Thus Hegelian theory postulates a force that transcends the interests and volitions of the individual, and yet deduces, as did the Classical analytic of history, a process of reason realizing itself. Except that in the Hegelian case, the bearer of reason is not the individual but the state; the state conceived as a reasoning, self-interested, transgenerational being. The bearer of reason is no longer Man, but Synthetic Man. State and nation are, in Hegelian conception, species of Synthetic Man.

Classical and neoclassical thought placed the state outside the viable community of individualized choice, purpose and action. Hobbes justified the sovereign power of the state because it would satisfy the need for a rule-maker outside of and detached from the game. The liberals were above all concerned with keeping that rule-maker from intervening upon the liberties of the game-players. To that end they excluded the state from the community of choice and purpose. For Hegel the state was not outside that community. Rather it expressed the community. It was the Idea, the purpose, the morality, meaning, spirit, truth of the community and its people. Hence for the individual to deviate from the purpose and rule and service of the state was, for Hegel, to deviate from morality, was to be immoral, was to betray one's own essence and meaning. Such deviation was, for Hegel, not an expression of freedom but an aberration from the path of freedom. Freedom, for Hegel, was in the capacity to realize one's truth, to express one's Idea, to know and become one's meaning. Since all these were as emanations of the state, freedom could only mean service and submission to its rule.

The Marxist State

Karl Marx (1818–1883) saw the social landscape as a field of battle and history as a panorama of conflict between economic class and economic class vying for shares in the economic product.

In brief the Marxist dynamic starts with a prevailing technology optimally expressed in a mode of production that differentiates the functional roles of those participating in the economic process. Those so differentiated form the economic classes. Role conveys power. Relative shares are determined through the exercise of that power. The class able to dominate through its possession of economic power, institutionalizes and reenforces that dominance, particularly through its control of the instrumentalities of ideological indoctrination and of the coercive force exercised through the state.

An advance of technology, exogenous to these class relationships, changes the mode of production, transforms roles, and changes the power that inheres in function. But the ruling class, displaced from functional preeminence, clings to an institutionalized position of dominance, using that heritage to prevent those immanent changes which, in enabling the emergent potentialities of the new technology to be fully realized, would deprive that class of its established advantages and privileges.

A new class, become functionally preeminent, awakened to the power that inheres in its role, aware of the unrealized but potential advantages to itself that the transformation of social structure could bring, takes up cudgels of change and becomes the spearhead of revolution. Thus the struggle. The old rulers possess the instruments of coercion and are supported by the habits of culture, but the logic of history is on the other side; the rising tide of these inherent economic powers insures the eventual triumph of the revolutionary class.

Marx saw an ascending series of class struggles approaching its culmination with proletariat pitted against bourgeoisie. The laws of history, the rationale of industrial technology, and inherent economic power were on the side of the proletariat. But the bourgeoisie had control of the state. The state, for the Marxist, was the executive committee, the general staff of the ruling class, an agency of coercion with counter-revolution as its mission; repression of enemies of the established order as its task. The first objective of the revolutionary class was to capture the state. Then, under the "dictatorship of the proletariat," the state would serve to neutralize or remove the class enemy, install a socialist economy where, since all would work at the same level, there would no longer be any class differentiation, class conflict, class rule, class coercion, and where the state therefore would wither away and vanish from history.

It is no longer as for Hegel a struggle between Idea and Idea with the peoples and the nations as their carriers, but for Marx, between class and class. Yet the

difference between the two is not so great as might first appear. For a class, awakened, aware, and consciously engaged in that titanic struggle, must be a clustering
of individuals around, and their expression of, a shared Idea. Marxist class is a
community of commitment to an ideology that charts path and goal. So, in the end,
class struggle too is a struggle of Idea against Idea, though the bearers of the Idea
are not now the nations or the peoples, but functional classes. For Marx as with
Hegel it is an evolutionary struggle. For Marx as with the liberals, it is ascent of
reason realizing itself; for each successive wave of revolution ushers in a more
productive technology and a higher social potential. Except that for Marx, the
protagonist of evolutionary advance is not the autonomous rational individual ener-
gized by self-interest, but class; and yet in Marxist conception, class, proletariat or
bourgeoisie, is conceived in the image of the self-seeking, reasoning individual, blown
large and rendered immortal, engaged in a foresightful and aware pursuit of the
interests implicit in the circumstances of a functional role. Again, Synthetic Man.

Anarchism and the State

There is another body of thought with roots in that same Nineteenth Century
psychic construct, expressed in the work of Marx and Darwin, where imageries of
strife and struggle, violence and death, culminate in utopia; that of the *anarchists,*
Blanqui, Saint Simon, Bukharin, Kropotkin.

Still of the world that glorified autonomous man and put its hope in enlightened
self-interest, the anarchists (in something of the spirit of Rousseau) differed from the
others in that they saw the ultimate region of reason realizing itself, not at the end
of history but at its beginning, not after man progressively had learned and in the
light of his learning, had rid himself of obscurantism, superstition, oppression,
exploitation, coercion, but before man had been lied to and deceived, made cruel and
afraid, his prejudices inculcated, his greed aroused. And who had done these things
to man? What culprit was responsible for this brutalization and exploitation? The
State! The state, for the anarchist, was the prime agent of corruption and coercion.
And the state (for Kropotkin) was the ally and the instrument, supporting and
serving the purpose of the priest, the police officer, the soldier, and the capitalist.
Eliminate the state and all of its cohorts would fall. Therefore an end to the state!
Eliminate it. Destroy it so that man can return as he naturally would, to a life lived
wholly within the zone of reason. Let him be rid of the capitalist, and man would
appropriate and enjoy the fruits of his labor. Let him be rid of the soldier and become
free of the delusions of glory and the fevers of patriotism, and man would see at last
the faces of those alleged to be his enemies, and know that they are men as he is
himself. Let him be rid of the police officer and the judge and their obscene body
of law, and man would seek and would find a human community based on voluntude
not servitude. Destroy the state and its force, and all its cohorts would topple. Then
man, in autonomy and freedom would regain himself. Autonomous man? But it was
not the Eighteenth Century landscape of reasoning and self-interested individuals
interacting and interlinked, man in a world of men, that the anarchists saw. It was
the vision rather of man in a nightmare world of dragons and beasts, nearly immortal
and disguised as man, Synthetic Men; police officer, judge, capitalist, priest in a
conspiracy of evil, alike under the domain of the state.

In their attitude towards the state, there is a curious link between liberalism, Marxism, and anarchism. In a sense anarchism carries the liberal and Marxist logic to its clear and unequivocal conclusion. For liberalism as for anarchism, the state is the natural enemy of liberty and reason. But liberalism dare not be rid of its enemy. Rather it would keep the state as a monster in chains, with its ferocious, imbecile might unleashed against the foreign foe, and used at home to protect the power and privileges of property—for it is in property that the liberal finds the essential space for the exercise of liberty. Whereas the anarchist would be rid of the state, and of property and nationhood along with it.

Marx too found the state to be the universal instrument of oppression, coercion, and the enemy of man, with a nationless, propertyless, stateless anarchy as the ultimate communist condition. But Marx would not yet surrender the state, for it was to be the forceps in the birth of a new and better world.

Perhaps it is an affront to the ultimate freedom the anarchist assigns to man, to ask what form of association, what mode of organization would replace the state since, to preconceive the future's design is itself to constrain and compromise the future's freedom. Still that nagging doubt remains as to whether or not it is possible for a world community to produce the wherewithal of life and to confront the problems to which we all are heir without institutions and without organization, hence without powers, hence without rule, hence without coercion.

The Neo-Marxist Theory of the State

No system of discourse has been so continuously and intently concerned with the character of the state as has the Marxist. Understandably so, for the idea of the state is central to Marxist theory and essential to its strategies of revolution. How has it fared, this classical Marxist conception of the state as the simple instrument of the ruling class, its formidable force for coercion, its best defense against revolution, that, once captured, would serve as the means of ushering in a classless communist society; and thereupon, having done that deed, would wither away?

Exiled from Germany, forced from France, in London with his motley discipleship, caught in the intrigues of conspirators on the fringes of the world, Marx wrote of a great and violent birth of socialism that would in its maturity attain the ultimate communist brotherhood. But all that was for him a dream, a fantasy for, in the foreboding realities of the Nineteenth Century, there was no socialism. All Marx observed of the concrete, the whole of his experience, was of capitalism, aggressive, powerful and triumphant, conquering, encompassing, and transforming what remained of the ancient, decrepit civilizations of the world. And Marx's theory was specifically a critique of capitalism, with the capitalist state as its target.

That has changed. Now Marxist socialism organizes a third of the earth's population. But socialism did not come, as Marx predicted, through the manifest will and conscious intent of an organized working class confronting the vested powers of the bourgeoisie. It took root not in mature capitalist economies but in technically backward peasant societies. In Russia it was installed in a power vacuum created by the collapse of czardom, out of the struggle of revolutionary elites to capture the autonomous power of the state. In China it was installed by the peasant army of a warlord carrying the banners of a new faith. Nor did the state wither away. In the world that calls itself Marxist, the state is the nexus of all economic and social choice and activity. And it remained an instrument of coercion, indeed coercing the working class in the interest of a credo enunciated by the state. What then has been the impact of Marxist thought upon and its value for Marxist societies?

It has had an impact as ideology for the elite, and as credo, ethic and popular religion, with its haunting paradigm of class conflict as omnipresence, with its anathema on private property, with its idealization of the proletariat, with its real if distant commitment to equality and brotherhood.

As in high aspiration, so too in its gross perversions, socialism has borne the stamp of, and found its justifications in the Marxist ideology and outlook, even as the horrible collectivization of Soviet agriculture was staged as a class war against the kulak. Withal, Marxist theory remained strictly a critique of capitalism, wholly focused on the capitalist state, without relevance to the deep and unresolved problems of every socialist regime, for example, in the reconciliation of individual with collective values, in the organization of creative change, in the recruitment and selection of leadership and the transference and control of power, or in the development of effective planning and of a rationale for collective choice.

Nor have events in Western Capitalism followed Marxist prophecy and expectation. When parties of organized labor gained and maintained political control of the state they did not displace private property or replace the capitalist mode of production. And after the Great Depression and World War II, in all technologically advanced capitalist societies, the state ceased to be dominated by the precepts of laissez-faire liberalism. There emerged instead, the welfare state, which curbed the capitalists, guaranteed the development of industrial trade unionism, and transformed the status of the "dominated" classes. Correspondingly the Marxist conception of the capitalist state is changing. Based on a study of current work in the Marxist tradition, I would propose the following as an emerging Neo-Marxist conception of the state.[3]

The state in capitalism today is a power center that, though operating in the context of class interests, possesses nevertheless, a significant degree of autonomy.

As an autonomous system, the state is composed of differently endowed, differently motivated, differently oriented parts. And it evolves quite different policy sets and institutional formations in response to the needs, pressures, and crisis of those different sectors of the economy, each with a distinctive mode of production, to which its functions, responsibilities, and power lines relate.

The state has this as its central function and responsibility: to maintain the coherence, cohesion, and stability of a complex and multi-faceted economic system. Because the capitalist state is committed to maintain the operating integrity of a system in which the bourgeois capitalist plays a dominant and essential role, *ipso facto* this state is committed to protect and preserve the dominant position and powers of the bourgeois capitalist, even when the state is not controlled by that class, and when the purposes and policies expressed through the state run counter to the manifest will and expressed interests of the bourgeois capitalist.

---

[3]Robert Solo "The Neo-Marxist Theory of the State," *Journal of Economic Issues* Vol. XII, No. 4 (December, 1978) pp. 829–842.

   The capitalist state functions as field of power balance and conflict-resolution, and as an instrument for achieving cross-class equilibrium. With the legitimacy of its authority based on universal suffrage, it obtains the consent of the governed, hence the acquiescence of the dominated as well as of the dominating classes by seeking to satisfy at least the essential or minimal needs of all functional groups, in part through income transfers and welfare guarantees. It also obtains consent through an apparatus of acculturation, socialization, and education that inculcates ideologies of individualism and nationalism; and through the juridical system that emphasizes the values and focuses on private rights and prerogatives—engendering thereby a consciousness of the individual in a world of individuals, and of individual rather than collective, group, or class values. Thus reinforced are the imageries of the world of man, of individuals interacting competitively as the natural and necessary condition of economic life, with the values of the collective conceivable only in the unity of nationhood.

   This theory of the state, certainly a significant advance in Marxist thought opens avenues of analysis as well for those with other than a Marxist orientation. More than that, it crosses a threshold into another (a properly postmodern) landscape of thought. It leaves the idea of the state as the instrument of class, where class is conceived in the image of Synthetic Man. And it conceives the state as a complex, many faceted system in a universe of systems.

From the World of Synthetic Man to the Universe of Systems

   The Nineteenth and then the Twentieth Centuries saw a world swept by great storms of change; a world whose institutional groundwork heaved and fissured and whose high structures crumbled under the force of social and political revolutions, industrial revolutions, technological cataclysms, the incredible, upsurging, outpouring of new wealth to new persons, the incredible down-falling, terrible impoverishment of depression, and war of incredible breadth and bloodletting with weaponries rising to a satanic crescendo of terror. It was of necessity a time of uprootedness, of alienation, of profound uncertainty; a time when private destinies were swept up in forces beyond individual control or comprehension.

   The psyche took refuge in familiar imageries, in ideas formed by another time; projecting upon the turbulence the face of man, imputing to those powers that encompassed and transcended the individual volition, the reason, the interest, the purpose, the character of man; creating in that way a synthetic artificial race, colossal, overpowering, immortal, before whom the individual with his will and reason became only a flyspeck, an insubstantial flicker.

   Synthetic Man, as a psychic device, is two pronged. It is a passive means of conceptualizing, comprehending, and explaining observed phenomena in the way that Marx understood class and Hegel conceptualized Spirit. It is also an active instrument for the uprooted, lost, and alienated, seeking a haven in the turbulence and finding identity in and salvation through submission to the created image of a synthetic superman, projecting upon some small mortal the form of a giant endowed with marvels of omniscience and the gift of miracles, so the Germans endowed

Hitler; so the Russians, Stalin, false colossi who then led peoples into abomination and madness. By the mid-Twentieth Century, the world was weary of their ilk. And when the guise of Synthetic Man was stripped away there appeared a tangled mass of diverse volitions manifesting nevertheless a degree of behavioral regularity, that could be analyzed and made explicable as a system. Into these systems it is possible to introduce rationality and purpose; it is possible to plan relationships; it is possible to organize volitions. But the rationality that can be introduced is not that of the individual volition and of private choice. It belongs to another, collective order. The planning of such a system is itself an open-ended shifting and vastly complex system. Postmodernity ushers in the universe of systems, infinite in variety and complexity. There the problem has its locus. And the questions arise: What am I? Where am I? What should I do in this universe of systems?

It is in that light that the work of Max Weber who lived and worked through the first quarter of the Twentieth Century should be understood. Max Weber did not write about the state as such. He wrote about political authority and power, of which he recognized three forms: the traditional, the charismatic, and the bureaucratic.

It should be noted that in this prospectus of choice and behavior, there is nothing there of autonomous individualism, neither of a "general will" arising from the consensus of reason, nor of social contract implying a rational individual commitment, nor of the "pluralism" that sees the state as a kind of market, an ordered arena for individual self-seeking, where the vote is equated to the dollar. Max Weber's horizon is beyond the world of man.

In Max Webber's three pronged topography of power and authority, the traditional or patriarchal is simply antiquarian; it belongs to Max Weber's study of origins. There remains for him, the charismatic and the bureaucratic. Charisma is the very stuff of Synthetic Man. Bureaucracy belongs to the universe of systems.

Charisma and Synthetic Man

For Max Weber

> There are three pure types of legitimate authority. The validity of their claims to legitimacy may be based on:
>
> (1) Rational grounds—resting on a belief in the "legality" of patterns of normative rules and the right of those elevated to authority under such rules to issue commands (legal authority).
>
> (2) Traditional grounds—resting on an established belief in the sanctity of immemorial traditions and the legitimacy of the status of those exercising authority under them (traditional authority); or finally,
>
> (3) Charismatic grounds—resting on devotion to the specific and exceptional sanctity, heroism or exemplary character of an individual person, and of the normative patterns or order revealed or ordained by him (charismatic authority).[4]

---

[4]Max Weber *On Charisma and Institution Building—Selected Papers*. Edited with an introduction by S. N. Eisenstadt (Chicago: University of Chicago Press, 1968), p. 46.

And charisma is understood as:

> a certain quality of an individual personality by virtue of which he is set apart
> from ordinary men and treated as endowed with supernatural, superhuman, or at
> least specifically exceptional qualities. These are such as are not accessible to the
> ordinary person, but are regarded as of divine origin or as exemplary. . . .[5]

Thus the charismatic leader formed in the image of man is endowed with
qualities beyond the reach, inaccessible to the ordinary being, possessing something divine, godlike, supernatural, superhuman whom others are obliged to obey, to follow
and submit, as a matter of duty, as a matter of right. He is, of course, Synthetic Man.

> The holder of charisma seizes the task . . . and demands obedience and a
> following by virtue of his mission . . . It is the duty of those to whom he addresses
> his mission to recognize him as their . . . leader.[6]

Weber puts great store in charisma, this "gift of grace"; it seems to be, for
Weber, even the sole innovating force, the only energizing source able to shatter and
transcend the groove of tradition and the inertia of the routine.

> The provisioning of all demands that go beyond those of everyday routine has
> had, in principle, an entirely heterogeneous, namely, a charismatic, foundation; the
> further we go back in history, the more we find this to be the case. This means that
> the 'natural' leaders—in time of psychic, physical, economic, religious, political
> distress— . . . have been holders of specific gifts of the body and spirit; and these
> gifts have been believed to be supernatural. . . .[7]

But note, beyond the supramundane, superhuman quality of the charismatic
being, a "time of psychic, physical, ethical, religious, political distress" is stressed
as its essential precondition. Again—

> The subject may extend a more active or passive 'recognition' to the personal
> mission of the charismatic master. His power rests upon this purely factual recognition and springs from faithful devotion. It is a devotion to the extraordinary and
> unheard of, to what is strange to all rule and tradition and which therefore is viewed
> as divine. It is a devotion born of distress and enthusiasm.[8]
> It is the recognition on the part of those subject to authority which is decisive
> for the validity of charisma . . . consisting in devotion to the corresponding revelation, hero worship, or absolute trust. But where charisma is genuine, it is not this

---

[5]*Ibid.,* p. 48.

[6]*Ibid.,* p. 20.

[7]*Ibid.* pp. 18–19. A younger contemporary of Max Weber, Joseph Schumpeter, in his seminal work
The Theory of Capitalist Development, published in Austria in the early 1920s, also held that innovationary change was brought about always by the rare and singular qualities of the "innovator." Schumpeter
lived to a later generation than did Max Weber, and in his *Capitalism, Socialism and Democracy*
published after World War II, Schumpeter abandons the reliance on his species of Synthetic Man, and
conceives innovation as a function of impersonal organization (of system).

[8]*Ibid.,* p. 23.

which is the basis of legitimacy. This basis lies rather in the conception that it is the *duty* of those who have been called to a charismatic mission to recognize its quality and to act accordingly. Psychologically this 'recognition' is a matter of complete personal devotion to the possessor of the quality, arising out of enthusiams, or of despair and hope.[9]

The perfect example of Weberian charisma is the relationship that the most disturbed, disordered, disoriented, lost, and despairful of human creatures, those confined to the asylums for the insane, have with their physician, or that those tortured, disturbed, and neurotic souls on the couch, have with their psychoanalyst. This is the critical example of pure charisma, *because* it is outside of history and hence outside of the vast and varied complex of forces that generate the phenomena of leadership and followership within the stream of history. Sigmund Freud, after all, systematized this relationship in the phenomenon of "transference," and made it the key instrument in the psychoanalytic treatment of the neurotic.

Thus Michel Foucault describes the role of the physician in the asylum for the insane, first created by Tuke in Great Britain and Pinel in France.[10]

> ... However, and this is the essential point, the doctor's intervention is not made by virtue of a medical skill or power that he possesses in himself and that would be justified by a body of objective knowledge. It is not as scientist that *homo medicus* has authority in the asylum, but as a wise man. If the medical profession is required, it is as a juridical and moral guarantee, not in the name of science.[11]
>
> It is thought that Tuke and Pinel opened the asylum to medical knowledge. They did not introduce science, but a personality, whose powers borrowed from science only their disguise, or at most their justification. These powers, by their nature, were of a moral and social order; they took root in the madman's minority status, in the insanity of his person, not of his mind. ... The physician could exercise his absolute authority in the world of the asylum only insofar as, from the beginning, he was Father and Judge, Family and Law. ... And Pinel was well aware that the doctor cures when, exclusive of modern therapeutics, he brings into play these immemorial figures ... the medical personage, according to Pinel, had to act not as the result of an objective divinition of the disease or a specific classifying diagnosis, but by relying upon that prestige which envelopes the secrets of the Family, of Authority, of Punishment, and of Love.[12]
>
> It is from these that the physician derives his power to cure; and it is to the degree that the patient finds himself, by so many old links, already alienated in the doctor, within the doctor-patient couple, that the doctor has the almost miraculous power to cure him.[13]
>
> ... it is by wearing the mask of Father and Judge that the physician, by one of those abrupt shortcuts that leave aside mere medical competences, became the almost magic perpetrator of the cure, and assumed the aspect of a Thaumaturge; it was enough that he observed and spoke, to cause secret faults to appear, insane

[9]*Ibid.,* p. 49.
[10]Michel Foucault *Madness and Civilization* (New York: Pantheon Books, 1965), p. 270.
[11]*Ibid.*
[12]*Ibid.,* pp. 271–273.
[13]*Ibid.,* p. 274.

presumptions to vanish, and madness at last to yield to reason. His presence and his words were gifted with that power of disalienation, which at one blow revealed the transgression and restored the order of morality.[14]

In the patient's eyes, the doctor has become a thaumaturge; the authority he has borrowed from order and morality, and the family now seems to derive from himself; it is because he is a doctor that he is believed to possess these powers, and while Pinel, with Tuke, strongly asserted that his moral action was not necessarily linked to any scientific competence, it was thought, and by the patient first of all, that it was in the esotericism of his knowledge, in some almost daemonic secret of knowledge, that the doctor had found the power to unravel insanity; and increasingly the patient would accept this self-surrender to a doctor both divine and satanic, beyond human measure in any case, increasingly he would alienate himself in the physician, accepting entirely and in advance all his prestige, submitting from the very first to a will he experienced as magic, and to a science he regarded as prescience and divination, thus becoming the ideal and perfect correlative of those powers he projected upon the doctor, pure object without any resistance except his own inertia, quite ready to become precisely that hysteric in whom Charcot exalted the doctor's marvelous powers.[15]

. . . there remains, beyond the empty forms of positivist thought, only a single concrete reality: the doctor-patient couple in which all alienations are summarized, linked, and loosened. And it is to this degree that all nineteenth-century psychiatry really converges on Freud, the first man to accept in all its seriousness the reality of the physician-patient couple, the first to consent not to look away or to investigate elsewhere, the first not to attempt to hide it in a psychiatric theory that more or less harmonized with the rest of medical knowledge; the first to follow its consequences with absolute rigor.

. . . on the other hand he [Freud] exploited the structure that enveloped the medical personage; he amplified its thaumaturgical virtues, preparing for its omnipotence a quasi-divine status. He focused on this single presence—concealed behind the patient and above him . . . all the powers . . . of the asylum;[16]

This purest charismatic relationship, observable in the numberless, systematic and instrumental use of charisma and nothing else, inherent in the patient-physician coupling of the insane and the doctor, and of the neurotic and the psychoanalyst, demonstrates that charisma is in no sense an emanation of the personal magnetism and unique qualities of the charismatic leader. If in the eyes of his patient he is omniscient, magical, possessed of daemonic and marvelous powers, all others will know the physician and the psychoanalyst as ordinary, even less than mediocre men. It demonstrates that charisma is always a function and consequence of the disorientation, alienation, despair, distress, and need of the subject or victim of charismatic power.

That disorientation, distress, alienation, extreme uncertainty, and despair that opens the individual to charismatic power, and that obliges him to seek for and to create the Synthetic Man upon whom he can anchor his hope and find a haven from unease and uncertainty, is most pronounced in the pathology of insanity and neuro-

[14]*Ibid.*, p. 273.
[15]*Ibid.*, pp. 275–276.
[16]*Ibid.*, p. 277.

sis. But all men can know despair, distress, disorientation, alienation, and correspondingly can be rendered vulnerable to the charismatic power and driven to seek for and ultimately to create Synthetic Man as their haven and hope. And this will happen, as Weber said, "in time of psychic, physical, economic, ethical, religious, political distress."[17]

We take issue with Weber on two grounds: first that the charismatic power (with Synthetic Man as its corollary) is a constant in history "the further back we look in history, the more we find this to be the case";[18] and second, that charisma is the sole or essential energizing force of innovation "provisioning all demands that go beyond those of everyday routine."[19]

Not all periods of history are, or are equally "times of psychic, physical, economic, ethical, religious, political distress." The Nineteenth and Twentieth Centuries with the impact of revolutionary and rapid changes, the erosion and collapse of tradition, the breakdown of habituated status, the explosion of expectation, the release of aspirations, the new powers of communication, the extraordinary increase in social and spatial mobility, were, even in their most beneficent and liberating aspects, a time of individual disorientation, alienation, uncertainty, of psychic distress without parallel. Correspondingly this was the day of charisma and the reign of Synthetic Man. Thus, aside from those he draws from the mythologies and the quasimythologies of ancient history, Weber's only clear and unequivocal examples of charismatic leadership are the first Napoleon and Joseph Smith and his Mormons, both products of the early Nineteenth Century. From the Fourteenth through the Eighteenth Centuries, during the Renaissance and the Enlightenment, ages replete with innovation and with heroes, adventurers, nation-builders, and geniuses, I can find not a single instance of "charismatic" leadership. Max Weber's conceptualization, though he projected it over the whole span of history, belonged to his own time; and the force of his perception was not in interpretating the past but in predicting the future. It was the strange and terrible phenomenon of three little men, a backroom manipulator, a psychopath, a blowhard, Stalin, Hitler, Mussolini, inflated into colossi by the force of charisma strutting the stage of history that, in the period of after his death, validated Max Weber's vision.

Bureaucracy

Ideological liberalism finds the source of all efficiency, all coherent social energy, all ingenuity, all reason, in the self-seeking individual operating from a base of private property; and condemns bureaucracy as the opposite of all that—as inherently slothful, irrational, inert, parasitical. Such has been the very credo of American politics. We glorify free enterprise and denigrate bureaucracy, failing to see that in the modern economy, they are the same.

Max Weber was the first, and the greatest organizational theorist. He wrote not of the modern nation state as such, but about bureaucracy, as the universal element of all large and complex modern organizations. And he celebrates bureaucracy as

---

[17]Op. cit., p. xxiii.
[18]*Ibid.,* p. 18.
[19]*Ibid.,* p. 18.

the epitome of efficiency and rationality. In his search for its laws and constraints, he naturally took as his prime exemplar, the Prussian State, which was in fact the first great modern organization. It was in the state, through the state, and not in the firms of the market economy, that systematic recruitment and promotion by the test of merit and skill were first designed and installed to match training and talent to task and responsibility. It was there that authority was first

> distributed in a stable way, delineated by rules[20] . . . [creating] a firmly ordered system of super and subordination . . . [which] offers the governed the possibility of appealing the decision of the lower office to a higher authority in a definitely regulated manner . . . [with its] management based upon written documents (the files) . . . [where the] executive office is separated from the household, business from private correspondence, and business assets from private fortunes . . . [where] management presupposes thorough and expert training . . . demanding the full working capacity of the official . . . [following] general rules, which are more or less stable, more or less exhaustive, and which can be learned . . . [where] office holding is a 'vocation.' This is shown, first, in the requirement of a firmly prescribed course of training, which demands the entire capacity for work for a long period of time, and in the generally prescribed and special examinations which are prerequisites of employment.[21]

Bureaucratization, which Weber considered to be virtually synonymous with rationality and systemization, begins with the state and is shaped by the functional focus of the state. It is not, however, confined to the state, but signals a general and basic transformation of the whole social order, of the character of behavior, and in the quality of life. It is, for example, to be identified with "modern mass democracy" in contrast to the "democratic self-government of small, homogeneous units."[22] Bureaucratic judgment will not be judgment case by case, but through the application of abstract principles, for example, "rule by law," hence "the demand for 'equality before the law' " and the "horror of privilege"[23] whereas, according to Weber, "The nonbureaucratic administration of any large social structures rests in some way upon the fact that existing social, material, and honorific preferences and ranks are connected with administrative functions and duties."[24] Control in such nonbureaucratic structures is exercised by those with powers and privileges extraneous to the functions they perform. As De Tocquiville before him, Max Weber saw modern mass democratization as a "leveling of the governed in opposition to the ruling and bureaucratically articulated group, which in its turn may occupy a quite autocratic position, both in fact and in form."[25] Bureaucratization and mass democratization, as complementary and parallel processes evidently produces a tension between the prerogatives of representation and participation with its demand for bureaucratic answerability on the one hand, and

---

[20]*Ibid.*, p. 66
[21]*Ibid.*, pp. 67–70.
[22]*Ibid.*, p. 70.
[23]*Ibid.*, p. 70
[24]*Ibid.*, p. 70
[25]*Ibid.*, p. 73.

the capacity and need for bureaucratic responsibility and for administrative *cum* technical initiatives on the other.

Later, in developing our own theory of the State, we will come back to Max Weber, in order to further examine certain of his arguments, to take issue with some of these, and to suggest the limitations of his approach. For the moment let it suffice to commend an original vision that conceptualizes and probes the conditions of post modernity, in a world that is neither of the autonomous individual nor of Synthetic Man, but of vast and complex systems wherein the face of man is lost.

3

THE STATE AS AN ORGANIZATION

The state is an instrument of group or collective action, but different from other instruments of group or collective action, different than the university, the corporation, the trade union, the church, in that it expresses and exercises the sovereign power, the ultimate temporal authority over individuals and other groups within a domain bounded by the sovereign power of other states. The state is the instrument of a client group or groups outside of itself; but also those who participate in the activities of the state may themselves constitute a group or a set of interacting groups; and these indeed may be most powerful in directing the exercise of its sovereign powers. In that sense and to that degree the state is autonomous. The modern state is the greatest and most complex of all organizations, and inasmuch as there are laws of organization, it is subject to those laws. It is to the consideration of the state as organization, subject to the laws and constraints of organization, that we now turn.

Weberian Bureaucracy

For that we go back to Max Weber and his theories of bureaucracy. Weber's central experience of bureaucracy was in the observation and knowledge of the Prussian State. He generalized from that experience to postulate bureaucracy as the essential quality and character of all modern organizations, including, of course, modern corporate enterprise," . . . in the private economy . . . in the most advanced

institutions of capitalism."[1] where "the modern entrepreneur . . . conducts himself
as the 'first official' of his enterprise, in the very same way in which [Frederick II,
"the Great" of Prussia, who mounted the throne in 1740] . . . spoke of himself as
'the first servant' of the State."[2]

For Weber, state, church, and corporate enterprise are all bureaucracies, with
that of the state different from the others only in its higher degree of development.
Variations are otherwise to be accounted for by the vanishing residuals of traditional
authority and the shrinking locii of charismatic power.

Bureaucracy is characteristic of all modern organizations. But Max Weber was
wrong in supposing that all bureaucracy must display the selfsame characteristics
he found in that of the Prussian State.

The character and quality of modern organization, and the behavior of their
bureaucracies, will vary greatly depending on the kind of power exercised, the scope
and nature of external constraints, the purposes served and the nature of the functions performed, and the cultural and cognitive context of the operation.

Corporate versus Public Bureaucracies

The power exercised by the Prussian State, and by every state (but certainly not
by every organization), was that of the sovereign: a terrible, ultimate temporal power
of life and death. That power, because is is inherently unbounded, will (to a degree
depending upon the cultural context) be carefully and rigidly constrained through
convention and rule. The corporate power, because of its intrinsic limits, requires
no such safeguards; and hence operates with no comparable constraints.

Resting upon the limited claims of property, the powers of the corporation are
constrained by the countervailing claims of organized buyers and sellers (including
the trade unions), by the competition of its rivals, and by the mobility of its personnel
(the ease and opportunity of "exit"), in what is essentially a voluntary association
for mutual gain. In contrast to the state, the corporate organization is flexible and
self-directed, free to change stance and shift direction, but constrained by the coun-
terplay of other organizations. Withall, the corporate bureaucracy exercises an
autonomous power that is real and considerable, an often formidable power that (in
contrast to that of the state) is inherently irresponsible and arbitrary in the sense that
its bureaucracy is not systematically and in principle responsible for the effects of
its choice, nor answerable to those who know the consequences and feel the impacts
of its action. Consider, for example, advertising. The corporate advertiser shapes
social values without concern for, nor consideration of the consequences, be they
good or evil, on the cultural system. Nor is the corporate bureaucracy considered
responsible, nor does it consider itself responsible, nor is it answerable to society or
to any part of society for those consequences. The corporate advertiser reshapes the
cultural system without any value objective beyond that of playing and winning the
corporate game play. The agencies of the modern western state, on the other hand,

---

[1]Max Weber *On Charisma and Institution Building—Selected Papers.* Edited with an introduction
by S. N. Eisenstadt (Chicago: University of Chicago Press 1968), pp. 66–68.
[2]*Id.,* p. 68.

are continuously subject to an elaborate machinery intended to insure answerability to those within the national domain, who bear the costs or are subject to the impacts of choice and action. The state bureaucracies must be continuously prepared to answer, to explain, to justify before the bar of public inquiry, their choices, their actions, and the consequences of these.

Duty and Play

Max Weber writes:

> . . . the position of the official is in the nature of a duty. This determines the internal structure of his relations . . . office holding is not considered as a source to be exploited for rents or emoluments. . . . Nor is office holding considered a usual exchange of service for equivalents, as is the case with free labor contracts. Entrance into office, including one in the private economy, is considered an acceptance of a specific obligation of faithful management in return for a secure existence . . . it does not establish a relationship to a *person*. . . . Modern loyalty is devoted to impersonal and functional purposes. Behind the functional purpose . . . ersatz for the earthly or supramundane personal master are such ideas as 'state,' 'church,' 'community,' or 'enterprise' . . . thought of as being realized in a community. Bureaucratic rule becomes 'ideologically hallowed.'[3]

It is hardly this sense of duty, this "acceptance of specific obligation . . . in return for a secure existence" that generates the energies and guides the behavior at every, or at any level of executive (bureaucratic) power in the American corporation. Rather, the corporate executive (bureaucrat), in the American context at least, at best is captured and driven by the dread of losing and the need to win in a game that is played within the corporate structure, as well as *vis-a-vis* those outside of it. The source of corporate coherence is no dedication to duty where duty has a common vector, but is rather the partisanship of the team.

Though ignored by social science, game playing is one of the great universals of social behavior. It is omnipresent as a need of the psyche. The energy and ebullience in the young animal and of the child find outlet and meaning in the playing of games; and in games, the energies and ebullience of the adult continues to find outlet and meaning. Perhaps the greatest satisfactions in the common life are realized in the comradeship of the team. It well may be that thin, synthetic, solidarity, and partisanship of fans, huddled together in the stadium on a Saturday afternoon, or with eyes fixed on the TV screen, signifies a more massive, continuous, and enthused involvement than is evoked by religion or by politics in the modern world —childish, ersatz, empty if you will, but undeniable. The modern corporation and its bureaucracies turn on the axis of gamesmanship; and their effectiveness will continue so long as the game entices.

The corporation cannot base itself on dedication and duty. The state cannot operate as a game. The state, in the work opportunity it offers, has the potentiality of satisfying another level of human need, and tapping a different source of motiva-

---

[3]*Id.,* pp. 69–70

tion. The need is deep, and the motivation can be powerful, as Max Weber saw—the craving for dedication, the pride in service, the clean clarity of duty, the sense of community. As no other agency, the state can offer these, and with them security and honor. It can, but it need not. If it fails to capitalize on this potential, then the state, *qua* organization, will be deprived of the high competence it could acquire and of the energies it could have mobilized.

The Antistate Bias of American Liberalism

Americans, imbued with the antistate bias of ideological liberalism, have never recognized the need to cultivate and employ that capacity for dedication, except in times of war; nor has there been any concern for that which is required to induce it. Nor has the American state offered its officialdom careers of security, responsibility, and honored dedication, except for the judge, the diplomat, and the professional soldier. Instead, in a curious *kowtow* to the idols of the market, we have, in the instance of the military-industrial complex, produced a set of nominally private companies that are in fact agents of the state, but outside the reach of public answerability or responsibility. And we have converted agencies of the state into imitation corporations, like that pitiful AMTRAK or the unfortunate new Post Office, so as to exclude the potentially powerful appeal and motivating force of public service, without the ebullience of corporate gamesmanship in its place.

The Social System as Context

It is not simply that the corporate bureaucracy and the state bureaucracy operate under different principles of motivation and constraint, and require correspondingly different forms of organization. States themselves, *qua* organizations, are subject to fundamental variations. It is the image of the nationalist *qua* military state that shines through Max Weber's theory of bureaucracy. Thus he writes:

> Once it is established, bureaucracy is among the social structures which are the most difficult to destroy . . . bureaucracy has been and is a power instrument of the first order—for *the one who* controls the bureaucratic apparatus. . . . (Italics mine)
> The individual bureaucrat cannot squirm out of the apparatus in which he is harnessed. In contrast to the honorific or avocational 'notable' the professional bureaucrat is chained to his activity by his entire material and ideal existence . . . he is only a cog in an ever-moving mechanism which prescribes to him an essentially fixed route of march. The official is entrusted with specialized tasks and normally the mechanism cannot be put into motion or arrested by him but only from the very top. The individual bureaucrat is thus forged to the community of all the functionaries who are integrated into the mechanism. They have a common interest in seeing that the mechanism continues its functions and that the societally exercised authority carries on.
> The ruled for their part cannot dispense with or replace the bureaucratic apparatus of authority, once it exists. For this bureaucracy rests upon expert training, a functional specialization of work, an attitude set for habitual and virtuoso-like mastery of single yet methodically integrated functions. If the official stops working or if his work is forcibly interrupted, chaos results. This holds for public

administration as well as for private economic management. More and more the material fate of the masses depends upon the steady and correct functioning of the increasingly bureaucratic organizations of private capitalism. The idea of eliminating these organizations becomes more and more utopian.

The discipline of officialdom refers to the attitude-set of the official for precise obedience within his *habitual* activity, in public as well as in private organizations. This discipline increasingly becomes the basis for all order . . . [a] compliance [that] has been conditioned into the officials on the one hand, and on the other hand, into the governed. . . .

The objective indispensability of the . . . apparatus, with its peculiar, 'impersonal' character means that the mechanism . . . is easily made to work for anybody who knows how to gain control over it. . . . [It] continues to function smoothly after the enemy has occupied the area . . . because [its continued operation] is to the vital interest of everyone concerned, above all to the enemy.[4]

To what corporate organization does the above apply? Indeed to what states? Few modern organizations, public or private, are anymore designed to transmit and enforce the command of "the one who controls." The modern organization itself, of itself, can and must be a decision-taking, policy-producing, even an innovating, change-making entity. The issue is not simply the transmission of and obedience to the word that descends from the top, replicated faithfully and followed precisely throughout. The issue is rather whether the word (as information, as command, as demand, as question, as reply, as data, as suggestion, as forewarning, as objection, as stimuli, as response) moves up as well as down, laterally as well as crosswise on the matrix of power and responsibility. Rather than command/obey, the task may be of the order of communicate, convince, verify, clarify, interpret, challenge.

Beyond Self-Interest

Neoclassical economics assumes self-interest as the force that motivates and explains behavior throughout the economy. Here self-interest is understood without sophistry, as the choices and actions of the individual directed solely and simply to the gain of the greatest possible advantage over any and all other individuals, in order to acquire and possess or consume all that can possibly be acquired, possessed, or consumed, balanced only against the sacrifices inherent in the process of acquisition. In this analysis, possession or consumption is equated to preference/utility/-satisfaction/well-being/ even happiness. And the drive to acquire is equated to efficiency in the allocation and utilization of resources. Admitting that more than simple self-interest is involved in the motivation and behavior of actors on the marketplace, nevertheless, the neoclassical assumption can be justified on the principle of Occum's Razor, since self-interest is a universal element in the human psyche and since it does suffice to explain the operation of an economy of autonomous individuals engaged in market exchange. It is an assumption that suffices to explain the operation of the neoclassical economic model of pure competition.

---

[4]*Id.,* pp. 75–77.

That assumption, however, cannot explain the operation of an economy of collective (group) choice and complex organization. This is not to say that simple self-interest in the grab for advantage and the greed for possession does not obtain in such an economy. Certainly it does. Sometimes and to some degree, such simple self-interest can be and has been deliberately integrated into the organizational plan, and mobilized, monitored, channelized as a positive force in the achievement of organizational objectives. The economy of planned organization can and sometimes does collapse into a morass of private bargains in a continuous and individual pursuit of self-gain, variously called graft, skimming, bribery, kickback, payoff, corruption. What self-interest cannot explain is the source of coherence and the prerequisites of effectiveness in collective choice, in group activity, in complex organization.

For that we must go beyond simple self-interest. And again this is not to say that considerations of self are absent from even the most high-flown ideological commitment. The worker who becomes a faithful and devoted member of the Communist party and suffers for his faith, may believe that the transformation of society to which he is dedicated would open up for himself the possibilities of a better life. The rich man who surrenders all of his possessions and joins a mendicant order may believe that in so doing he will save his soul. The unemployed Italian student who joins the Red Brigades and shoots the knee caps off of hapless civil servants may believe that in so doing he is pushing open the gates to a world in which he will enjoy a new kind of human brotherhood. A sense of self-betterment, yes: but for us what is important is that in each case a particular and complex set of ideas, images, and values, an ideology, whose source must be accounted for and whose basis of acceptability must be understood, has intervened to integrate the individual into a group volition, and has determined the pattern of collective behavior.

It is our purpose now to explore the territory beyond self-interest in search for that which might motivate and could explain the motivation of bureaucracy, the force of organization, and the patterns and parameters of collective behavior.

Craftsmanship

There is, as Thorstein Veblin saw, a drive as basic and universal as that of simple self-interest, in the instinct of workmanship, man's need to work, and pride in the skill of the hands, and in the product they fashion, in the agility of the mind, and in the problems it solves, in the sensitivity of the ear, and in the music it creates, in the strength of the limbs, and in the race they run, in the powers of the imagination, and in the inventions it produces. In the work itself, in its intrinsic character and the mark it makes, regardless of external rewards or market values, the individual is likely to find his worth and through his work, establish his integrity and safeguard his honor. Work itself satisfies a psychic and possibly a physical need. The work ethic, the idea of time as a work space, presumably implanted by the cultural system that nourishes such pride and honors that integrity, can be a powerful organizer of energies in any economic system. It does not, however, explain the formation of collective choice, nor can it provide a blueprint for organizational policy.

Duty

The sense of duty also is a powerful, fundamental organizer of energies. In doing his duty, the individual finds respite from the prods of conscience. This sense of duty is less instinctual, more specifically moral, more totally an implant of the cultural system than are the calls of craftsmanship and the work ethic. The devotion to duty is at least peripherally ideological, for there inheres in it the questions: duty to whom?, duty to do what? It contains the notion of a legitimate order to which devotion is due, and of a rule that is as it ought to be. Max Weber's bureaucratic model requires for its operation no more than a pervasive sense of duty faithfully transmitting and exactly implementing commands descending "from the top." But the sense of duty cannot explain the formation of collective choice nor the blueprint for organizational behavior.

Enlightened Partisanship

The modern corporation is a vast and complex association for mutual gain. The gains that can possibly accrue to the shareholders, workers, craftsmen, salesmen, executives, engineers, R&D scientists, and anyone else so associated, must necessarily depend on the earnings, the "winnings" of the enterprise, which in turn depends on the quality of the collective performance and on the skills and strategies of corporate gamesmanship. With rare exception there is no visible, ascertainable, let alone measureable relationship between the effort, efficiency, devotion, imagination, contribution of an individual within the organizational complex, and the "winnings" of the whole, from which some share is the due of that individual. And yet the performance and effectiveness, and the "winnings" of the whole will depend on individual perceptions of (and commitment to) the relationship between what the individual does and what comes back to the individual as a consequence of what is done by the corporate whole. That such a perception will in fact prevail requires that a complex *idea* of the relationship of cause and consequence be inculcated (it is not self evident), accepted, and shared. Hence the performance of the organizational whole will depend on the enlightened (or deluded) partisanship of those so engaged.

The Instinct of Gamesmanship

More important than enlightened partisanship, which is a species of self-interest, in the dynamic of corporate bureaucracy, is the instinct of gamesmanship, the addiction to gameplaying, and the identification with, and pride in the team.

The Technological Imperative

Organizations, even more so than individuals, protect, promote, and perpetuate the doing of what they know how to do. Especially this is true for those organizations that recruit for, train for, and are engaged, and isolated in the performance of the tasks of a highly complex "advanced" technology where, for that reason, they alone are likely to possess and contain the body of expertise that would be needed to evaluate the worthwhileness and dangers of their endeavor. In the learning from the experience they generate, in the careers they install, in the recruits they attract, they replicate (and develop) a vectored competence and a continuum of vested interests in the protection and promotion of the given line of activity, establishing a techno-logical fix into the future in a movement that can draw the whole social culture, sometimes disastrously, in its wake, extending streams of outputs, either of nuclear reactors, automobiles, manned bombers, ICBMs, of somniferics and tranquilizers, with effects malignant or benign, and no power able to pull the brake or force a change of direction.

Ideology

Ideology is the sole source of group or collective coherence. The state is always the instrument of groups, and for a group, any group, ideology is at the root of choice and behavior. The technological imperative and enlightened partisanships, consti-tute ideologies of a sort. Duty vectors into ideology. The coherence and rational basis for policy in the state derives from the ideologies of the groups who participate in its process of choice, that is, who are represented in "governance." The stability of the democratic state (and the seeming viability of democratic participation) depends on the extent that a common ideology prevails as the basis of a consensus and a common response to questions and issues by the elected representatives and those they represent. Where different groups with conflicting ideological commitments share power in the process of choice, consensus is not possible. There is then no "general will." And the stability of the state is likely to rest on the precarious condition of domination. And when ideological commitments disintegrate, as they have, then common guidelines vanish; inertia replaces coherence, the link of a common response between those who represent and those who are represented is broken and the illusion of democratic participation dies; and the agencies of the state drift in the course of *ad hoc* expediency. Save that those agencies may have their own ideological core.

Among those who constitute a group, there will be great variations in the degree of ideological commitment. There are laymen in the Church and there are priests, those who attend the service and those who say the holy mass, those who confess and those who give absolution, those who pray for saints and those who seek sainthood, those who contribute funds and those who give their lives. So also with the ideologies vectored upon the state. Thus, for example, there are many who profess an allegiance to the nation, but also there are professional nationalists, and priests of nationalism, and professionals with careers of service to the credo of nation.

Simple self-interest, the call of craftsmanship, the sense of duty, the technologi-cal imperative, and the force of ideology, not one but all of these simultaneously determine choice, policy and the structures of organization in the state.

4

IDEOLOGY AND INTERESTS IN THE FORMATION OF THE AMERICAN STATE

Authoritative and Composite Choice

The behavior of the organization, like that of the individual, is many faceted. What we find out about it, will depend on what we are looking to discover. Since our emphasis here has been on the ideological, we have tried to understand, and in this chapter we propose to say something concerning the role of the ideological in contrast to that of the non-ideological, (that is, of the interplay of interests) in determining organizational behavior; particularly with respect to the state *qua* organization. Having formulated an analytic, we will use it to explain the behavior, policy-formation and development of the American State.

In any organization, there are those decisions or choices that are made by an individual in authority on the basis of that authority *for* an organization; call such choice, *authoritative.* But also policies may emerge and practices develop, not as the consequence of any deliberated and purposeful decision, but rather through interactive processes that compound and reflect the diverse drives and interests of those who participate in the operations of the organization and/or who can influence or exercise pressures upon those within it. Such behavior-producing processes, which may be structured or unstructured, will be called here, *composite.*

Though authoritiative choice is made by the individual, it is not at all the same as the "individualized" choice of libertarian imagery like that, say, of the entrepreneur of neoclassical economic theory where the activities of the firm are to be understood as the proprietor's self-interest. Between such individualized choice and the choice of an individual in the exercise of authority, there is this critical difference. Individualized choice is made independently. It is self-responsible. Individualized choice is not answerable whereas those who choose in the exercise of authority are answerable to those upon whom they must rely, directly or ultimately, to support their authority and/or to accept and act upon their word. Since authority is answerable, it must be prepared to answer, with its choice justifiable before those upon whom its authority depends. In order to choose what can be justified, it must choose within a zone of the acceptable. The boundaries of that zone are determined by the idea shared by those to whom authority is answerable as to what is and what ought to be with respect to the relevant field of choice and action—this is to say the boundaries within which the choice of authority operates are fixed as a function of ideology. In their authoritative choices the plant manager, the army officer, the catholic bishop, the trade union official alike are answerable to those who support and/or accept their authority, but each to a different group operating from a different ideological base, hence for each the zone of the acceptable, determining the range of possible authoritative choice, will be very different as well—even in universities.

As a visiting professor teaching in a French university, I called on students to come to the front of the class and solve problems on the blackboard, as is the normal practice in the United States. They pounded their desks. They stood on their chairs. They threatened a riot. It wasn't, they shouted, "the French Way!" It was as though I had demanded they come forward and expose their private parts. Evidently my idea and theirs of the role and relationship of student and teacher were not the same. I had transgressed their boundaries of the acceptable, and my professorial authority came to naught.

An effective authoritative choice must have as its base and operate within the frame of an ideology that links its exercise to the support and acceptance of its imperatives. Composite choice is quite another matter.

Composite choice, emerging out of a diversity of interests and pressures, is without a specific point of reference save in the weight of counterbalancing forces. It need not be justified. It is geared to no process of explanation or rationalization. Its effective expression is in the nature of an event and a becoming.

It follows that ideology will imprint itself on organizational behavior most strongly through the agencies of authoritative choice. Expediency will more likely prevail for the composite. Authoritative and composite choice can be compared in the instance of the American State through contrasting the Supreme Court with Congress and the Executive agencies.

The Supreme Court, nine justices, each with life tenure, with immense prestige and enormous power, each justice exercising powers of choice independently, individually but not as an individual acting upon his own and answerable to no other. Rather each chooses for American society and each is responsible for his choice to American society. In each decision, the judge explains, justifies, pleads his case before the great bar of social opinion. The field of each justice's discretion is wide, but it is surely bounded. The support for its authority and the willingness of society to accept and to implement the Court's decisions requires that there be some social concurrence with the norms it articulates; the Court must operate within (changing) boundaries of a zone of the acceptable.

The Court is small. Each justice says what he intends, and envisions the impact of what he decides. The decisions of each justice and the choices of the Court are products of the reasoning mind, of an integral set of values, of an outlook on past, present, future. In contrast, the agencies of the executive are enormous, encompassing pressures, influences, interests of thousands, incorporating a vast diversity of opinion. The information, knowledge, expertise that enters into its processes are widely dispersed, with fragments monopolized. Each of these great agencies and each of their component parts is geared to the service, and relies on the support of different clients all expressing a diversity of interests. Within the halls of Congress there exists a wide diversity of interests, opinions, angles of outlook; and Congress interacts with, and merges into an amalgum of the political parties, the political machines of states and cities, the lobbies, patrons, clients, partisans, piper-payers and tune-callers, and the organized and the anonymous elements of the electorate. Congress and the executive agencies top a seething system open to, and bringing into play elements of the whole vast social universe, where an individual's word sinks onto the wide sea of verbiage, and where no choice, no act, no opinion, no input of an individual can know its full effect or eventual destination. Out of the ceaseless grouping and regrouping of power relationships, the strivings for comparative advantage, the gaming and counterpoise of strategies, emerge directions of activity, collective rules, policies. Such is the composite choice in the American State. Though the constraints and currents of belief, the waves of fanaticism, the fervor of orthodoxies are among its inputs, the processes of composite choice cannot be the expression of a unitary purpose, a reasoning mind and an integral ideology.

Thus two forms of organizational choice: composite and authoritative, neither the equivalent of nor to be understood by analogy to the individualized choices of those self-sufficient self-seekers, responsible for and answerable to no other than themselves, who inhabit the landscapes of libertarian thought.

Qua forms of organizational choice, the composite and the authoritative each has a particular set of strengths and weaknesses.

Consider. A system of composite choice like that of the Congress and the Executive Agencies of the United States *represents* a universe of real needs, preferences, pressures, ideas, values, with all the contradictions and conflicts thereof. It gives expression to demands, aspirations, discontents, crises as these exist whether or not they fit into an established frame of thought or are explicable by reference to the ideology that prevails. Composite choice responds to loci of pain and desperation without the need for an intervening rationale. It provides for an interplay where contesting forces can find a state of balance so that the social organism survives in spite of irreconcilable conflicts and contradictions. Flexible, representative, responsive, pragmatic—such are its virtues. Its vices are the vices of expediency; meandering, aimless, wasteful, without focus, without foresight, without hindsight, without logical consistency, without vision. It reacts to crisis but not in anticipation of crisis. It has to be kicked into motion. Such is the character of composite choice, and such is the usual quality of choice by the American Congress and Executive.

Authoritative choice, based upon and justifying itself by reference to an ideology that links governed and governor, is capable of hindsight and foresight, of rationality, of coherence. It expresses a logically consistent system of ideas and values that can evolve, that can develop through experience, through learning. It contains a

vision of the desirable as the blueprint for the deliberated creation, or transformation, or preservation of institutions and the organization of social activity. It is
purposeful, focused, knowing of where it is and where it is going. Such are its
strengths and values. Its vices and weakness are in the inescapable inability of the
mind and its constructs to comprehend the social whole or of ideology to encompass
all the flux and complexity of the universe to which it would refer. Philosophies must
simplify. Ideologies must exclude. Elements of reality escape its purview. Authority
is locked into ideology, at once a system of thought and a focus of inquiry that sifts
out the extraneous and defines the visible. Once embedded in the psychic system of
the individual and in the cultural-cognitive systems of society, ideology is difficult
to escape, even impossible to discard, resistant to the most violent onslaughts of
experience. And an ideology, developed through and perpetuated in the cultural-
cognitive systems of society, is the cumulative product of a whole history, bearing
the weight of ancient encounters, with current experience infiltrating only at the
margin. Since the world that is need not replicate that which was, a vision shaped
by the experience of the past need not comprehend the present. In times of rapid
change and of fundamental social transformation, the gap will grow between encountered reality and the imageries of ideology. Then, more and more of the experienced will escape the conceptual net of authoritative choice.

We are developing here a particular analytic of the state. Certainly there are
others. According to Cone, Cole, and Easterling,[1] the established approaches to the
analysis of collective behavior and political event comprehends four "viewpoints,"
(1) the economic, (2) the political, (3) the organizational, and (4) the legal. Consider
these four.

The "economic viewpoint," conceives or judges the state as a rational, economizing entity, a species of Synthetic Man who is or ought to be optimizing a net
social product by reference to a given set of priorities or values. It is according to
this "viewpoint," justifiable that such optimizing choice should be made by the state
rather than by individuals or corporations inasmuch as the values held by individuals
in their capacity as consumers on the market differ from the values they hold in their
capacity as citizens of the state; for example, in relation to national security or with
regard to the well-being of future generations, or inasmuch as the market-generated
distribution of income gives undue weight to the demands of the rich, or inasmuch
as the market organization of production fails to take into account (externalizes)
relevant costs and benefits. In order to correct such inequities or to offset such
distortions, or to give voice to those values that cannot be expressed appropriately
through consumer demand on the price-competitive market, the state has available
a number of instrumentalities to transfer income and variously to influence entrepreneurial choice.

The "economic viewpoint" is of no use in comprehending and analyzing the
process of collective choice and political action. Conceiving of the state simply as
an adjunct to the market with the task of supplementing and correcting certain
malfunctions of the market, it does provide a critique of, and a guideline for political

---

[1]Burce W. Cone, Roland J. Cole, and James Easterling, "A Theoretical Approach to Analyzing
Incentives for Energy Production," *An Analysis of Federal Incentives Used to Stimulate Energy Production*
(Richland, Washington: Battelle Northwest Laboratory, 1978), pp. 17–34.

behavior. Its viability as an explanation of political phenomena and its effectiveness
as a guideline to political policy will depend entirely on the force of the ideological
commitment that links those who exercise political authority with those to whom
they are answerable. The "economic viewpoint" is thus simply one possible basis for
authoritative choice.

From the "political viewpoint" the relevant universe is the field of pressure and
maneuver where

> individuals, groups, and organizational participants inside and outside of govern-
> ment bargain with each other to obtain government actions that will favor the goals
> they independently seek. The federal government . . . is a collection of political
> groups that together with nongovernmental groups, forms a . . . bargaining arena.
> . . . Because resources are scarce, not all groups will get everything they want. Since
> bargaining power is unequal, some groups will get more of what they want than
> others will. . . .[2]

This idea of a universe of choice and action may be coupled with a "democratic
ideology" which would take full representation, that is, the capacity of all groups
or individuals to participate in the political free-for-all, and the resolution or muffl-
ing of conflicts between participants, as intrinsic values and self-sufficient political
goals. Thus understood, the process validates itself simply by perpetuating itself, and
thereby presumably abetting the continuity of the society of which it is a part. From
this point of view the process of representation and conflict-resolution is its own
justification. No handle is offered to deduce or to evaluate specific outcomes, when
these are external to the political process.

The "political viewpoint" relates to and lays out the format of *composite choice*
where it is the balance of interests and not the force of ideology that shapes political
event. But even here, it should be remembered, the groups who participate in this
process of pressure and maneuver, are themselves always communities of ideological
commitment. It is through ideology that they share a perception of the field of choice
and action, and through ideology they find their common goal.

Unlike the great work of Max Weber, in its current American incarnation the
"organizational viewpoint" focuses on the corporation; postulating a corporate
model of essentially mechanical rule-making, problem-searching, goal-forming,
decision-taking, complete with information flow and feedback. Its recognition that
neither the corporation nor the political agency is or can be understood by analogy
to the self-seeking individual is indubitably a virtue. But alas, as an analytic approach
to political phenomena, it has not been rich with substantive insights, nor has it
evolved a theory capable of explaining complex events or of predicting nontrivial
political outcomes. It neither provides an ideological criterion for the evaluation or
formulation of policy, as the "economic viewpoint" does; nor can it take into account
the field of pressure and maneuver, as the "political viewpoint" does; nor does it
comprehend the formative role of ideology and authoritative choice.

The "legal viewpoint" conceives of the state as an instrument for the resolution
of conflicts-at-interest. The resolution of these conflicts produces rules. These rules

---

[2]*Id.,* pp. 24–25.

form the parameters of choice and behavior, and define the boundaries of individual, group, and property prerogatives. Within parameters thus formed, new conflict-of-interests arise, new conflict-resolution must be made, producing new rules, within whose parameters new conflicts of interest arise, and so on ad infinitum. The ethical-ideological reference base of authoritative choice, and the weight of the forces engaged in composite choice, the tasks of creative organization and of planning for complex social and economic outcomes, are all outside the scope of the legal viewpoint. The value objective implicit in this viewpoint, its "idea" of what ought to be, is confined to the perfecting and extension of advocacy procedures and the enforcement of established rules. In fact, ideology is expressed through the decisions and interpretations of the judges in the exercise of their authority, and the law itself is a variable in the pressures and maneuvers of those who participate in composite choice.

Authoritative and Composite Choice in the American State

Authoritative choice must be independent and isolated. Inasmuch as nominal authority interacts with and is responsive to the pressures, interests, preferences of those upon whom it exercises authority, it becomes to that degree an element of the composite, with the weaknesses and strengths thereof. And in actual organizational choice there is always some such interaction. Authority is never pure. So, too, in such systems as we might designate as composite, there will always be elements and instances of the authoritative. Our generalizations concerning authoritative and composite choice like all such generalizations, simplify and exclude. We suppose them to be useful nevertheless in explaining policy and choice in the organizational context. In their terms we will survey the development of function and policy in the American State.

Inasmuch as we have correctly understood the nature of authoritative and of composite choice and have properly designated the Supreme Court as characterized by the former and the Congress and the Executive Agencies of the American State by the latter, this can be deduced: that during such periods of history when there exists a strong and prevailing ideological commitment and where that blueprint is not yet realized in the structure of institutions or in organizational arrangements and practice, and when at the same time there is no disequilibrium in the balance of established interests; then the Congress and the Executive Branch, bound into that equilibrium of interests, will remain inert, a force for the status, resistant to the disturbances of change, whereas the Supreme Court, agency of authoritative choice that can speak and act only by reference to the ideological blueprint, will spearhead the transformation of institutions towards the achievement of ideological goals. For the realization of ideology, look to authoritative choice.

But when existing institutions, established policies, and organizational practice are all in harmony with and express a prevailing ideology and yet when untoward social drift and rapid circumstantial change opens wide a gap between ideology and experienced encounter? And when as a consequence of that, policies fail, expectations are not met, problems proliferate? Then Congress and the Executive agencies of composite choice will sputter and explode in responses to felt miseries and rising frustrations, reacting to problems and realities outside the reach of accepted belief and established outlook, producing pragmatic, ad hoc change. The Supreme Court, its authority rooted in the prevailing ideology, will resist such change as contrary to reason and contrary to belief, constituting itself as a bulwark of the status quo.

This is an argument that must run counter to the grain of judicial self-conception. Lawyers and judges see themselves as applying laws which they did not make but that are given to them, with the supreme law of the Constitution beyond juridical discretion. But still, when the judge interprets the grand phrases of the Constitution, he supposes those words to reflect a sound reasoning and a rational intent, which is to say a reasoning that he in his time would consider as sound and an intent he would deem rational. He takes the words to mean what they must mean if they are to make good sense (to him, in his day). And when he knows that his judgment will deeply affect his society, inasmuch as he can, he will render judgment by reference to what he thinks best for his society. In all of these ways, for all of these reasons, the Court's choices will reflect an ideology that prevails.

The Development of a National State

The development of the American State falls into three critical periods. The first begins with the War of Independence and ends with the Civil War. For that period, the overriding issue was whether the excolonies could make it as a nation, exercising a single sovereign power through the Federal State. This struggle to achieve an American nationhood parallels that which had already occurred in France and Great Britain, and would come about later in Germany and in Italy. For decentralization, for dispersion, for fragmentation, were the forces of tradition, of loyalty and allegiance to the excolonies and their existing and effective governing institutions, and the cultural differences, religious differences, differences in the forms of economic organization and in economic concerns that separated them, and all the powerful interests vested in those established excolonial structures of power: precisely the array of centrifugal forces that stood and would stand against the struggle for sovereign nationhood elsewhere. In each case the centripetal force for sovereign nationhood was simply an idea and its promises.

The sense of an American "weness," the commitment to American nationhood, aroused and writ in blood in the War of Independence, was dimmed by the defeat and departure of the Other across the great ocean. The future of the institutions and political arrangements which would integrate or separate the former colonies was left to improvised instruments of composite choice, to *conventions,* with representatives from the separate states. Successive conventions produced first the Articles of Confederation, and then, jogged by failure and crisis, the Constitution of the United States. Both documents were intended to permit only the minimum surrender of the sovereign power vested in the separate states. Thus the field was prepared for the critical confrontation in a struggle for the national state. On the one side, the array of traditional loyalties and allegiances, of habitual practice, of effective and responsive instrumentalities of established governance, cultural, religious, economic differences and the whole complex of vested interests, and on the other the ideological commitment to sovereign nationhood. At once the Supreme Court abrogated to itself the authority to rule on the distribution of power as between the federal government and that of the separate states,[3] and in a series of critical decisions[4] turned topsy turvy the compromises arrived at in the constitutional convention, spearheading the creation of a sovereign nation state. The new born Court could do this only because, whatever had been produced out of interacting interests in the processes of composite choice, an ideological commitment to American nationhood did prevail and the revolutionary decisions of the Court spoke to that commitment. The issue would be ultimately settled of course, and the great depth of the nationalist commitment as well as the power of the interests it had to overcome, would be demonstrated on the battlefields of a terrible Civil War. During this first period when ideological design, confronting the array of established interests was as yet unrealized in the power structure of the political system, the Supreme Court as the agency of authoritative choice spearheaded change while composite choice in the other branches of government remained inert.

Industrialization and Ideological Lag

The second critical phase in the development of the American State occurred between the end of the Civil War and the Great Depression of the 1930s. The threshold of nationalism was passed; the nation state established. Ideological liberalism was the unchallenged blueprint for social and economic organization. Established institutions and the internal structure of the political system conformed well and truly to that blueprint, with political power constrained by its laisser faire imperative. It was during this period that American society and the American economy were industrialized, urbanized, with that rapid and fundamental transformation creating a great and unbridgeable gap between the universe of encountered reality and the imageries of ideological liberalism. The new conditions of industrialization and urbanization produced loci of desperation, times of deep distress, dreadful victimizations, enormous wealth, incredible inequalities, vast corporate agglomorations that displaced the competitive, price-directed markets of another day, and the catastrophes called depressions. All of this was beyond the conceptual grasp of the ideas and imageries of ideological liberalism.

Whether or not comprehensible in the format of ideological liberalism, whether or not explicable in its terms, the distress, the outcry, the desperation, the outrage had political impact; politicians could not remain indifferent to the voting force of the disemployed, the impoverished, and the victimized. Crisis and breakdown had repercussions, produced responses. The legislative and executive agencies of composite choice responded with real, though no doubt sputtering, ad hoc and directionless efforts to protect and ameliorate, with such measures undertaken never as contradictions of, but only as exceptions to the laisser faire rule of ideological liberalism. Throughout the period, for more than half a century, the Supreme Court, bastion of an established, prevailing ideology, enforced the rule, striking down nearly every intervention, preventing any significant action by the State to ameliorate the

---

[3]*Marbury v Madison* 5 U.S. 137 (1803)
[4]Especially *McCulloch v Maryland* 17 U.S. 316 (1819) and *Gibbon v Ogden* 22 U.S. 1 (1824)

miseries or to deal with the crises of an industrialized economy or to countervail against the powers of property,[5] with this single exception. Within a tightly bound area the state was permitted antitrust prosecution of monopolies and conspiracies "in restraint of trade," and, in the absence of competion it was allowed a very limited right to regulate pricing by monopolies considered "natural," hence inescapable. In what it allowed, as in all that is disallowed, the Court was acting in strict accord with ideological liberalism. That it could so impose those idealogical precepts as constitutional law required that his ideology was, in fact, prevailing.

Thus in this second period of the development of the American State, when industrialization drove a wedge between encountered reality and prevailing ideology, the position of the Court is reversed. Whereas before the Court, bearing the banner of the still unrealized nationalist aspiration, spearheaded reform and transformation, while the agencies of composite choice stood pat; in this period the Court, its rule rooted in an ideology that is realized in organization and in practice, becomes the bulwark of the status quo. It resisted and aborted the occasional, ad hoc yet persisting efforts of Congress and the Executive, agencies of composite choice kicked into action by misery and crises, to protect the victimized and ameliorate their miseries.

Across the Threshold

The 1930s saw another threshold crossed in the development of the American State, onto our own time of fundamental and unfinished transformation. The Great Depression, broke the grip of ideological liberalism on American thought and policy. For governments throughout the Western world in these days of disaster, it was sink or swim. Some sank. Others thrashed about without direction, without design, ignoring the nay saying of their sages, doing what had to be done to stay afloat.

In the United States, the Congress and the Executive in the Administration of Franklin Roosevelt, exploded in a multidirectional, stumbling onrush of responsive actions, without any coherent ideological design, but energetic, pragmatic, and necessary. In the first instance the Supreme Court, citadel of ideological liberalism, declared constitutional anathema on the entire New Deal program,[6] throwing it out kit and kaboodle. But no longer was the ideological underpinning of the Court's decision acceptable to those upon whose support the Court's authority depended. Its independence, its autonomy was threatened and was almost lost. Nor were the justices of the Court blind to the events of the day, to the absolute failure of liberalist policy and libertarian expectation, to the mortal peril and enormous suffering that could be confronted only through the powers of the state, but never by a state held in the harness of laisser faire liberalism. Perforce, between 1934 and 1942, in a series

---

[5]*See* for example (with respect to child labor) *Hammer v Dagenhart* 247 U.S. 251 (1918) and *J. W. Bailey v. Drexel Furniture Co.,* 259 U.S. 20 (1922); (with respect to the states' power to ameliorate working conditions) *Lochner v New York* 198 U.S. 45 (1905), *Bunting v Oregon* 243 U.S. 426 (1917) *Adkins v Children's Hospital* 261 U.S. 525 (1923) *Morehead v New York ex rel Tipaldo,* 298 U.S. 587 (1936) (with respect to limits upon the power of regulation) *Lemke v Farmers' Grain* Co., 258 U.S. 50 (1922), *Ribnick v McBride* 277 U.S. 350 (1928).

[6]*Schechter Poultry Co., v U.S.* 295 U.S. 495 (1935); *Carter v Carter Coal Company* 298 U.S. 238 (1936).

of the most dramatic reversals in its history the Court abandoned the citadel of ideological liberalism.[7]

The instruments of composite choice could and did transmit and project into law and action, the impulses deriving from the whole crisis-torn social system, without the intermediary of an ideological concensus and without the need for ideological transformation. Not so for the Supreme Court. Once the justices abandoned the old citadel they had to find another ideological base. They could not face their task and formulate their choices and write opinions justifying their decisions so that the rational implications of what they decided today could stand up as a viable guide to behavior tomorrow, without a coherent idea of what is and ought to be over the whole range of their responsibilities. They needed an ideology, a new outlook appropriate to the time. And so perforce this agency of authoritative choice has become again the spearhead in articulating and implementing a new ideological basis for social policy, in the direction of a positive and responsible state. If the record of the Court in this period of ideological and institutional transformation, demonstrates the values and the strength of a form of authoritative choice at once autonomous and yet systematically answerable to the society that it serves, it also demonstrates something of the inherent fallibility of that or any form of choice operating from ideological imperatives. Ideology simplifies, excludes, and much of reality will escape its net. Thus we must credit the Court with destroying racial barriers and driving towards the goal of a racially integrated society, as the instrumentalities of composite choice never could. But, is there evidence that the Court has taken, or can take into account and respond to the actual impact of its directives on the character and quality of the educational system or on the complex realities of racial relationships and of social organization and order?

It is curious to contemplate the prospects or the process of ideological transformation in this time of vast systemic complexity. With thought fragmented into narrow, specialized grooves, one may wonder from whence, or whether a new, integral and, encompassing outlook can arrive. Old ideologies displaced from the seat of power never seem to die. They sink back into deeper, more obscure layers of consciousness, awaiting recrudescence. They withdrew into enclaves, small and large, temples where their celebratory rites continue, their priests prepare and their partisans await the moment of return. Though pushed for awhile from center stage, ideological liberalism has never been lost from sight. It never ceased to be celebrated in corporate boardrooms, nor taught, elaborated and perpetuated in the ivied halls of academe, nor to motivate and guide the antitrust agencies. The New Deal itself was not intended as an assault on ideological liberalism or upon the ingrained imageries of the World of Man. On the contrary, in its Keynesian incarnation it was put forward as the savior of the competitive market and free enterprise capitalism.

[7]*Nebbia v New York* 291 U.S. 502 (1934); *Townsend v Yoemans* 301 U.S. 441, (1937); *Currin v Wallace* 306 U.S. 1 (1939); *Mulford v Smith* 307 U.S. 38 (1939); *U.S. v Rock Royal Cooperative* 307 U.S. 533 (1939); *Sunshine Anthracite Coal Co., v Adkins,* 310 U.S. 318 (1940) *R. R. Commission v Rowan and Nichols Oil Co.,* 310 U.S. 573 (1940); *NLRB v Jones & Laughlin Steel Corp.,* 301 U.S. 1 (1937); *NLRB v Freuhauf Trailer Co.,* 301 U.S. 58 (1937); *NLRB v Friedman-Harry Marx Clothing Co.,* 391 U.S. 58 (1937); *Steward Machine Co., v Davis* 301 U.S. 548 (1937); *Helvering v Davis* 301 U.S. 619 (1937); *Wickard v Filburn* 317 U.S. 111 (1942).

Never mind that these old imageries remained; there were critical shifts in outlook, changes in habitual expectation, and an infiltration of value elements into the prevailing mode of thought. The poor were no longer considered (entirely) to blame for their poverty. Unemployment was not (wholly) explicable as due to sloth, or as a "preference" for leisure. The state was held to be responsible for the condition of the economy, for the level of employment, for the stability of price, for the advance of productivity, for the rate of growth, for inequities and injustices in the distribution of income, for the condition of the environment, even for the quality of life.

In spite of these expectations, implying responsibilities that only a powerful and positive state could meet, in the United States at least the habitual and contemptuous denigration of the state and its "bureaucracy" and all its works, continues. The old utopian dream of the golden city in the World of Man did not die.

Keynesian Revolution and the Welfare State

It is with all this that we associate the Keynesian revolution. How revolutionary was that revolution? This much can be said. It was the first grand theory in economics not built up from individualized choice in competitive exchange. The individual self-seeker is without a place in it. It is a theory of systems, and a first departure from the imageries of the world of man.

Neither Keynes nor the Keynesians proposed or developed new policy, nor did they design and install new techniques for implementing established ones. Their achievement was of another order. They rationalized pragmatic actions undertaken by the state under the dictate of necessity, so that economists could accept and participate in the systematic inflation of a collapsed level of aggregate demand without abandoning their vision of individualized choice and price directed markets. Keynes allowed them to suppose that in the bowels of the economy, in the details of production and consumption, in all the interrelations and interactions that constitute the web and woof of economic realities, nothing is changed. All that needed no correction. The old verities prevailed. In allocating resources, in organizing production, distributing income traditional theory remained for them the living image of reality. Keynes asked the economists only to draw back, to see the economy from another perspective, from a distance taken as a whole, as an econosphere floating, so to speak, like a balloon adrift in currents of aggregate spending. Depending upon the pressure of those expenditures the balloon would rise up to the stratosphere of inflation or be sucked down into the slough of depression. Thus the state was assigned its task; by manipulating fiscal and monetary levers to maintain the pressure of aggregate spending at precisely the level where the econosphere would float with employment full and prices unchanging. Supposedly it all could be done, it all would be done from *outside* the econosphere. There was no need for the state to disturb the relationships within, no need for the state to control business entities, no need for the state to regulate economic activities, no need for the state to manage and plan and be concerned with the specifics of technology and organization. Within the econosphere all that would spontaneously be optimized in accord with established verities under the beneficent control of the invisible hand. Within the econosphere —in the domain of microeconomics—all was as before.

This outlook was not particular to economics and economic policy. That it all could be done on the outside with no need for the state to control, to regulate, to restructure, to manage, to plan the relationships within, nor to change the system itself characterized the whole new landscape of thought. All that had to be done could be done, illfare dealt with, and the range of social problems resolved by simple offsets, transfers and grants, fiscal and monetary manipulations, subsidies and tax incentives, and an occasional change in the parameters of private choice and in the rules of the competitive game. The interior relations of the sociosphere as the econosphere could remain unsullied by bureaucratic intervention. That was the ideological blueprint made manifest in the Welfare State.

No need to denigrate the Welfare State, and the Keynesian interlude. They provided the Western world with a period of growth and prosperity and the compassionate amelioration of some of the insecurities that afflict industrial society. But now they have come to the end of the line. They no longer suffice for the tasks at hand. They cannot in their own terms comprehend the great problems that confront us. And to this confrontation with problems and phenomena outside the ken of established competencies and habituated conceptualization, there has been this same twofold response, alienation or anger without issue, alternating with a resurgence of the old orthodoxies, a fervent reembrace of ancient verities, a search for roots, for stability, for coherence, for order in the comfort of familiar values and resurrected theories. With time dimming the memory of its catastrophic failures, ideological liberalism is back in the saddle. Travail and disillusion will surely be our portion before we regain our path into the future. The path that we will take or, rather, that, after failures, bitterness, and turmoil, the path along which we will of necessity be driven is in part prefigured in cause and consequence of the Keynesian demise on the thickets of stagflation.

Keynesian Demise and the Positive State

Keynes succeeded, Keynesian thought was welcomed because it enabled the economist to think that he could have his cake and eat it; that no matter what external manipulations were needed, internally the econosphere would work according to the neoclassical book, with the optimizing magic of competitive markets intact. This is a falsehood. Between the imperatives of Keynsian thought and the requisites of liberal (neoclassical) theory, there has always been an absolute and fundamental contradiction. They cannot both be true. That the contradiction remained for so long covert is a monument to the colossal power of disciplinary self-deception. Evidently the shielded illusion, the unfaced falsehood always comes home to roost; individual and society alike pay a price for self-deception. Today we are paying the price.

The (microeconomic) theory that allegedly explains the inner workings of the econosphere absolutely requires and turns upon the axis of free moving price. The Keynesian system absolutely requires and will not work without inflexible, fixed, rigid prices. Beyond the blind eye that it turned to this fundamental contradiction, the Keynesians avoided the logical implications of their own assumption. If, as indeed was the case in the Great Depression, prices and wages were fixed and inflexible, that must mean that prices and wages were controlled as a function of trade union wage and corporate price policy. Since prices and wages were unaffected by the most catastrophic decline in aggregate demand ever recorded, the power of these autonomous organizations to determine prices and wages must be beyond the reach and outside the control of any public management of aggregate demand. Hence prices and wages, determined as they are through the political-cum-sociological processes of organizational policy formation, can only be understood and must be explained by reference to those processes. One self-evident truth about such organizational policy is this: it can change. Organizations can learn. Over the years corporate and trade union organizations have learned; and their policies, reflecting expectations of continual income advance and economic betterment, have changed with prices raised and wages raised, year in, year out, irrespective of the level of demand, the level of unemployment, marginal costs and excess capacity. That is the saga of stagflation. The crux of it is the *arbitrary* power of the great modern corporate organization and trade union; arbitrary in the sense that neither is it held to the straight and narrow by competitive market forces on the one hand, nor by any systematic answerability to the larger society that feels its impact on the other: an arbitrary power exercised far more than control of prices and wages.

What if this arbitrary policymaking power is used as it has been used in the matter of wages and prices in a manner detrimental to the interests of society at large? It is a power that, as we have seen, cannot be controlled by fiscal monetary manipulations external to the econosphere, designed to control the level of aggregate demand. It is a power that cannot be destroyed without destroying the technological hub of the modern economy. What then?

There is simply no way of reaching that arbitrary power of great modern business and labor organizations, no way of assuring that their policies will roughly conform to the public's interests, save through some form of participation by agencies of the state in the formation of those policies.

We will in time arrive at a system of wage and price control. Indeed no recent presidential administration whatever its ideological commitment, no matter its declared abhorrence of the very thought of such control, has managed to avoid some form of acquiescence to the pressures of necessity. Eventually, after more failure, more travail, because there is no other option, because there is nowhere else to go, there will evolve a viable system of public participation in the process of wage/price policy formation. The experience of failure is driving us, and will continue to drive us beyond the region where goals are sought through simple welfare transfers and gross fiscal and monetary offsets, into the realm of the positive state. This in turn requires fundamental structural and ideological transformation. Consider the competence, entirely absent now, that must be built into the political system as prerequisite to viable, coparticipatory planning and the formation of policies affecting industrial organization and technology and the allocation of resources, and (more difficult to achieve) the ideological consensus that would be required of the people, for the electorate to accept with tranquility a given distribution of income and wealth (via the determination of prices and wages) when this becomes a function of collective policy rather than of random chance and the play of autonomous forces. It is not only stagflation (and recessflation) that carries us towards of participatory planning.

In each of its great responsibilities, to stem the incredible, even absolute decline in American industrial productivity and, through advancing technology, to accelerate economic growth, to deal with a chemical revolution come home to roost with its poisons upseeping through the earth, with air and the waters even the life-enabling biosphere threatened, to dissolve the hard-backed, parasitical, crime-ridden poverty enclave that grows like a cancer, to resolve the crisis of bankrupted, corrupted, burned out cities and the condition of spatial disorder, to maintain and develop the critical, sometimes collapsing systems of the infrastructure, of health care, of transportation and especially now, in the face of resource closure (the once bottomless well is running dry) of energy, the American State is driven in that same direction.

In the United States as in every advanced industrial society, there is already an enormous public sector, the locus of the world's most advanced technologies, where choice, and where planning and programming are entirely a function of the state. At least at the federal level in the United States, this sector was developed almost entirely as the consequence of the nature of post-World War II weaponry and of that other accounterment of cold war, competitive space exploration. The new weaponry and space exploration required a base in academic science and a vast R&D establishment and production capabilities developing in entirely different directions than might arise spontaneously in civilian industrial markets. Civilian-industrial preeminence ceased to be, as once it had been, transformable into military prowess.

The activities of this sector, fueled by the passions of patriotism, veiled by the xenophobic imperatives of security, operates outside the zone of rational choice and public scrutiny. It relies upon, and is dominated by corporations that are public agencies in effect but without public answerability and accountability. It has absorbed the bulk of the nation's science-trained, research brainpower and thereby drained the civilian-industrial side of an ingredient essential in the process of technological advance and real growth. To control, to manage, to hold accountable, to operate efficiently, to accelerate the advance of technology, to capitalize upon the potentialities and to realize upon the values of these and other activities within the public sector, must certainly require the positive development of the positive state.

Underlying such change in the character of the state is a fundamental transformation, from the world of man, to a universe of systems. Those systems are of a complexity and vastness beyond the compass of those who occupy their niches, powerful and rudderless, driving into the future with a enomous inertial force. In this universe of systems, there is only one that is, or can be made specifically answerable for consequences and effects, that can be made to answer for the configuration of the whole. And that is the state, locus of the sovereign power. Yet this state (in America at least) perforce positive, is only dragged by necessity, pulled kicking and screaming by the seat of its pants, to perform tasks of great responsibility and infinite complexity, for which it is perpetually unprepared and unequipped. It is without the competencies it requires. It is without (and we are without) a conceptual frame that can encompass and comprehend the phenomena with which it must deal. It lacks (and we lack) an ideological map with which to chart its (and our) voyage through dark and dangerous waters.

NATIONALIST STATE, LIBERAL STATE, POSITIVE STATE, GLOBAL STATE

We propose in this chapter to integrate, generalize upon, and further develop arguments made in the preceding chapters. Let us recall that earlier:

Ideology was defined as a (coherent) set of ideas as to what is and what ought to be with respect to some field of choice and action.

A *group* was understood as a community of ideological commitment, sharing ideas of what is and ought to be with respect to some field of choice and action.

The *nation* is such a community, delineated and given coherence by a set of shared ideas. There is a "nation" only when and inasmuch as individuals share a common ideology—an ideology of the genus *nationalism*. What is the character of nationalism? And of the various nationalisms? To what field of choice and action do they relate?

What is the nature of this ideological commitment that forms the nation? What is it that determines the weness of nationhood? When is the collectivity a nation rather than a grouping of another sort? What determines the Frenchness of France, and what causes that Frenchness to dissolve into the domains of Breton, Provenciale, Norman, Savoyard, Alsatian, or causes it to be swallowed up into a viable European Community? What determines the Canadianness of Canada, and can cause it to dissolve into the domain of Quebecoise and other fragments? What has determined the Americanness of America, and what once dissolved it into the Virginianess, Carolinaness, Georgianess of the Confederacy? What makes the nation?

The nation is not an association organized for and finding its coherence in the expectation of mutual gain like a corporate enterprise is. It is not a community of belief shared in some supermundane reality like a church is. It is not held together by ties of blood, like a tribe is, nor by a network of established allegiances like the feudal entities were. The nation is a body of those who hold together because they feel themselves alike. It is a communality of resemblance. The nation projects an image in which each loyal son and daughter sees him/herself mirrored. Nationalism is, therefore, a kind of self-glorification. Patriotism is a species of self-love. That dedication which solidifies the nation is a self-dedication, or at least a dedication to an idea of the self.

Nationalism conceives its universe as a set of distinct entities, of nations, each a generational continuum of those who feel themselves alike, bound together by sensed affinities; each closed and sovereign, threatening and threatened. Such is the landscape of nationalism.

This social grouping we call the nation is a recent arrival on the scene of history. It establishes itself as a basis for political association only in the Fourteenth Century; coincidental with that transformation of thought that, departing from the region of traditional allegiances, of faith and authority, asserted the absolute primacy of the individual, conceiving the single, isolable one as beginning-and-end-all, monad of social reality, entering upon what we have called the world of man. As a form of political association, the nation belongs to the world of man. Given the rational, the self-seeking, the entirely autonomous individual, in a universe of such autonomous self-seekers, what other form of political association would be feasible except between those who come together because they hold themselves alike, so that the group is a projection of the self, and each sees self mirrored in the image of the nation. Given the apotheosis of self-interest, given that responsibility, purpose and value begins and ends with self, alikeness must be of a very great worth, and the swollen and immortalized superego projected in the nation becomes a proper object for dedication. The nation is to be found in the love of that which is like myself, wherein my very own qualities are projected, where I find myself reflected, and immortalized, fusing egoes into a superegoism that admits no rule and no right beyond its own.

Not brother, not twins, not anyone born on this earth has ever been exactly like any other. Alikeness is never absolute. It is always relative to that which differentiates us from the Other. We are alike only in contrast to the Other. We know our kinship in that which sets us apart from the Other. It is from the Other that we learn of our alikeness. The presence of the Other sharpens that awareness. It is above all the threat of the Other that unites the community of resemblance and solidifies the nation. It is in the Other that the nation discovers itself and in the Other that nationalism finds its object. Otherness is inseparable from weness.

This sense of alikeness in nationhood has been a powerful mobilizer of energies, of a force and character that was largely determined by the force and character of the Other—as threat, as oppressor, as conqueror, as prey, as victim. It was the invasions of Italy by the Spanish and by the French that roused Machiavelli's yearning for nationhood. When the armies of Napoleon conquered Europe, they displaced archaic institutions and the yoke of ancient privilege, and introduced a new level of enlightenment, of liberty, of law. And yet everywhere they went they sowed the seeds of nationalisms that would be turned against them. By their power, by their presence, by the juxtaposition of their difference, they aroused an awareness of alikeness that had not before been sensed or harnessed as an energizing force and a basis for political association.

We have spoken of the nation as a group, united by an idea of alikeness. In what ways alike? It is a community of sensed affinities. What sort of affinities? Erich Kahler specifies the shared "stock of instinctive memories which we call tradition," "a special folk character, . . . a homogeneous way of life," "special customs, institutions, and cultural forms evolving from the interaction of specific popular stocks and the specific nature of a country."[1] And yet nationalism does not need such "popular stocks" nor the "instinctive memories" called "tradition." None of these, indeed, can explain the sense of American nationhood, which, rather than from a sense of common rootedness, derived from the experience of a shared uprootedness.

In sum those affinities can be anything, or nothing. They can be bogus. The sense of the difference that separates us from the Other can be bogus, trumped up, delusory, systematically cultivated. Whether or not those affinities are false or real, what must be real for the viable existence of the group we call a nation, is the feeling of affinity. So long as there is an idea of alikeness (and of difference), of weness and theyness that can suffice to create, to delineate, to cohere, to solidify the nation.

Nationalism

Need this felt affinity be coupled to an ideological commitment? Must it become the basis for vectored action and political prescription? Certainly not. One can sense affinities without becoming a nationalist. Sensed affinities can be no more than a source of psychic satisfaction, (or disatisfaction), of self-revelation (or self-disgust), providing the basis for ease of (or unease in) discourse—that, and nothing more. One can accept the existence of the nation, of "my" nation and of the nations as fact, without ideological commitment. To be a nationalist means more than that.

An image of a universe of nations, where each is a generational continuum of felt affinities, where each is closed and self-seeking, and all perpetually are poised for confrontation, is the *what is* of nationalism; its underlying idea of how things are. *Qua* hypothesis that image can be tested through observation and experience and accepted as well by those who are not committed to nationhood. Nationalism implies a commitment to an idea of what *ought to be.* Nationalisms have their moral content; moral, not in the sense of what is good, but of what, be it good or evil, is valued. For the individual, for sets of individuals, for the norms of nations, the value commitment and moral meaning of nationalism will range over the pathologies of hatred, all the macho postures, and the varieties of love as well. There was Abe Lincoln's deep and abiding nationalism, and there was Hitler's.

As obsession, as barbaric cult, as the prototype of the malignancy to which the ideology of nationalism is everywhere prone, consider the moral content of National-Socialism in Germany in the regime of Adolph Hitler. The felt affinities of the

---

[1]Erich Kahler, *Man the Measure* (New York: Meridian Books, 1967), p. 339.

German nation were deified as Blood and Soil, setting a mark upon those entitled to enter the sacred circle, and excluding all others. An abominable program of racial purification had as its objective to purge out every taint of Otherness. Before the projected Nordic-Aryan self-image, ecstasies of self-worship were performed. Thus:

> Now he stands before us (wrote Professor Adam of Tubingen) he whom the voices of our poets and sages have summoned, the liberator of the German genius. He has removed the blindfold from our eyes, and through all political, economic and social and confessional covers has enabled us to see and love again the one essential thing—our unity of blood, our German self, the *homo germanus*. [2]

This German nation turned with awful fury upon a small population, marked out as the Other, that had by historical happenstance been dwelling for a thousand years in its midst.

> Just as primitive man's concept of God presupposed the existence of the Devil, so the German's progressive self-deification during the Third Reich depended upon the demonization of the Jew. The white outline of the German's image of themselves —in terms of character no less than color—acquired definition only via the moral and physical darkness of its Jewish antitype. Metaphysically as well as materially, the roots of German heaven were deeply embedded in the Jewish hell. [3]

With all their variations, the nationalisms that have come and have gone, from the Fourteenth Century until today, have shared at least these values.

All have asserted that the interest of the nation is above all other interests. They have demanded the subordination of all other groups to that group. There are reasons in history for this absolute imperative and this total demand. The threat of the Other was, or might be a total threat, a threat to survival; and survival took precedence over all other interests and considerations.

And all modern nationalisms have aspired to a political domain operating autonomously, accepting no command, no rules, subordinated to no interest other than its own; and, within that domain, imposing one law, providing one coin of the realm, assuring an integral and uninterruptable zone of intercourse.

The Nation State

The nation is united by the commitment to an ideology that asserts its right *qua* group, to collective autonomy and to a political domain where its power is ultimate, where its rules are final. Nationalism demands sovereign power for the nation. And the nations, formed as the possessors of and sole claimants to sovereign power, exercised that power through the state.

It must be reiterated, Nation and State are not the same. The state, as we have shown, is the instrumentality of sovereign power, those agencies and processes

---

[2]Richard Grunberger, *A Social History of the Third Reich* (New York: Holt, Rinehart & Winston), p. 439.

[3]*Ibid.*

related in the exercise of an ultimate temporal authority. The nation need not be sovereign. The sovereignty exercised through the state, need not belong to the nation. The nation can exist without nationalism, as the Jews did through centuries of the diaspora. A nation of nationalists yearning for but without autonomy, can exist without a state, as the Poles did during the times of partition. And, for millenia, sovereign power has been exercised by emperors and kings, by tribal elders, by chieftains, by war councils, by high priests, by popes and cardinals, unrooted in any nationalist commitment. In the course of modern history, nevertheless, those generational continuua bound by a felt affinity called nations have emerged as the key entities of the world polity exercising sovereign power through an institutional complex called the state—hence, our universe of Nation-States.

The modern state, in the exercise of its sovereign power, has come to perform numerous, important social tasks, and indeed some instrument of sovereign power is indispensable in the performance of those tasks, and for the fulfillment of responsibilities that have nothing to do with the relationships of nation to nation or the commitment to nationhood. Even though the community, bound by sensed affinities and committed to nationhood, should disappear, the modern state, or its proxy, *qua* process of collective choice, *qua* locus of residual responsibilities, *qua* sovereign power, would still be necessary, would still be valued, would still be supported, and would continue to exist. Thus the nation, as an historic and habituated boundary of convenience, can continue to exist for the sake of the state, rather than the state for the nation.

Nor is it clear in today's universe of nation-states, whether or how far the commitment to nationhood remains as the cohering and energizing force of that which is called the nation. Nor is it certain when and where the state, as nominal instrumentality of a nation, requires or reflects a national commitment. Those tribal conglomerations, created in Africa in the wake of imperial rule, are hardly nations bound by the inner bonds of felt affinity. They nevertheless operate within, and require a state endowed with sovereign power. The ideological underpinning of the sovereign power in Eastern Europe and Soviet Russia, be it nationalism or communism, is equivocal and in transition. Nor does the commitment to nationhood in Western Europe and the United States have its former fervor and force. But if the nation diminishes, the state increases in its functions and responsibilities.

The state is the locus of an enormous latent power; and it is an instrument that can serve any set of purposes. What will determine then the purposes served by the state?

Self-interested individuals, of course, will always seek to manipulate its machinery for the sake of personal advantage. And certainly, what the state does or fails to do will reflect a mass of petty, self-interested manipulations, coalitions, trades and arrangements. Especially in a time of ideological bankruptcy, of failure of collective aspiration and of the end of large hope, there may be nothing else but the flux and play of those interests to energize the instrumentalities of the state.

The state also serves the purpose of the groups that participate in its processes of choice. The "nation" defined and united by the nationalist ideology is one such group. There are many others, coextensive with, or fragmented within, or conflictual within, or transcending the nation. Every one of these groups is a community of ideological commitment; and when ideologies change, the purposes of the state will be changed. And when the weight of the groups in the process of choice is changed, the purposes of the state will change. And with its purposes, its structure.

The state, as a complex set of agencies and institutions, is to a degree autonomous. It is itself an actor in the process of social choice. There are interests particular to the state, and ideologies built into the core of some of its agencies.

Nationalism and the State

In sum these attributes of nationalism constitute the root and focus of the national state.

1. All nationalisms are based on a sense of affinity between individuals, on an idea of alikeness, on the projection of a shared self-image. All nationalisms are a species of collective egoism, and, as is congruent with the swollen and unfettered ego, the nation as a group will accept of its own volition no rule, no law, no authority beyond its own. It would be as it calls itself, sovereign.

2. All nationalisms emerge, and the ideology of nationhood takes form in relation to an idea of the Other. Those who identify with the nation find their alikness in what differentiates them from the Other. And, as a collective existence, the nation derives its character, finds its energy and solidarity, its purpose and meaning in the response to the Other. That engagement with the Other which most encompasses, absorbs, and solidifies commitments to the nation, is that of war. It is in war, or in the threat, prospect, or possibility of war that the absolute sovereignity of the nation is rooted.[4] The state in the first instance is the means of making manifest an ideology of nationhood.

Outer and Inner

The ideologies of nationalism vector to the outside only; as an outlook on things, it must be insisted, nationalism turns entirely on dealings with the other, the foreigner, the alien. So far as internal relationships are concerned, with respect to the institutions, organizations, goals, and policies as these might prevail domestically, nationalism has nothing to say. It provides no basis for such choice except and only inasmuch as internal relationships might or must be controlled and organized for external objectives in the strategies of war and power.

One cannot explain by reference to nationalism, the character of organization and control *within* the nation. Such choice must have a different ideological reference. The collectively chosen internal order will reflect some other, additional ideological commitment of a group or groups, coexisting with, and encompassed by the nation.

Just so, the nationalist can also be a socialist, or a communist, or a feudal monarchist, or a liberal democrat. Whatever might be the ideology that dominates

---

[4]Max Weber, *Economy and Society* (New York: Bedminster Press, 1968). For a different but important conceptualization of the nation, see pp. 385–398.

and determines *domestic* policy and the formation or relationships *within* the society delineated by the boundaries of nationhood; that ideology impacts upon and operates through the instrumentalities of the state.

Why not? The state, once established, as the sovereign instrument of collective choice and action will be useful and necessarily will be used to obtain the intranational purposes of whatever group or group can command or influence its decision processes. And, in the world of autonomous man, from the Renaissance to the threshold of the first world war, it has been *ideological liberalism* that progressively came to dominate and give shape to the *internal* policies of the state. The modern state was formed under the dual impulsion of an other-directed nationalism, and an inner-directed liberalism.

There have been thus two faces to the modern state, or two states have coexisted, the one that expressed the idea of nationhood, and the other that operated under the imperatives of liberalism. Compare the pure and total nationalist state with its liberal counterpart.

The Nationalist State

The pure nationalist state expresses the idea of a people who know that they are one and indissoluble, instinctively bound together, recognizing their alikeness in their difference from the Other, and with a national spirit that gives to each a pride, a significance, a meaning. One people, one land, one law, one coin, one sovereign.

The interest of the nation is the supreme interest, and every national shares a common danger and a common destiny *vis a vis* the Other. In the threatening, uncertain, unstable world of nation states, all who are of the nation must be subordinate to the national interest. To that end all within the national domain must be continuously available, mobilizable, and controllable; or mobilized and controlled for the national purpose. The achievement of this national purpose *vis a vis* the Other must, in the end, depend on the power of the nation to wage war. In war or through the threat of war, in the conquest of or defense against the Other, the nationalist state finds its definitive meaning. The pure nationalist state develops its strengths, organizes all of its resources, directs and controls the energies of all of its people, in a perpetual readiness for, preparation for, or engagement in war. The pure nationalist state is therefore a maximal state that encompasses every private purpose and all the resources of society. A maximal state and as well, a military state; the one and essential professional competence it requires, and upon which it relies, is that of the soldier, and at his side the diplomat-statesman to negotiate for the national advantage from a basis of military power. The virtues proper to the nationalist state are soldierly virtues of obedience, duty, and courage.

The Liberal State

Liberalism envisages a world of private worlds, the social universe conceived as a flat and endless plain, divided as a grid, a vast checkerboard, with each of an infinite number of private spaces reserved for the sovereign volition of the self-interested, self-responsible one, where individuals are free to engage or to disengage in trade or any other form of social intercourse, and the supreme social value is *liberty,* the right of the individual to choose for himself in controlling what is his own; that right preserved through the sanctity of property. For in property, the power of choice is individualized and a space for individual autonomy is preserved. Such are the imperatives of ideological liberalism.

What kind of state would be shaped under those imperatives? Almost exactly opposite to the nationalist prototype. There would be no overriding national interests, only individual interests. There is no national spirit, only individual spirits, only individual feelings and volitions. Happiness, satisfaction, fulfillment must be sought for and can be only obtained by the individual in his own way, by reference to his own preferences, needs, and potentialities. The social well-being is simply the sum of individual satisfactions, and the social purpose is no more than the aggregation of individual purposes. Hence the liberal state has no purpose and no value other than to facilitate and protect the individual pursuit of personal values and of private ends. The liberal state is a minimal state, subordinated to and intended only to protect and to facilitate the individual pursuit of private purposes and personal values. To enable and to facilitate that pursuit, the state must protect the security and the property of the individual. It must lay down and enforce rules for the exercise of the property power lest the freedom of one transgresses upon the freedom of another. It must draw boundaries on the rights of property, lest the claims of one trespass on the prerogatives of another, resolving the endless conflicts between ownership and ownership, between claim and claim. It must provide for the interpretation and enforcement of contracts voluntarily entered into by private parties in the matrix of exchange.

All these tasks are juridical. The pure liberal state is a juridical state. It can do without kaisers and kings, without prime ministers or presidents, without parliament or congress, but it cannot do without a judiciary. In the words of the great Blackstone:

> . . . The rights of mankind . . . may be reduced to three principles or primary articles; the right of personal security, the right of personal liberty, and the right of private property; because there is no known method of compulsion or of abridging man's free will but by an infringement or diminution of one or other of these important rights, the preservation of these, inviolate, may justly be said to include the preservation of our civil immunities in their largest and most extensive sense.[5]

For the judicial function—through the work of judges, juries, prosecutors, and defenders, advocates representing interests before the bar, and the police who enforce the rulings of the courts—is essential to the operation of the market economy. The single skill proper to the servant of the liberal state is the skill of the lawyer.

Thus the two—the maximal nationalist state, outer-oriented, command-based, requiring the skills and dominated by the outlook of the soldier; and the minimal

---

[5]Quoted by M. M. Clark, *Social Control of Business* (2d ed.; New York: McGraw-Hill, Inc., 1939), pp. 95–96.

liberal state, inner-oriented, providing the juridical frame for private transactions, requiring the skills and dominated by the outlook of the lawyer.

In the tension between these polar norms, all modern states have been formed; the closer to the one or to the other, depending upon an historic preoccupation with war.

The Nationalist State In Prussia

At one extreme, closest to the nationalist norm, was the Prussian state; for centuries invaded, threatened by invasion, invading, east, west, south, north, on the path of ethnic unification and imperial glory, vectored toward the Other in postures of aggression or defense, continuously preoccupied with war. With its nationalist objectives steady and unceasing, its military and diplomatic strategies were varied and flexible, depending on the flux of circumstance. Accordingly, it operated in response to the whiplash of the central command, geared to the precise transmission of orders and exact, immediate obedience, imposing controls upon and mobilizing the resources within its domain into such complex arrangements as strategy demanded. At the power core was the Reichswehr, self-perpetuating military elite, center of military command. The Prussian State, truly formidable, powerfully efficient, was the first great modern organization. It created a general system of education that produced the first top-to-bottom literate population. It systemically inculcated a range of industrial skills and managed an industrial revolution. It established the science-industrial linkage of R&D. And all of this was for the purposes of war. The Prussian State organized as a command center was dominated by the soldier with the statesman-diplomat at his elbow.[6] And the Prussian culture was shaped in the mold of the soldierly virtues, patriotic obedience, discipline, and duty.

---

[6]According to Erich Kahler (*op. cit.,* pp. 404–404), the Prussian state represents a perfect, gapless functioning, in which everybody is tied to his special job within the whole working process. On the one hand, it corresponds to the scheme of a Lutheran community, on the other, it is the archetype of the total state, not only because it claims control over every sphere of public and private life, but also because its essentially unideological, indeed anti-ideological character. It was devoid of any substantial principle, of any idea of life, of the glory of God or the glory of a nation. Prussia was no nation in her own right, neither did she stand for German nationality and greatness. She was a perfect collective, but a collective that did not derive from the consensus and common will of a people, nor aim at the palpable well-being of a people. Her sole obsession was the dynamic functioning, was the ever-expanding, ever more powerful working process of the collective, the sport of building up power as such, a power that in reality was enjoyed by none, not even by the rulers, that was not meant to be enjoyed but to be followed as a "damn duty," an infinite, chimerical ideal in itself.

This original idea of the state was established and carried out by the Prussian monarchs in its purebred, artificial form. It was like an experimental preparation, a social homunculus, constructed of whatever stock of people was available, provided they proved fit for the task. The original form later swallowed and assimilated other intellectual, economic, and social elements in the course of its expansion over Germany. It fused with the national movement of the wars of liberation against Napoleon, in which Prussia took the lead, and with the romantic and idealistic philosophy of the epoch—in this period, Hegel furnished the first theoretical formula of the state. It fused with the industrial revolution and incorporated the effects of the broad economic developments of the Nineteenth Century. The result was the Reich of Bismark. . . .

The American Liberal State

At the other end of the spectrum, was the American state in a country that was never invaded or threatened by invasion, flanked and protected by two great oceans, and hence, during its formative years, least preoccupied of all nations with war. Not that the American State was without its nationalist phases and facets. Its Revolutionary War was a nationalist uprising asserting an American nationhood, the sense of an American weness against the otherness of what had been the English motherland. The great political issue for the first half century of the republic's existance was as to where the sovereign power would find its locus; a struggle that opposed the centrifugal forces of traditional allegiance, cultural disparity, economic difference, and interests vested in established autonomies against the centripetal force of the nationalist ideology. And among the agencies of the American state, from the beginning there are those that represented and constituted themselves as temples of nationalism—the Departments of State, of Navy, of War, designed and installed following European elitist models. The American service academies at Annapolis and West Point produced an officer class trained to command and obey and inculcated with the soldierly virtues. But these had only a standby role, existing as an enclave apart that never touched the heady course of events and of dynamic change in American affairs, at least until the threshold of the two world wars.

The American civil state was a lawyer's state. The judiciary exercised a power without precedent in history. The Supreme Court, oracle of a written constitution, in interpreting the fundamental law, formulated basic policy. In Congress and the executive branch, lawyers governed. Congress and the civil departments of the executive were themselves juridical in character, functioning as advocates of interests; regional for Congress, and functional for the executive departments, that is, agriculture, labor, commerce. Meanwhile, Congress operated to formulate as law parameters of individual behavior and commercial intercourse.

Even the peripheral economic controls, installed during the epoch of liberalism in the effort to maintain competitive markets or to regulate natural monopoly, operated under advocacy procedures as functions of the judiciary.

Thus the American state, shaped by the blueprint of ideological liberalism, was profoundly *juridical* in character, subordinated to and serving to facilitate the operations of the market, and the competitive pursuit of private advantage. And the American liberal state was *minimal.* Until the catastrophic breakdown of the Great Depression, the American State, in fact and by constitutional fiat, was quite literally impotent, without the autonomous power to intervene, control, organize, plan, direct, or in any way significantly affect the course of internal event, or the structure of relationships, or the distribution of wealth and incomes, or the output of industry, or the character of life, or the nature of the economy.

In the American mythos, rational choice belongs exclusively to the private entrepreneur. Ingenuity is supposed to be uniquely the quality of the free-acting, self-interested, profit-seeker. Efficiency is considered inherent in the operation of the competitive firm. And the state and its minions are relegated, in that mythos, to the opposite category of the necessarily corrupt, sluggard, and inefficient. But if the state and all its minions are held in contempt, curiously, the judge has been looked up to with awe, the lawyer is respected, and the American does not question the integrity and dedication of the military officer, with never a thought that these are precisely the professionals, the sole professionals trained specifically for and alone offered the opportunity of secure, responsible, and honorable career opportunities in the service of the American state.

From a Liberal to a Positive State

Change is underway. The liberal state, with its essentially juridical function, is being transformed as part of the greater transformation of the social and economic structure and the structures of culture and cognition, associated with industrial revolution, organizational revolution, and urbanization. At base it is a consequence and reflection of the crossing over from that world of man where the individual knew an approximate autonomy and self-sufficiency, expressing his wants and will through his own word and private choice to the universe of systems, where the once private being is encompassed by the group, and the personal volition by organizational policy, and where the individual is suspended within and is dependent upon a complex of coexisting and fast-moving systems of a vastness beyond the scope of his comprehension or control. Nor are these systems self-adjusting and self-equilibrating, as the matrix of innumerable individual transactions on the price competitive market was alleged to be. Generations, masses, classes are swept, as by a tidal wave to the depths of despair, or to unknown golden shores. More than a century ago, David Ricardo postulated the existence of a complex of forces working through and below individual volition, outside the individual's conception and beyond his control, that would carry the world to universal poverty poised on the edge of mass starvation. Karl Marx discerned a system of history that captured and enmeshed the generations, masses, and classes in a perpetuum of exploitation and conflict, moving inexorably towards cataclysm, prophesying the coming of a new rationale to harness and direct those transcendent energies.

What brought home to America at least, the perilous nature of the rudderless systems in which the individual was enmeshed and totally vulnerable, was that catastrophic collapse of Western capitalism during the late 1920s and the 1930s, called the Great Depression; a catastrophe that cracked ideological liberalism, and forced important changes in the character of the state.

The change in the role of the state is associated with the Keynsian "revolution." What was the contribution of this "revolution"? It recognized that the economic system was not self-equilibrating and self-adjusting, and it found the cause of the economic collapse in a self-perpetuating insufficiency of aggregate expenditure. Hence aggregate expenditure must be controlled and held at the level where labor would be fully employed. Who was to manage aggregate expenditure? The state, of course. No other agency had the power, or would bear the responsibility.

It was not unusual for the state to bear a *residual* responsibility for doing what the free market left undone. During the long epoch of ideological liberalism, with its anathema on positive action by the state, the state nevertheless came to perform a host of functions, doing what the market left undone; in supporting elementary education, in providing water and sewers, fire protection, roads, bridges, harbors, parks, sometimes electricity and gas, information of many sorts, public health protections, and so forth, nearly always as the ad hoc response to local initiatives to service the local needs the market did not satisfy. But now the sovereign power of the federal state was called upon to manage an essential dimension of the whole economic system; and the federal state was to stand responsible for the general level of employment. And a new professional or quasiprofessional competence was joined to that of the lawyer and the soldier exercising the powers of the state: that of the economist whose prime task was to manage the system of aggregate spending.

After the Great Depression came the Second World War, where a civilization itself was tested. With survival at stake, there had to be, and there was a recrudescence of the maximal and the military state directing the course of technology, mobilizing and controlling all the resources of the nation. After the war in spite of its victory, the American State did not, perhaps could not, as it had done before totally relinquish control of resources of production, and of technology-generating systems rooted in research and development, surrendering those to the realm of civilian industry and the free market. This was so for two reasons; first, because the American state was now continuously and intensely preoccupied with war, with communism identified as the Other, increasingly taking a nationalist form. Secondly, because weaponries had evolved that were of a level of technological advance beyond the reach of civilian-industrial systems, requiring sets of science inputs and a line of technological development entirely outside the call of consumer demand. This, plus space exploration as part of the muscle-flexing of the cold war, made the American state into the direct or indirect employer of the bulk of all the R&D scientists and engineers in American society, and the locus of the most complex and advanced technological operations in the world.

The Keynsian "revolution" succeeded, its doctrines were accepted because it evaded and obscured its own self-evident truth. It said hallelujah to the mythos of free enterprise. It managed to change the policy prescription without offering any challenge to ideological liberalism. It yea-said the conception at the heart of neoclassical economics, of a universe of individual self-seekers in competitive interaction, with resources and preferences optimally equilibrated by the guiding light of free-moving price; with free-moving price as the visible finger of the invisible hand; with free-moving price as the perfectly attuned index of scarcity; with free-moving price as the sure indicator of priorities and preferences; with free-moving price mobilizing energies, guiding allocation, directing production, balancing savings and investment, determining value. The Keynsian "revolution" left that idea unscathed and unchallenged. It carved out a narrow niche for the new activity of the state, always peripheral to and supportive of the supposed operation of the competitive, price-directed market, namely that of managing aggregate expenditures by encouraging/discouraging private investment through central bank manipulation of money supply and interest rates, and by the judicious budgeting of surplus/deficit at the source of public spending. Thus the Keynsian "revolution" offered a neat, simple formula to cure the ills of contemporary capitalism.

Following the logic of that Keynsian analytic, the Great Depression was the consequences of a downward shift in aggregate spending, producing mass unemployment, *because* price did not move freely. Price did not, automatically and spontaneously, equilibrate available resources to output preferences. Price did not register the index of real scarcities. The key, and cherished, indeed the indispensable mechanism of a neoclassical theory did not work. At the core of the modern industrial capitalism, price was administered and controlled. It was administered and controlled because the industrial economy is constituted not of a multitude of self-seeking individuals in competitive interaction, but of enormous organizations, trade unions, and corporations. These organizations possess the power of controlling and administering price, and indeed they have absolutely no option but to control and administer the prices within their cognizance. Hence price becomes a function of organizational policy, but of a policy that is not responsible to, nor answerable for, impacts upon other than those within the small circle of the organization itself. Hence prices and wages become the function of an autonomous and arbitrary power not answerable for their effects nor responsible for their consequences on the economy and society. And it is through the exercise of that autonomous and arbitrary power that the neat simple formula that the Keynesians offered as a cure to capitalism's ills, has been shattered. The state increases the levels of aggregate spending to absorb pools of unemployment. Those increases in aggregate spending are absorbed by higher wages and higher prices raised at the behest of organizational policy, leaving untouched the pools of unemployment. With massive unemployment and excess industrial capacity, prices and wages continue upward at the behest of organizational policy. It is called stagflation. Beyond stagflation, at the root of it, is an arbitrary power that extends to every phase of the organization's behavior. Who can monitor and harness that power, or hold it accountable, or fix parameters upon its exercise, or participate to represent the public interest in the formulation of its policies? Only the state. There is no other possible instrument or agency.

The powers of the state have evolved following essentially the same sequence everywhere. The terrain has changed but the maps have not been redrawn. After the traveler slams into a boulder, tentatively and timidly a way may be found around it; and again the traveler sets off with his obsolete map until again he falls into a pit or sinks in a swamp. Bit by bit, crisis after crisis, because no other power than that of the sovereign is sufficient, because there is no other system of general answerability and responsibility, the state is driven by society's needs and expectations, to undertake more and more central and complex responsibilities. And, in this world of organization, the issue for the individual ceases to be the liberty to choose and decide, and becomes instead, the means, the character, the possibility of participation in organizational choice.

It has become incumbent upon the state to assure a stable national energy system. It has become incumbent on the state to assure a rationally organized, upgraded national transportation system (by road, railroad, and air). It has become incumbent upon the state to install a rational and universally available national system of health care and protection. It has become incumbent upon the state to provide security for the aged. It has become incumbent upon the state to protect the environment and to upgrade the "quality of life." It has become incumbent upon the state to offset urban deterioration and to deal with the crisis and despair of the cities. It has become incumbent on the state to sustain and accelerate the rate of economic growth, hence to deal with the very rapid decline of key American technologies. Incumbent upon the state, for there is no other instrument or agency available to do what needs to be done. The *positive state* emerges because it must.

It is not prepared for its new role. In spite of the enormity and complexity of what must be done, no thought is given to recreating and developing that which must do the doing, no thought is given to an overhaul of the archaic system of governance, no thought is given to building into the state the competencies absolutely needed to diagnose and cure the technological *cum* managerial ills of failing industries; to monitor the performance and to participate in the formulation of the critical policies of the great autonomous organization; to organize, develop, and install rationally ordered low-cost infrastructural systems of energy, transportation, communication, health. The state is a perennial scapegoat of large mouthed politicians and political ignoramuses. We heap upon it abuse, contempt, and gigantic new tasks, in equal measure. By our behavior we insure that it will remain a haven of mediocrity, timid and muddled before the mounting agenda of social needs. Above all it lacks, and we lack a clear and encompassing idea of what is and ought to be, an ideology that makes sense and provides us with a shared vision and the frame for a rational, foresightful, collective choice.

From a National to a Global State

Can nationalism, should nationalism, *qua* ideology, continue to provide the basis for the sovereign power in a world of nation states? No doubt high mobility, shrunken distances, instant communications, cultural homogenization and transnational organization, reduces those felt affinities that defined the weness and set us off from, apart from, and against the Other. The very notion and sense of national distinctiveness, national identity, national (patriotic) commitment, are called into question.

Who is the Other, enemy, fearsome menace, or tempting prey by whom the nation finds and defines itself? French against German? Austrian against Italian? English against French? Those oppositions, once total and definitive, have lost their old force and meaning. During the cold war decades the conflict between political entities ceased to have a specifically national character. It became rather an ideological confrontation expressing the missionary fanaticism of zealots with the message —convert or die!, socialize or die!, free enterprise or die! That fire too is burning down, with the ideologies at issue, both communism and capitalism bankrupted and the sacredness of their imageries lost.

Moreover the sovereign power, now broken into national fragments, confronts phenomena and must deal with systems that transcend the nation, or nations. The economic entity, the corporate locus of economic choice, is increasingly transnational. Transnational too are the great systems of the infrastructure: energy, transportation, communication, health care, and disease control. We depend now on a common, diminishing natural heritage, drinking from the same well where the thirst of each determines what will remain to sustain the rest. Global, transational too is the science-discourse, which has become absolutely essential in the process of technological creativity and advance, and for solutions of problems implicit in our shrinking resource base.

Security in the old sense of protection against the other's force of arms, cannot any longer be provided by the counterforce (the "strength") of the nation, but depends absolutely on transnational arrangements to avoid the final nuclear blastoff. And the provision of security against those other threats, of the biosphere shattered or befouled, of animal species forever destroyed, of atmosphere radiated and poisoned, all transcend the reach and rationality of the nation-state.

How then to create a viable base for sovereignty in the universe of organization? Hardly by a supernation united by the universal commitment to a single sense of identity. It is perhaps more likely to evolve (barring and instead of a revolutionary response to global catastrophe) in piecemeal accommodations to concrete needs, creating transnational, even universal locii of sovereign power, supported as the necessary instrument for doing tasks that must be done.

EPILOGUE TO PART ONE

I had just given a paper titled "Faces and Phases of the Modern State" to the philosophy colloquium, summarizing some of the arguments made in Part One of this book, and had invited the young professor of philosophy who had introduced me at that session to my disordered little office to share with me what remained of the afternoon coffee pot, and to discuss my paper. He was a Marxist and I waited for a Marxist critique, possibly for a crossing of intellectual swords, for a challenge. All that came forth was a kind of cross-muttering between us. Hearing him, and listening to myself I became aware of the different constructs of mind within which each of us was isolated. We didn't agree or disagree. We didn't have that upon which we could agree or disagree. Each of us, he and I, were looking for causation, explanation, clarification in different worlds of thought. It is as a reflection on that difference in basic orientation that this epilogue is intended.

He was a Marxist. His two keys to understanding (and he searched my argument in vain for the keyholes in which to insert and turn those keys) were "capital accumulation" and "class conflict." There is in the whole flow and development of historical change conceived and described in this book, nowhere any place for the consideration of class conflict and capital accumulation. One could dismiss the significance of class conflict and deny the explanatory value of capital accumulation. There remains nevertheless that larger genra of thought within which such notions as these belong, instead of class read interest groups, or monopolies, or trade unions, or developing countries, or military industrial complex, or political machines; instead of capital accumulation, read profit maximization, or power seeking, or imperialistic ambitions, and so on. It is a genra of thought that sees a mechanism of change and development in the drives, the interplay, the tensions, the coalitions, the confluence, the conflicts of discernible, identifiable actors on history's stage. Who can deny the drama of drive, conflict, adaptation, accomodation, response? Not I, certainly. And yet, if the reader will think back, there is none of that in the history of the development of the state as it unfolded in the preceeding chapters. No wonder my Marxist friend muttered and mumbled and could find no intersection of mind in dealing with my paper.

What I have written belongs to another genra of thought. My isolated wanderings have landed me in a different camp, among a melee of disciplines and a confusion of tongues, where, rather to my surprise, I find those of a similar cast of mind. Some identify themselves as "structuralists," while other abjure that title.[1] At least we are alike in this essential. Our inquiry focuses not on the conflicts and interplay of the actors but on the structures of mind expressed in the acts. We interpret histories and we understand societies by reference to successive or varient structures of mind that contain, constrain, and impose their patterns on thought and on behavior. We emphasize those tensions and conflicts produced when transformed structures of mind confront and are contained within institutions, practices, installed hierarchies, and established powers that represent and express another, earlier irruption of thought, or those tensions and conflicts that arise when circumstances change and realities are transformed but habituated imageries and deeply ingrained, laggard structures of thought remain.

Is there a name for the cast of mind, the larger genra of thought to which that of the Marxist belongs? Let me invent one—actodrama. Actodramist and structuralist. The one watches the interplay of interests; the other looks to the underlying structures of the mind. Their aims are not in contradiction. There is no necessary conflict between them. Nor, as yet has a means of integration and synthesis been found. It may be helpful nevertheless to understand why we do not see eye to eye; why we fail to find a common ground for discourse; what it is that separates us.

---

[1]*See* Robert A. Solo, "What Is Structuralism? Piaget's Genetic Epistemology and the Varieties of Structuralist Thought" *Journal of Economic Issues* (December, 1975), reprinted in *The Chicago School of Political Economy* (East Lansing: Michigan State University, 1976).

Part

2

OPTIONS FOR THE POSITIVE STATE
STATE

FOREWORD TO PART 2

I would suppose, for reasons that will be suggested in Chapter 6 that two very particular kinds of contributions to the system of collective choice should be peculiarly the province of the university community. The first of these is in exposing, critiquing, challenging, and developing the cognitive framework of thought (call it episteme or outlook or paradigm or ideology) in terms of which society or some part of it would comprehend and act upon the world. Such that was the intention of the first part of this book, to expose and critique the ideological basis for current policy and, reaching beyond that, to begin to construct a different framework for thought. It sought to show from whence we have come, where we now are, and where we should be going.

The second category of contribution, peculiarly suited to the academic in the process of collective choice, is to formulate concrete and specific policy options for policy choice, thereby to broaden the base and widen the range of alternatives open to public choice. And that will be our objective in this second part of the book. Having demonstrated its emerging configuration, we will propose options, concrete and specific, for choice and action in the context of the positive state.

We choose the term "option" to suggest that what is offered are possibilities merely, intended for discussion, perhaps worthy of consideration. They are as seeds thrown on the grounds of thought, ideas cast into the hopper of discourse. They are not programs finished and ready, not the end products of weighing up and evaluating given alternatives. Rather than conclusions they would be provocations, beginnings, that may end by adding to the alternatives open for political choice.

I will speak, it is true, from a base of limited knowledge and massive ignorance. Who doesn't? I speak, it is true, before all the facts are in. Are they ever? I am a tenured professor without an iota of power to implement or require any choices that I might propose. I have no clients to please or whom I fear to offend. I am answerable to no electorate and to no authority. My time is my own. I follow my curiosity, sniffing out the information that interests me. Old and very heterodox, I am no more concerned either with the sacred cows of my profession or with the ideological hangups and sensibilities of my colleagues. And if all of this diminishes the authority of my words, it does allow me a freedom of imagination in the invention of options, that is not granted to many.

Let this be the start of a discourse. Collective choice after all is or should be a cooperative endeavor. Where there are counterarguments, let them be made. Where there are lacunae, let them be filled. Where there are mistakes, let them be corrected. How else can we open and extend the boundaries of choice, or develop new alternatives, new opportunities for social action?

Chapter

6

WHERE WILL THE OPTIONS COME FROM?

The State and the System of Collective Choice

What we have meant by "the state," are those agencies and processes related to or deriving from the exercise of the sovereign power. The state can also be understood as an instrument of collective choice; within the domain of nationhood, it is perhaps the sole, consciously articulated, and purposefully developed instrument of collective choice. And yet the whole system whereby society chooses this direction or that, this instrument or that, and forms its policies, and changes its character *qua* society, *qua* community, far transcends the state. It would certainly include activities of the press, the schools, the churches, the trade unions, the corporations, and of households as well. What gives coherence, cohesion, and direction to the groups who participate in political choice is always an ideological commitment. The boundaries upon the choice of those who act with authority, and the linkage between those who exercise authority and those upon whose support they must rely, again is ideology. Hence that which forms, reforms, deforms ideology is also fundamentally a part of the system of collective choice. And choice itself, even within the frame of an ideology is always between a finite set of alternatives. Whence come these as options? And when neither alternatives *A, B,* or *C* suffice, solve or satisfy, then how and by whom will new options, *D, E,* and *F* be devised? All that relates to the creation, communication, elimination of options, all that narrows or widens the spectrum of alternatives, is critically a part of the system of collective choice. So also, and more fundamentally, whatever acts upon the ideological framework of thought is a part of the system of collective choice.

71

There can be no end to ideology, in the sense that we have used the term; but certainly when Daniel Bell proclaimed *The End of Ideology,*[1] he was reflecting upon an indubitable truth—the dilution, the diminution, the disintegration, the loss of faith in those all-encompassing ideologies, communism, facism, liberalism, catholicism, that, a few decades ago, dominated history. We live in a time of ideological bankruptcy, and of ideological transformation, of search and groping for a unified and coherent idea of what is and ought to be in our universe of choice and action.

And even in confronting very concrete problems, in seeking for quite specific objectives, we suffer the poverty of options.

The Poverty of Options

Choices are made, policies are formed within the frame of a limited set of option, that is, of ideas existing in men's minds as to the feasible, practicable, acceptable, workable, alternatives for choice and action. It is a paradox of our time that though the human and material resources at the disposal of the American State are vast and its powers are great, its established options create boundaries upon its actions so narrow that meaningful choice virtually ceases. Like an inverted pyramid, the mass of political activity concentrates down to a pin point at the locus of choice. The interests, pressures, turmoil, despair of the vast electorate reduces to the realm of the clerks, polltakers, statisticians, experts, busy as bees buzzing in a thousand places to gather in and carry like honey to the hive, data to those who, in their endless office cubicles, project, predict, calculate, respond, feeding information and answers to politicians, officials, executives, managers who justify, challenge, explain, assure, affirm, deny, document, communicate, manipulate, reorganize, forever on the run from crisis to crisis, self-promoting, conferencing, budgeting, supervising, operating, with powers and energies all concentrating down to the point of decision, of choice —locked there into the deep, narrow, unchanging rut of the available options.

Mr. Johnson succeeds Mr. Kennedy. Mr. Nixon succeeds Mr. Johnson. Mr. Ford succeeds Mr. Nixon. Mr. Carter succeeds Mr. Ford. Mr. Reagan succeeds Mr. Carter. One administration after another takes their seats at the table and reshuffles the same old cards, with no prospect whatever of transcending time-tested patterns of failure. The crises of the positive state is precisely the poverty of its options, the acceptable, respectable, established options that set boundaries upon public choice.

This is the familiar scenario. The administration in office fails in one of the prime responsibilities of the modern state, to maintain full employment and stable prices. Soothsaying to the contrary, inflation continues or worsens, unemployment continues or worsens. Monetary and fiscal manipulations have become a ritualistic juggling, a painful sacrifice of burnt offerings, at the periphery of malaise. The election approaches, a time of testing. Denunciation rings out, indignations are registered, all in the election hulabaloo. In a flurry of promises and under a halo of hope,

---

[1]Daniel Bell, *The End of Ideology* (rev. ed.; London: The Free Press, 1965).

another administration is ushered in. Faces are different now; they speak with a different accent. Their tone is new. It may even be that honest men, earnest men, smiling, concerned, high-minded persons have replaced the tired old gang of crooks. But what is done, hardly changes. What is done remains fixed within the narrow, conceptually determined confines of what is thought to be doable. Policy is locked into the management of aggregate expenditures, with the choice between fiscal-dee and monetary-dum—two methods of skinning the skinless. And even at the level of the instrumentalities of control, the choice between deficit finance, open market operations, interest rate manipulation, is a choice between crude and costly techniques devised by earlier forgotten generations for other purposes entirely. Nothing within the meaningful range of choice reaches the heart of the inflation-unemployment phenomenon. The failure is a failure of ideas. On every front, with respect to each of its great responsibilities, the positive state is afflicted and its powers are held in thrall by the poverty of options.

Where Will the Options Come From?

Certainly it is not unusual to inquire into the interests that influence public choice, or into the breadth and significance of participation into that process, or into the effectiveness of the political system, or into the rationale of public decision. But the most crucial question is hardly asked at all. Namely, where do the options come from? When and from whence will new ones, extending the range of choice, arise? How are they to be created? By whom?

None of this was really of concern in the era of liberalism. What need was there to extend the options for collective choice, when so little was chosen collectively, and the state was without responsibility except to keep things secure and in order. But for the positive state, turning as it is in futility, the formation of new options is critical.

There are reasons why new options for choice have not been forthcoming, reasons that arise from the same transformation that has produced the positive state. Collective choice confronts the problems of systems that are so vast and complex as to be beyond the observational scope of the individual. As with the phenomena which are the concern of physics or chemistry, to comprehend these systems requires conceptualizations abstracted from the study of data that has been specifically researched and systematically organized; requires that is to say, the concentrated, focused, analytically skilled efforts of the specialist, one for whom such inquiry is a vocation and who works within a discourse where hypotheses can be tested and information exchanged.

This is not to say that those who have acquired the prerequisite analytic skills and who have access to the factual information needed to understand underlying phenomena and problems at issue will be motivated or will be able either to formulate and propose lines of approach different and devient from those of the established canon, or to challenge and change an accepted framework of thought. It is only to insist that the need to master a dense body of information and of analytic skills as a prerequisite to the formation of new policy options or to challenge and change the understructures of thought, excludes all but a few from the possibility of making that creative contribution to the system of collective choice.

Who and where are they, those who have the analytic skills and the knowledge required to formulate policy options or to challenge and reconstruct existing frameworks for the conceptualization of social phenomena? They are of two categories—the active and the passive. The active are those actually engaged in the processes of political choice and in the formation of public policy, as lobbyists and consultants, as advocates and defenders, as congressmen or senators and their staffs, as executives, officials, managers, scientists, technologists in the agencies of government. The passive, equipped with the requisite analytic skills and the necessary information base but entirely outside the circle of power, exist nowhere else I think, there is no other niche for them in the systems of modern society, than in the university. Of these two categories, the active are certainly closer to the critical phenomena and are under more pressure to concern themselves with and to find an effective resolution to the problems at issue. And they possess the power to venture, to experiment, to act. But, for the creative task of inventing policy alternatives and for the probing and restructuring of the framework of conceptualization and choice, they lack one essential ingredient. They lack the free time, they lack the time to wonder, to ponder, to fantasize, to imagine, to speculate, to philosophize, to discuss, to invent.

From where then will the new options come? Only the passive specialists of the university community are granted the essential pre-conditions for nurturing the new options desperately needed for social choice. There alone are there the requisite analytic skills and knowledge and the free time for reflective thought. There alone does there exist an organized discourse open to the critical testing of ideas. Sad to say in our time, only in the universities can a part of the population devote its energies and efforts to the pursuit of goals (the invention of policy alternatives, and the reconstruction of the critical frameworks of thought, among them) where there is no profit in it, nor interests of an established clientele to be served. Unhappily perhaps, the universities, given the complexity of our social systems, are or seem to be the only potential seedbed for the formation of new policy options and of another structure for conceptualization and thought.

Alas, pure science's ethos of social indifference, the powerful hold of archaic dogmas upon the social sciences, the societal insensitivity and political ignorance of the engineer, the vested interests of the academic authority in that intellectual furniture which is the throne of his authority, the vested interests of the disciplinarian in the paradigm of the discipline, all stand against the realization of that potential. Nor is there an effective dialogue between those who dwell in the detached space of reflective thought and those on the fast moving treadmill of policy choice and political action. To institutionalize such a dialogue is quite a different thing than pulling academics into the maelstrom of crisis management, making of them quasipoliticians playing the power game, and quite cut off from the realm of creative reflection.

While the university and perhaps only the university has the potential for becoming the seedbed of new options for collective choice, the university is without an awareness of that potential. It neither expects it of itself, nor does society demand it.

I would like in this book to awaken an awareness of the need to develop the universities as the natural, and the only possible seedbed and source of new options for the positive state, and as a fundamental component of the system of collective choice. What follows might be, perhaps, something of a model, or a first step in realizing upon this potential; for our approach will be to propose options for public choice and policy in the light of the problems and possibilities of the positive state. Not solutions but options, not intended as the final word but as the beginning of a discourse that aspires to open the spectrum of alternatives for the choosing.

THE INSTRUMENTALITY ITSELF

What the state will do must depend upon what the state, an instrument of choice and action, can do. Is the instrument itself appropriate for the task; for the enormous, crucial tasks of the positive state? The sword will not serve as a plowshare, nor conversely. And if the instrument is not suited to the task, then what changes can be proposed as options for its restructuring or for changes in the direction of its development.

To provide a framework for our suggestions, a model of the modern American State will be proposed; specifying the character of its electoral, representational, leadership, surveillance and accountability, operational, and jurdical functions, tying these with its ideological understructure, its organizational structure and its built-in competencies, all residuals of a long path of historical development. Intended as background, this model makes no claim to completeness.

The Functional Path to Policy Formation

The path of functional organization, starts with those who *elect* representatives to positions of power and responsibility. The electorate enters into the electoral process from three distinct yet always overlapping outlooks. They come into it as individuals whose concern is with the institutional context wherein they act, choose, and seek after their private goals; and/or they come into it as a party-at-interest seeking to gain some comparative advantage; and/or they come into it as ideologues committed to an idea of what is and ought to be. Mr. *X,* the individual, wants better protection for his property and less red tape in dealing with government; but Mr.

X, the farmer, demonstrating and "striking" for higher crop support payments, is a party-at-interest who would use the powers of the state to gain a comparative advantage *vis-a-vis* the consumer; and, Mr. *X.* qua nationalist, votes for those who favor a grain embargo against the Soviet Union, thwarting thereby his interests as a farmer.

The Electoral Function

The electorate votes for and selects its "representatives" on the basis of two rational, but often incommensurable criteria. Voters select or seek to select those in whom they see themselves, where they find their own responses, values, interests reflected, and whom they trust therefore to do as they would do if they had the opportunity to participate in public choice directly. When I face the mirror, there appears an image that is a very good representation of myself. It looks like I look, It winks when I wink. It jerks when I jerk. It represents me because it is like myself.

Or voters may select or seek to select those in whose abilities they have confidence and whose moral stature they respect, in the expectation of "leadership," and with a readiness to rely on the discretion of leaders whom they hold accountable for "results." I go to a lawyer because I believe in his competence to operate in a universe beyond my ken, because I think he has the ability and the honest commitment to pursue objectives that I consider to be in my interest. Whether I recognize myself in him, is quite beside the point. He is not a representation of myself, but he represents my interests. Both forms of representation have a place in the system of democratic answerability. With the positive state and its tasks, the latter representation takes on a new and critical importance.

In the first instance the representative represents in the sense that elector X equals elected $Y.$ In the second instance the representative represents in the sense that the elected Y is the agent of the elector X as his doctor or his lawyer or his minister or rabbi might be, with the latter giving advice, guidance, and allowed independent initiatives, but expected to deliver the results. In the first instance the ideal body of representatives is simply a reduction of the universe of the electorate to more manageable proportions. In the second instance, the representative body is ideally an elite that operates under delegated responsibilities, surviving in its power, through the character of performance and the consequences associated with that performance.

What are the tasks and responsibilities of "representation" in the formation of policy? For the constituency of individuals, it is to articulate a concern for the context within which they pursue their private lives.

For the constituency of parties-at-interest, to represent is to advocate, interest against interest. For the constituencies of the ideologically committed, representation also means an advocacy of value against value, outlook against outlook. But since there is a corollary and shared interest in social continuity and consensus, the representative would also seek compromise, containment, and the resolution of conflict. For this reason, and because he is involved in advocacy-processes other than his own, the representative will also act perforce as arbitrator and judge. In its "leadership" role, representation articulates and advocates before its own constituencies, ideas of purpose and priority as the base line to the exercise of controls, the specification of tasks, the devising of strategies, the allocation of resources, the imposition of constraints, and the establishment of agencies and instruments for the performance of tasks.

The Surveillance and Accountability Function

Governance consists of a series of delegations of power matched by systems intended to insure effective surveillance over, and to require accountability for the exercise of that power. Such, of course, is an objective of periodic elections.

The agencies of implementation established under the authority of representative bodies possess necessarily a considerable autonomy. They will recruit, select, and train operating personnel. They will choose between alternative forms and avenues of action by reference to some set of priorities. They will formulate policies, devise strategies, and impose controls and constraints by reference to some table of values. They will develop constituencies and represent interests.

These agencies established under the authority of systematic representation, moreover, through contractual relationships, in turn establish activities and engage organizations nominally outside the political system, which also exercise a considerable autonomous power in the choice of alternative modes, forms, and avenues of action.

Wherever power is thus delegated, or wherever an autonomous but subordinate power exists, as in the relationship between representatives of the electorate and the public agencies operating under their authority; and between public agencies and the corporate organization operating under contract to them; and between regulating agencies and the entities they regulate and control, surveillance is needed. Needed also is the institutional means of insuring that those exercising delegated or subordinated power are accountable for its exercise and the consequences thereof. Effective surveillance requires the systematic inflow of relevant information and the capacity of those to whom accountability is due, to comprehend it.

The Operating Function

Given rule and constraint, priority and resources, purpose and strategy, given representation, surveillance and accountability, there remains the critical operating tasks of futures planning, creative organization, and effective management. Under the circumstances of the positive state the operational task is liable to be of vast magnitude and great complexity, with the motivational base and the table of values, hence the calculus of cost and of benefit, of another order than would exist in the market.

Ideology and the Juridical Function

There is also the juridical function where individuals and groups enter into advocacy procedures as parties-at-interest without the intermediary of elected representation, wherein decisions become rules and parameters controlling individual activity, social intercourse, commercial exchange, and power relationships. The electoral process, which epitomizes what we earlier called composite choice, gives greater weight to the weight and balance of interests, whereas the authoritative choice of the courts more directly expresses the prevailing ideologies.

Corollary with the path of functional organization, converging with it at the point of collective choice in the formation and implementation of public policy are those (cultural and cognitive) systems that form and reform the tables of collective value and of social priority, and provide the motivational force of the political system and its agencies. The solution of problems depends on the comprehension of phenomena and the other elements of the capacity to problem-solve. Choice rides on ideological tides, and at every level is confined within a range of established options. This second path on the way to public policy and its implementation, is in the formation of cognitive and value structure, ideological development and collective awareness, and the creation of policy options.

Criteria for Functional Evaluation

By what criteria can we evaluate the electorial function leading to the formation of policy; policy implementation requiring surveillance over and accountability from loci of operations; operations encompassing planning, organization and management; and conflict resolved through advocacy procedures, with the courts formulating rules within the zone of the ideologically acceptable? The following are some of the criteria by which we might evaluate these functions of the state.

1. That the accepted, legitimatized rules of the electoral process, for example, one man, one vote, are not evaded.

2. That the elected are effectively answerable to, and responsive to the electorate; and are neither answerable nor responsive to any extra-electoral interest.

3. That the electorate is informed concerning and is capable of comprehending the problems that confront its political representatives, and the viable options between which they must choose. Here, as elsewhere, where education, communication technology, the capacity for discourse, the power of the media are all at issue, other systems converge with the political.

4. That the electoral process exposes and opens the widest range of available talents and the fullest spectrum of political outlooks to electoral choice.

5. That the full spectrum of ideologies and interests, as these prevail, are effectively advocated in policy formation.

6. That the process of representative governance, interest-advocacy, and conflict-resolution operate within accepted and legitimatized rules.

7. That there exists a sufficient balance as between the advocacy of particular interests and ideologies, and the general interest in social continuity, to enable the requisite compromise, containment, or resolution of conflicts.

8. That representative bodies develop and possess, and that public agencies recruit and through systematic training, develop the competencies required for the fulfillment of their responsibilities.

9. That public agencies capitalize on the potential for dedication to public service as a motivational force, and that they evolve on appropriate table of collective values as a basis for operating choice.

10. That there be a systematic accountability for plans, performance, and the consequences thereof between public agencies and representatives of the electorate, and between corporate contractors and public contractees, and between regulatees and regulators.

11. That there exist a systematic inflow of the relevant information, as a prerequisite to policy formation, to operational choice, to effective accountability, to surveillance and the monitoring of performance.

A Functional Critique

How then, given these criteria, shall we evaluate the instrumental character of the American State?

1. Our agencies (and system) of representation and accountability, including Congress, the Senate, and the numerous legislative bodies and elected assemblies, and those loose amalgams called political parties, and the lobbies and patrons, and finally the voting electorate itself now play a highly equivocal and uncertain role. Formed at a time when the tasks of the state were infinitely simpler, they are inadequate in their *accounting to* those whom they "represent," and also, even more fundamentally they are quite unable to take *into account* and to *account for* the immensely complex activities and crucial organizing and control responsibilities that fall within the domain of the modern state.

2. Our agencies (and the system) of moral surveillance and conflict-resolution including the judiciary, the police, the prosecutors, the prisons, the bar, and the juries, the echelons of public commissions are very powerful and, in part, highly respected, with a deep and continuous history, an invisible dynamic, a hierarchy with its apex in the Supreme Court. This is the only segment of our civil state with a professional competence and commitment (lawyer and judge) particular to itself. The authority of the judiciary, given its form of decision, constitutes necessarily a bastion of ideology (just as the system of choice associated with Congress and the other American agencies of accountability, give the greater weight to interests in the processes of composite choice). For that reason, in this time of ideological bankruptcy, the American Supreme Court has spearheaded the search for and formulation of an idea of what is and ought to be, that is, for an ideology appropriate to this age. But the judiciary and its advocacy procedure is intended in the first instance as an instrument of social discipline, punishing the marginal few who transgress moral norms embodied in the law, and secondly the

advocacy procedure is designed to enable the settlement of disputes and conflicts of interest that occur within a viable, accepted, legitimatized economic and social structure. What the advocacy procedure and the juridical system is not designed to do, and what is totally beyond the lawyer's rationale and the scope of his training and competence, is to get to the root of social deviance and turmoil and to act upon root causes or to take into account the costs and consequence of punishment, or to vector upon and to design and implement a strategy for the achievement of long range social goals, or to evaluate the performance of functional systems, or rationally to reconstruct those systems for the sake of better performance. And yet the phenomena of crime and deep social malaise and (for example, via the antitrust laws) the structuring of the economy, the upgrading and desegregation of the black underclass, have all, presumably as a consequence of an entrenched ideological liberalism and perforce because there exists no other more appropriate competencies built into the operations of the American State, been left to the judiciary and advocacy procedures designed for another order of task entirely.

3. Our agencies (and systems) of collective action, organization, innovation, and control ranging from the simplicity of the post office to the complexities of NASA, are in a general state of disarray. The latent powers of the state traditionally were brought into play only in war or absolute crisis. But now, under the pressure of residual needs and mounting public expectations and collective responsibilities, the traditional values and deep-rooted prejudices that long kept its powers in check have been violated. The state has extended its activities far beyond the scope of that for which society is ideologically prepared. With the agencies of accountability in their present form, quite incapable of taking into account or comprehending, judging, evaluating, or making any creative contribution in the development of policy and practice for vastly complicated activities, there is naturally a tension between the agencies of accountability and the agencies of implementation, as well as and between the universe of individuals and a state that is at once too weak and too timid to satisfy their demands or to solve their collective problems, and yet that annoys and irritates "the people" in violating ingrained proprieties of liberalism by the very presence of inevitable mechanisms of action and control. Hence we have been treated to the strange spectacle of a Washington that is resolutely anti-Washington, of Chief Executives whose stock-in-trade is to denigrate the efficiency and to denounce the execution of activities whose efficiencies are their responsibilities and of tasks the execution of which they are in charge. We witness the perverse demand, egged on by professional politicans, to dismantle and disperse the machinery of collective action and control as a matter of principle, without consideration of effects on task or function; and we accept the kowtowing to the ritual forms and symbols of liberalism that transform the organization of the agencies of the state into mock-ups of free enterprise, at once insulated from the force of market competition, and also deliberately detached from any identification with social purpose, removed from

the normal scope of public answerability, and deprived of the potentialities for rational planning; unique combinations of the worst of all worlds.

We are heir to a political system of decision, implementation, and control that evolved piecemeal in an ad hoc, mostly local responses to residual needs the market could not satisfy, during the long generations when the federal authority was kept impotent as a matter of ideological principle, under constraints sanctified by constitutional interpretation. The existing structure of political authority and control is hence a jumble of fragmented bits without any organizational rationale. And yet the perennial panacea is not to reorganize the state to utilize more rationally the sovereign power, but is rather to further fragment its apparatus and to deplete that power, by "returning government to the people." So, during the postwar decades, the size of the federal establishment has remained virtually unchanged while that of the state and local jumble has increased manifold, even while the sinking cities cry out to the federal authority to assume responsibilities that they are entirely unable to shoulder.

Harassed by professional politicans in this sure fire appeal to popular frustrations, saddled with the hangups of ideological liberalism, scapegoat to the popular wrath, adrift, without leadership or any coherent orientation, deprived of the force of ideological dedication, yet faced with vast tasks of the most critical importance; that is the dilemma of the action agencies of the American State.

The Nationalist-Libertarian Phase (1800–1930)

The structure of the American state is the product of a long history. Its development has been in layers, superimposed one upon the other. The nationalist component came first, for the American State was initially a loose association to organize rebellion against, to expel through war, to defend against, and then to deal effectively with the Other.

Made secure from foreign invasion by two great oceans, the American state developed under the imperatives of ideological liberalism into a libertarian state par excellence. By Constitutional intent its institutions and instruments were not designed to do anything but rather to insure that nothing could be done; and under the strict surveillance of the Supreme Court, the collective will expressed through the state was barred from any effective control upon or challenge to individualized choice clothed in the prerogatives of property. Until the 1930's the sovereign power of the Federal State was impotent to bring about significant change in the structure and organization of the economy or society.

While circumstantial context, role, responsibilities, tasks of the state were vastly different then than they are now, the constitutional design for inaction and impotence, has not changed in its essentials.

During the long epoch of liberalism the core operation, the effective arm of the American State was, of course, the judiciary, It formulated and imposed through its decisions, the moral parameters of individual behavior reflecting prevailing norms. In the resolution of conflict through advocacy procedure, it established and delimited property rights, interpreted and enforced contracts, and guaranteed the liberties

of individualized choice against collective intervention. The nonjuridical components of the state also acted upon the economy and society through advocacy
procedures in the juridical mode. It was thus with the independent regulatory
commissions and under the antitrust laws where the Department of Justice acted
upon economic structures under the aegis of the courts. Like the courts, Congress
and the Executive formulated and imposed the moral parameters of individual
behavior reflecting prevailing norms, as statutory rather than common law. Through
a species of advocacy procedures, Congress and the Executive adjudicated conflicts,
usually over shares in the social increment. Congress was the forum for the representation of regional interests while the key federal agencies (before World War II, the
Departments of Agriculture, of Labor, of Commerce) were advocates of functional
interests in a perennial "dividing up the pork."

With federal powers rigidly constrained under the laisser faire imperative, during the long epoch of ideological liberalism, it was necessarily through their local
governments that communities acted to supply services not to be obtained through
the market, in education, in public health care and sanitation, in police and fire
protection, in the building of roads and sometimes in the operation of transport
facilities. This organically evolved ad hoc jumble of fragmented public activities at
state and local levels, could and can find some measure of coherence only through
superimposed linkages.

During this epoch of liberalism the state was as housekeeper in a house of
many rooms. She swept out the corridors, she locked the gates at night and kept
a dog to defend against intruders, she maintained house rules, settled disputes
between the roomers, and collected the rent. If tickled or tipped, she might indulge
the pleasure of a favored few. On festive occasions, the pig that grubbed in the
yard was slaughtered and the pork was divided up, with those who had the longest
reach and the fastest grab getting the biggest chunks. But otherwise, barring any
hanky panky, each one lived in and tended his private space and went about his
business as he pleased. Such was, such is, the *housekeeping function* of the liberal
state.

The Welfare State

The Great Depression put in train a transformation and redesign of the political blueprint. Added to the housekeeping function of the nationalist/libertarian
state was the offset function of the welfare state. It became the task of the state
through fiscal and monetary manipulations, through transfer payments, through a
very occasional change in the rules of the market game, to offset instabilities,
insecurities, inequities of the free enterprise economy. To the libertarian rights that
sanctify individualized *vis a vis* collective choice, were added welfare rights in the
social guarantee of opportunity and security. There was as well another category
of rights: organizational rights, (as those laid down by the National Labor Relations Board) defining, delineating, securing the prerogatives and the autonomies of
the niches occupied by individuals or categories of individuals in an organizational
matrix.

To the professional competencies of the lawyer and the soldier, trained for and geared specifically to the service of the nationalist and the liberal state, was added now the professional competence of the Keynesian economist trained to the task of offset management.

Again change is in the offing; again, with the failure of Keynesian and welfare offsets, the questions: what structure? what competencies? what policy options for the positive state?

Borrowed Doctrine

The economist was sought for and admitted into the policy-formation process of the political system to become along with the soldier and the lawyer the third of the triad of professions trained to the service of the state. His training equipped him to manage aggregate expenditure, and perhaps also to manage fiscal gadgetry intended to influence market outcomes, and other sorts of market offsets (loans, transfers, subsidies, tax incentives). Such tasks no doubt, will continue to require the services of the professional economist. With events demonstrating the inadequacy, the insufficiency of a simple policy of welfare offsets, and with the sheer management of aggregate spending seesawing the economy between recession and inflation (recession until it becomes unbearable, then inflation until it becomes unbearable, back and forth, ad infinitum) moving now to a new phase of recession plus inflation, another question arises. How relevant is economic doctrine to the political economy of the positive state?

There is a certain presumption that the economist of certified skill and authenticated reputation must be an expert on all matters economic, a presumption quite in accord with the conceits of practitioners who are ever ready to pronounce upon the responsibilities and policies of the positive state. In fact, the skills acquired and the outlook ingrained through conventional economics in no way prepares the practitioner to contribute to the formation or implementation of those policies. Given the unfortunate but alas general proclivity of the expert to deny the reality of that which his theory does not explain, and to reason by false analogy from that with which he is familiar to that which he is not, the ingrained outlook and accepted doctrines of the economists have served as a profoundly distorting lens through which the role and tasks of the positive state are seen and evaluated.

The economist has no theory of collective behavior, no theory of the state. There is no place in the economics paradigm for the conceptualization of the state, hence of an economy with state as its nexus of evaluation, organization, motivation. Economics was born of an argument against any "intervention" by the state, with the antistate bias inextricably ingrained. For the economist the state is X, a dark and dangerous outside force, bearer of residual burdens, actor of the last resort. The preoccupation of the economist is and has always been to draw, and then redraw, and to draw again the precautionary line (for the past half century, in a continuing retreat before the state's spreading responsibilities and new found tasks), "This far, but no further." Observing that perforce and under pressure the state is obliged to undertake this task or that, the economist then rationalizes and explains this and that as exceptions to the fundamental laisser faire rule. That rationalization is never with reference to what the state can, but to what the market cannot do. Such is the substance of public choice economics.[1]

The economics paradigm has to do not with the state, not with collective choice, but with the market and, with certain marginal asides, only a particular market, that of pure competition. Anything else is deviation and distortion. The corporation and trade union in the organizational sector, incomprehensible in its terms, are subsumed into the imagery of individualized choice and the proprietary price-directed firm, where ownership links power and volition, volition and efficiency. For economics has not only no theory of the state; it has no theory of organization. It is therefore without the framework to conceptualize the key economic entities, public or private, of our time. Herbert Simon was awarded the Nobel Prize in Economic Science in 1978 for his contribution to decision theory, and in his speech of acceptance[2] complained bitterly and at length that such inquiry as his was excluded from the "economic heartland."

When economists have ventured to critique, conceptualize, or to offer a schemata for the organization of the activities of the state, it seems always a projection of the imageries of purely competitive markets. When Lange and Lerner offered their prescriptions for socialism in the 1930s, it was as a set of instructions to socialist managers, to act strictly according to the rules and canons of pure competition.[3] So it has been throughout. Allow a single example, to illustrate both the character and the fallacy of this kind of projection.

This is the problem. How should it be decided whether to divert resources through taxation or otherwise into a given public project? Economists belonging to a variety of schools agree on the following criterion: that the rate of return on the resources used (invested) in the public project should be equal to or greater than the rate of return on investment earned in the market. The controversy has only been as to which of a number of possible market rates of return would be appropriate.[4] In the words of William Baumol:

> We may now establish a rather obvious criterion to test the desirability of the proposed resource transfer. If the resources in question produce a rate of return in

---

[1]The work of Mancur Olsen Jr., Ronald Coase, E. J. Mishan, Gorden Tulloch, Kenneth Arrow come to mind. For a literature review and general bibliography, see Peter O. Steiner, *Public Expenditure Budgeting* (Washington: The Brookings Institution, 1969).

[2]"Herbert A Simon, "Rational Decision Making in Business Organizations" *American Economic Review* (September, 1979). Actually Professor Simon in replacing the notion of optimizing with that of satisficing did not create a theory of organization. He simply proposed a different goal (and one so equivocal that it could not possibly be refuted through empirical test). But this satisficing is still pursued through the same rational, self-seeking individualized volition as imputed to the entrepreneurial firm.

[3]Abba Lerner, *The Economics of Control* (Fairfield, N.J.: Augustus M. Kelley).

[4]William J. Baumol, "On the Discount Rate for Public Projects" in Robert Haveman and Julius Margolis *Public Expenditure and Policy Analysis* (2d ed.; Skokie, Ill.: Rand McNally & Co., 1977). Baumol's essay includes an extensive bibliography to which might be added J. Hirshleifer, "Investment Decisions Under Uncertainty: Choice-Theoretic Approaches," *Quarterly Journal of Economics* (November, 1965); "Investment Decisions Under Uncertainty: Applications of the State-Preference Approach," *Quarterly Journal of Economics* (May, 1966); Kenneth J. Arrow and Robert Lind, "Uncertainty and the Evaluation of Public Investment Decisions," *American Economic Review* (June, 1970); Paul A. Samuelson and W. Vickery, "Discussion," *American Economic Review* (May, 1964).

the private sector which society evaluates at r percent, then the resources should be transferred to the public project if that project yields a return greater than r percent. They should be left in private hands in their potential earnings if the proposed government investment is less than r percent. The logic of this criterion is self evident. It states no more than the minimal dictate of efficiency; never take resources out of a use where they bring in (say) 9 percent in order to utilize them in a manner which yields only 6 percent![5]

Consider. What is this rate of return on resources invested in the private sector? Where does it come from; what does it represent? In the imagery of economics, it represents profits, as the margin of difference between the price of what is sold and the cost of what is produced, including the imputed "costs" of management or entrepreneurship. It is the share of market-produced income that accrues to that small part of the community as a consequence and as a measure of the pure power of ownership. The current market worth of this power of ownership is indicated by what will be paid in interest or dividends for money claims on resources that can be used to extend the powers of ownership:

1. Taxation channelizing resources into a public project diverts not resources that would otherwise have been invested in the private sector but a crosscut of all forms of private spending.

2. The rate of return earned in the private sector may be a measure of the benefit received by those few in possession, but that rate of return in no sense measures benefits equivalent to those sought for in utilizing resources in the public sector, for example, it is no measure of what is added to GNP or of any positive impact on productivity. Thus the highest rates of return are frequently to be found in societies where there is no growth and no increments to productivity.

3. The rate of return is directly related to the powers of ownership *vis a vis* the powers of other actors in the economic game. It is a measure of the monopolistic, monopsonistic power of ownership to exploit, by raising price and pushing down wages. What has such "return" or such "lost opportunity" to do with a criterion for utilizing resources on public projects?

4. The rate of return is based on the difference between selling price and cost, between S and C. Is there an equivalent S for the outputs of programs and projects in the public sector? There is rarely a sales price for outputs in the public sector, nor, if there is, it is determined by exogenous forces of a market. Nor can the social/collective evaluation of benefits be equated to market pricing.

5. Nor from the point of view of ownership, and from the social point of view, does "cost" have an analogous meaning. On the table of private accounts,

---

[5]Id. p. 163.

everything else remaining the same, higher wages raises costs and reduces the rate of return, hence making the investment less desirable. Would it be the same if wages in a public program (say the pay rates of privates in the armed forces) were raised as a matter of policy choice? Not at all. Evaluated from a general and social perspective costs would not have been increased; income would have been redistributed.

Thus the rationale of costing is not to be compared. The rationale of output evaluation is not to be compared. For public projects there is no ownership interest inherently motivated to squeeze wide the margin between what is paid out and what is paid in; there is indeed nothing analogous to the market rate of return. The market rate of return is in no sense an index of values to be compared and measured against (as the opportunity cost of) benefits sought for and received in public projects. In sum, no matter the modifications and qualifications that might be made, no analytic that approaches the public sector through the projection of (and by analogy with) the price-competitive market of neoclassical imagery can be anything but a distortion. The doctrine is not to be borrowed. The positive state requires a theory and an analytic proper to itself.

The Borrowed Businessman

Thus a framework of thought, a theory, a table of values, an ideology that comprehends the phenomena and that can give a common direction to collective energies, are needed for the effective organization of the positive state. It is essential also that a set of competencies particular to its needs be built into the instrumentalities of that state. The two are indissolubly related; competence implies and requires an appropriate framework of thought and table of values, and in allowing the necessary competence to develop, with learning through experience and in the exercise of responsibility, there must be a corresponding development of the requisite knowledge and outlook.

To be a most excellent cashier does not require or imply the competence to organize and run a bank. To be a most successful banker does not require or imply the competence to organize and run the monetary system. Nor need those who are capable of organizing and running a monetary system have what it takes to be a successful banker. Nor need the successful banker have the skills of a good cashier. We can think thus of a related but distinct set of competencies: of *technique,* skills in the specific task (the cashier), of *operations,* in competence to organize and manage an activity (the bank), and *systemic* in the ability to comprehend and control the integrity of diverse operations (the monetary system). It would seem axiomatic that the competence in technique is the most easily transferable from the private to the public sector, that the operational competence is less so, and that the systemic is the least transferable from the one sector to the other. There would, for example, be no problem in transfering one with a skill in keeping neat and accurate accounts from a firm in the private sector to a job in a public agency, or conversely. But an acquired skill in knowing what has to be taken into account and accounted for, hence in the devising of an accounting system, cannot be directly transferred from the private to the public sector, where different effects must be taken in account and different values accounted for.

The positive state engages and must engage increasingly in devising, planning, organizing, activating, managing, or monitoring and exercising surveillance over systems with a large, complex technological component. For those tasks, neither the competencies of the soldier, the lawyer, the economist (the only professionals trained to the service of the state), nor the administrator or the politician are appropriate. And the state in such a case has relied on the guidance and called in the competence of the *borrowed businessman,* filling its policymaking echelons with temporary transfers from Wall Street, former wheeler-dealers, bankers, and corporation executives on loan. It suffices to have made a million in "free enterprise," no matter where nor how, to take an honored seat in that critical policymaking circle.

This works badly. It is a perpetual source of fumbling and failure. To give a concrete example which will, moreover help explain why this is so, I have appended to this chapter excerpts from an article which was written in response to the Carter Administration's taking of the synthetic rubber experience as its model for development of an industry to produce synthetic fuel. This was, in turn, derived from an in-depth study of the establishment of the synthetic rubber industry in the United States, often touted as a shining example of achievement by the positive state, with borrowed businessmen at the helm.

We are not concerned with conflicts of interest, nor to question the integrity, the patriotism, or the ability of the American businessman. It is our contention simply that as a consequence of their experience, and as a prerequisite to their success, they acquire an outlook, skills, a set of reference values, a body of knowledge that is deep, dense, subtle and is ingrained as a basis for their choice and action. And that all this is of another order than that suited to the tasks of the positive state. It is easy enough to change official hats, but the thinking cap sticks to the skull.

Between the entities of the market economy and the systems that fall within the responsibilities of the positive state, there are fundamental differences in the appropriate reference values, in the value-indicators, in the criteria of evaluation, in the sense of what is essential and what is incidental, of what is variable and what is inviolable, in the form and character of power and in the constraints upon its exercise, in the imperatives of organization, in the processes of decision, in the nature of risk and in the means of comprehending risk, in the character of motivation, in the potential sources of energy and the possible incitements to action, and in the barriers to change.

The positive state *needs* a new kind of competence, one that does not now exist, wherein the essential grasp of relevant technology and a sensitivity to the table of collective values, is coupled with an outlook, skills, and a body of knowledge relevant to the political systems and to the tasks of the positive state, as deep, dense, and subtle as those acquired by the businessman through his experience with a different set of systems. That competence will develop *if it is allowed to.* There can be no doubt that a dedicated life in the public service is powerfully attractive to young men and women of the highest talent and energy, even without the lure of great material rewards as might accrue to those in private business.

Certainly that was evident to those who knew Washington in the New Deal days of Franklin D. Roosevelt, or during the short administration of John F. Kennedy, or have had dealings with recruits to the Peace Corp. In all the advanced nations of Western Europe, wherever the opportunities exist, the high civil service attracts the most talented of each generation. The "brightest and the best" can be recruited and they will develop the critical competence if they are allowed to: if, they are exposed systematically to the relevant challenges, if they are given the ideological go-ahead, if they have the chance to observe and learn through experience and to test themselves in the exercise of responsibility, and are tested in their perform- ance, if they are offered lifetime careers that lead to the echelons of policy-forma- tion and control.

Competence and commitment are, of course, the first requisite for any tasks of the positive state. Without them nothing will work. In what follows we must and *we will suppose* that there is the appropriate competence built into the instrumentali- ties of choice and implementation.

A Competence for Surveillance

Needed is a new competence not only for the agencies of the policy-formation and implementation, but also for Congress to monitor and to evaluate and to hold those in charge accountable for the performance of the tasks of the positive state. Technical advisors made available to Congressional committees through the Office of Technical Assessment is a recent step in institutionalizing that competence as part of the surveillance function. Let us propose another.

Consider the U.S. Senator, flooded with the demands of his constituents, know- ing no letup in the middleman function of representing regional and other interests in their struggle for protection and comparative advantage, ceaselessly mending fences, building bridges, infighting, wheeling and dealing as a prerequisite for politi- cal survival and Congressional effectiveness, with no space left for contemplative thought and disciplined learning. It is upon this Senator and the Senate, that "august body" of which every member perforce is a political ringmaster and a jack-of-all choices caught on a fast moving treadmill of decision upon decision concerning an unbounded universe of issues on the swift moving belt of the legislative assembly line, that we rely for the crucial surveillance of infinitely complex technological systems and for the anticipation of need and crisis in the context of these. It is upon this Senator and the Senate that we must rely for such massive redevelopment and turning around of technology as might be in the public interest. As a first small step in building into the Senate the competence for dealing effectively and foresightfully with the vital and technologically complex national systems of (1) energy, (2) trans- portation, (3) communications, (4) health, and (5) defense, I propose the following.

Let five committees of the U.S. Senate be created, each to take primary jurisdic- tion in all matters related to one of the aforementioned systems. Let five additional members be elected to the Senate, on a national basis, as are the President and the Vice President. They would be nominated not simply for a seat in the Senate but specifically for the chairmanship of one of the five aforementioned committees. One would be senator-chairman for energy, another Senator-chairman for transportation, and so on. Senator-chairmen would be permitted to cast a vote in the Senate only on matters within the jurisdiction of their committee. Their committee staffs would have the character of permanent secretariats. Leading staff members, appointed by the Senator-chairman, would be given the status of assistant secretaries in the regular departments of the executive branch. Senator-chairmen might be invited to sit with the President and his Cabinet when matters under the committee's jurisdiction are at issue. A Senator-chairman or his designate would be privileged to coparticipate in the investigatory, advisory, surveillance, and planning functions of the regular executive departments or of other public agencies in relation to matters of committee concern. After leaving their positions, neither Senator-chairmen nor committee staff would be permitted under the law to be employed with any private agency that had been or subsequently would come under the jurisdiction of the committee.

This proposal has several purposes. First, by focusing responsibility and narrowing tasks, there could be developed in Congress the high competence that is needed to deal creatively, foresightfully, and effectively with technologically complex areas of great national concern. Second, the public agencies and private corporations that are the operational entities of these technologically complex national systems would be made more effectively answerable to Congress and Congress more effectively answerable to the people. Third, this proposal not only would give the public a clear-cut locus of Congressional responsibility, but also would allow those who would stand responsible for the performance of these critical systems in the eyes of the public the status and exposure that would permit them to speak independently to the national constituency in order that they might provoke the public awareness, muster the political support, and find the electoral roots that would be needed in order to oppose the demands of great agencies, such as the Pentagon in the public sector or the regional and corporate interests of the private sector. Finally, by creating a bridge between them, the exchange of information and cooperative planning by the Congressional and executive branches of government in areas of crucial importance and great technological complexity would be facilitated.

It is a modest proposal after all; it would add but a handful to the membership of the Senate, and these would have no more power than do those who chair Congressional committees today. Modest or not, the great difficulties that can be anticipated in putting this or any significant proposal for Congressional reform into effect, bespeaks the need to reexamine the capacity (or incapacity) of the political system to change itself. At base the difficulty of reform lies not in Congress, the Constitution, or the political system, but in our own confusions.

APPENDIX TO CHAPTER 7

Synthetic Rubber and the Borrowed Businessman[1]

That which follows, summarizing American experience in the World War II development of the synthetic rubber industry, is intended to demonstrate the problems associated with relying on the competencies of businessmen and bankers borrowed from the private sector for the formation and implementation of the critical technological cum organizational policies of the positive state. The experience in synthetic rubber is especially germaine at his moment, as the development of an alternative energy source is being entrusted to the Synthetic Fuel Corporation which is designed to act in the model of the old Reconstruction Finance Corporation, as a private investment bank.

The synthetic rubber technology was not created by Americans or in America. The basic technology, believe it or not, is a prerevolutionary Russian invention. The particular synthetic rubber we use in the United States, Buna-S, was developed in Germany, and in their war preparations under the Nazis, the Germans created a massive industry to produce Buna-S rubber along with gasoline and a host of other synthetics out of low-grade brown coal deposits in Silesia. Standard Oil of New Jersey got the technology by chance, as part of a package deal to acquire I. G. Farben's catalytic engineering technology. Standard then adapted it to use petroleum as the raw material source.

In 1939, at the razor's edge of World War II, aware of the American vulnerability to a cut-off of natural rubber, Standard Oil became the champion of a synthetic rubber alternative. To this end, it exercised all of its influence on the new "defense agencies" to enlist governmental financing. But not until after the Nazis

---

[1]Exerpted from Robert A. Solo, "The Saga of Synthetic Rubber," *The Bulletin of the Atomic Scientists* (April, 1980). For other references see Robert A. Solo. "The Sale of Synthetic Rubber Plants," Journal of Industrial Economics (December, 1953); "Research and Development in the Synthetic Rubber Industry," *The Quarterly Journal of Economics* (February, 1954); "The New Threat to Natural Rubber," *The Southern Economic Journal* (July, 1955); and especially *Synthetic Rubber: A Case Study in Technological Development under Public Direction,* Study 18, Subcommittee on Patents, Trademarks, and Copyrights, Committee of the Judiciary of the U.S. Senate (Washington: U.S. Government Printing Office, 1959). This study, until recently out of print, has been updated and is now available under the title, *Across the High-Technology Threshold: The Case of Synthetic Rubber* (Darby, Penn.: Norwood Edition, 1980).

had destroyed the British army, overrun France, and were masters of the whole of Western Europe, with Great Britian isolated and under heavy bombardment, was there any response from the borrowed business executives who manned and controlled the defense agencies. Finally in July, 1940, the National Defense Advisory Commission (NDAC), a precursor to the War Production Board, recommended a government financed industrial complex to produce 100,000 tons of synthetic rubber—about 11 percent of projected rubber needs. Those corporate executives, on loan from business to run the NDAC, never thought to query the technology that would be used to produce the rubber or the material resources upon which it would rely.

In September, 1940, the heads of the National Defense Advisory Commission took their recommendation to the Reconstruction Finance Corporation which had the funds, hence the power, to support such a venture. That agency was run by Jessie Jones, a Texas banker, who was much appreciated by Congress as somebody who "made money for the government." Jessie Jones' edict was that if the Corporation was to give financial support, then the whole problem and responsibility must be put in his hands. Two months later Jones and his associates, without explanation, reduced the production goal to 40,000 tons. By January 15, 1941, proposals and building plans were in the hands of the Rubber Reserve Company, a subsidiary set up to take charge of the much reduced program. But on February 26, 1941, the whole laboriously developed plan was suddenly abandoned—Mr. Jones and his banker associates had decided that there was no danger, no emergency worth wasting the taxpayers' good money on.

Pressed by the oil and tire companies, by the new Office of Production Management, and above all by the disastrous course of events (Nazi submarine sinkings had reached new peaks, their armies had now swept through Yugoslavia and Greece and were advancing with uninterrupted success in North Africa), the Reconstruction Finance Corporation agreed again to the 40,000-ton synthetic rubber program.

On May 21, 1941, the details were settled. All plants would be financed and wholly owned by the government, but built and operated by private companies on a cost-plus-fee basis.

By mid-December, 1941—after the destruction of the fleet at Pearl Harbor and America's declaration of war on Japan, Germany, and Italy; after the Germans, now masters of Europe, had thrown their armies against Russia and were advancing through that country with terrible speed; after the Japanese, sweeping down the Asian coast through Malaysia and Indonesia, had cut off totally America's source of natural rubber—construction had not yet begun on a single plant to produce the critical feedstock, butadiene, needed to produce synthetic rubber. Nor had the government acquired a stockpile of natural rubber. Such was the quality of planning.

Forced by absolute necessity, the 40,000-ton output plan was rapidly increased. By March, 1942, approximately 700,000 tons of synthetic rubber were scheduled for production. But there were questions: How to produce that great quantity of rubber? With what technology? Using what resource base? How much of which rubbers should be produced? When would they be needed? To what timetable should production be geared?

Standard Oil's technology was not the only possibility—there was a wide range of technological options. All of the proven, established technologies, including the Germans', followed the alcohol-to-butadiene route. None had produced butadiene from a petroleum or natural gas derivative. In the United States, moreover, there were then enormous grain stocks in warehouses, owned by the government as a consequence of its farm price-support programs. These could be used to make alcohol with no incremental expenditures and with no strain on the war economy. And there were the whiskey distillers whose plant capacity could be diverted to the production of grain alcohol, again with no strain on the war economy.

The Reconstruction Finance Corporation and the Rubber Reserve, however, did not have the scientific or technological competence to take any such options into account. They were bankers, and like bankers they put their trust in the big customers, with substantial assets on hand. And the borrowed businessmen and company engineers who ran the War Production Board were in full accord. The entire program would be based on petroleum and natural gas derivatives. The Chemicals Branch of the Board answered all challenges and queries with the assertion that nothing else was possible. Alcohol was in critically short supply. There was no capacity available to produce it. None could be spared.

It was a time of apprehension and frustration. The Nazis were tearing Russia apart. A cross-channel invasion, it seemed, would be absolutely necessary in order to keep Russia in the war. The ultimate, decisive confrontation seemed very close at hand. Yet the sense of a planning failure ran deep through the country and in the Congress, especially with respect to synthetic rubber. There the sense of failure was augmented by repeated War Production Board and Resource Finance Corporation "brushoffs" of those who asked that alternative technologies be considered, and by suspicions of conspiracy. Congressional revolt was brewing. Rubber Reserve was under attack by the Truman Committee. Senator Guy Gillette of Ohio addressed a report to the Senate accusing Standard Oil of blocking the use of grain-based alcohol to produce synthetic rubber.

Under Gillette's chairmanship a Senate committee began hearings in March, 1942, and drove hard on the facts of the synthetic rubber fiasco. Under the accumulating exposures and the increasing pressures of this investigation, the company engineers and borrowed businessmen of the Chemicals Branch of the War Production Board suddenly found that instead of a critical shortage, there was a huge surplus of alcohol. They were "swimming in alcohol." Almost overnight rather than 280 million gallons a year of alcohol producing capacity, they had an annual capacity of 540 million gallons. Some discovery! And of the 700,000-ton planned synthetic rubber total, Rubber Reserve re-allocated 220,000 to alcohol, of which 180,000 tons would be grain-based.

In spite of this concession, Congress rose in full revolt. Under the urging of its key committees, it decided to take the rubber program into its own hands. On July 22, by a decisive vote, both Houses passed the Rubber Supply Act of 1942, designed to set up an agency independent of the Executive, directed to increase the production of synthetic rubber from alcohol "produced from agricultural or forest products," with the power of absolute priority in obtaining all that might be required to produce rubber for satisfying military and civilian needs. In a word, a separate executive agency would have been created, supreme within its own sphere, and answerable only to Congress. In his long veto message, the President pointed out that the bill would subvert the whole concept of materials allocation according to relative essentiality in prosecuting the war. But he did not defend the rubber program, conceding that there may have been "serious mistakes . . . based on misinformation, misconception, or even partiality." In August, 1942, he appointed a three-man committee—Bernard Baruch, James Conant and Karl Compton—to review the program and recommend an overall rubber policy.

The Baruch Committee blasted the planning and the organization of the synthetic rubber program, above all for the total lack of any independent technological competence in the administering agency, but indicated that it was far too late in the day to introduce substantive changes. And indeed the time of reckoning was at hand. By the military timetable, the program had to be vectored to 1943, a year "so critical for the rubber situation that the production of 100,000 tons more or less of Buna-S might be the determining factor" in victory or defeat. For now the Germans had cleared the Crimea and had pushed to the foothills of the Caucasus. In the north, the Russian and German armies were locked in the battle of Stalingrad.

During August, 1942, intelligence reports reaching President Roosevelt already conceded a complete German victory at Stalingrad and wrote off those Russian armies as lost. Since February of that year, the American-British Combined Chiefs of Staff had been basing their preparations on two alternatives: a limited invasion of continental Europe during 1942 should it be necessary to relieve the German pressure on the Russian front; or a full scale, cross-channel invasion of the continent in the Spring of 1943. Thus everything indicated an enormous demand for rubber-bearing equipment during the last half of 1942 and in 1943 to support military operations calling for limitless supplies of planes, tanks, trucks, and aviation fuel. A shortage of any one of these might spell disaster.

What happened? For the critical year 1943, Rubber Reserve promised an output of 400,000 tons of Buna-S. The Baruch Committee directed an output of 450,000 tons. Actual production was 181,470 tons. Against the Committee's call for 596,000 tons of all synthetic rubber, only 217,235 tons, or about 37 percent was forthcoming. By its own objectives, the program was a flat failure.

That catastrophe did not follow was due to a fortunate turn in world events. It was the German armies that were destroyed at Stalingrad; nor thereafter was there any doubt about the Russians' staying power. The cross-channel invasion was put off until June, 1944. The rubber program was thus afforded more than a full year of grace. It might have been otherwise. And if the crisis had come when expected, not only would supplies have been disastrously short, but no petroleum-based synthetic rubber could ever have been produced.

The Reconstructions Finance Corporation bankers, and the borrowed businessmen and company engineers who ran the War Production Board, did everything in their power to restrict the entire synthetic rubber program to petroleum-based butadiene. Only a Congressional revolt forced the inclusion of grainbased, alcohol-to-butadiene plants, and that very late in the day. Yet in the all-critical year of 1943, the alcohol-based plants produced 130,000 tons of butadiene, while those using a petroleum derivative produced a mere 20,000 tons. In 1944, out of a total production of 557,605 tons of butadiene, 361,731 were made from alcohol. Alcohol-based synthetic rubber carried the nation through all the critical phases of the war.

And why this disgraceful wartime performance of the petroleum-to-butadiene plants in contrast to those based on the use of alcohol? Precisely for the reasons that the critics of the program foretold. The latter technology was established, relatively simple, well understood; many of its essential components were already largely in place. The former was complex, untried, requiring a full line development of new plant and equipment. Above all, what blocked the production of petroleum-based rubber was that it required the same cut of petroleum as that which was essential to the production of high octane aviation fuel. The conflict was not only in the demand for butylene but also in the demand for the whole research apparatus and man and machine power of the petroleum industry.

All this was foreseeable. And it was foreseen by no one more clearly—nor did anyone protest more forcibly—than Chaim Weizmann, later President of Israel. A world-famous industrial chemist, Weizmann was known for his contributions to allied victory in World War I. Associated with synthetic rubber research since 1910, he had been sent to the United State by Winston Churchill in the hope that he might be of help. His prophetic voice was ignored, as was his offer of a technology that would produce a true substitute for natural rubber. In his autobiography, *Trial and Error,* he wrote bitterly that "to initiate a process which had not the approval of the oil companies was almost too much of a task for any human being."

In August, 1944, before the waning level of conflict and the diminished demand for high-octane fuel made it possible to bring petroleum-based butadiene on stream, and with the production of alcohol-based butadiene cut back deliberately, the alcohol plants, operating at almost double their assigned capacity, were producing at a rate of 412,544 tons per annum. This was only 163,000 tons short of the highest level of wartime output. At that level of production moreover, the supply of Buna-S was in excess of industrial demand for it. By July, 1944, inventories of Buna-S were far in excess of 100,000 tons. Clearly, the alcohol plants alone could have satisfied all butadiene requirements.

In terms of proper wartime planning, the enormous expenditure of the most crucial materials and of the most highly skilled technological and scientific manpower, devoted to building the plants and to the design and establishment of the petroleum-to-butadiene technology, was pure waste. It was taking much away from and adding nothing to the capacity to wage total war. One reason that industry could not use the butadiene produced was that the planning program had grievously erred in estimating the proportion of natural rubber that was necessary in tire construction, and especially for heavy duty truck and aircraft tires. Ignoring Weizmann's technology for producing isoprene as a natural rubber substitute, the program relied on large increases in the production of Standard Oil's specialty, butyl rubber, and on DuPont's neoprene. Both turned out to be useless for the purpose.

The intention here is not to rake up old scandals, certainly not to infer wickedness or corruption, but to demonstrate that the certified and proven skills, reference values, and practical outlook acquired through the working experience of the banker and of the business executive, is not transferable to the positive state, without grave peril.

Such was the quality of the wartime planning and organization of a synthetic rubber industry. . . .

Certainly there is this lesson to be learned from the synthetic rubber experience. . . .

Don't entrust the task of social planning, involving choices of scientific and technological complexity, to a financial agency modeled on the Reconstruction Finance Corporation. What is absolutely necessary, and what was critically lacking in the instance of the synthetic rubber programs throughout, is a high technological-scientific competence at the center of policy and program responsibility—one that is disinterested, that is adapted to the processes of public choice and political action, and that is sensitized to the table of social values. That is not the competence of the banker, nor of the borrowed businessman, nor of the company engineer. Their lifetime experiences have given their way of thinking a different orientation and have built other values into their judgment.

Why did those connected with the Reconstruction Finance Corporation and the War Production Board, regardless of corporate affiliation, strive so hard to reserve the butadiene program to the petroleum companies, even though a technology based on petroleum derivatives was so clearly untenable in an economy at war? Because in market terms, by reference to the values to which businessmen and company engineers were accustomed, petroleum-based butadiene technology was to be preferred. They could not readapt their thinking even to the simple criteria of war planning. It is easy enough to change official hats, but the thinking cap sticks to the skull.

A POLICY FOR THE
ORGANIZATIONAL SECTOR

The Organizational Sector

The Neo-Marxists are certainly right in supposing that within the national domain, there is not one market-based economy but several, and that the role of the state is different with respect to each. Thus, for example, parity price supports, government operated experiment stations, and a vast extention network relate not to the economy in general, but represent "agricultural policy" tailored to the particular needs of one of the economies that compose the whole. Economic policy should and tends to be in fact developed in relation to the needs and circumstances of constituent economies (call them sectors). Elsewhere[1] I postulate three market-based sectors, as parts of the American national economy: namely, "decentralized, price-directed sector," which would include agriculture, conforming more or less to the model of pure competition; and a "decentralized, market-segmented sector" with large numbers of relatively small firms competing in segmented markets under conditions analogous to those described by Edward Chamberlin as of "monopolistic competition," including, retailing, construction, professional services; finally the "organizational" or "corporate" sector, dominated by massive corporations and trade unions, whose autonomous and arbitrary powers were earlier discussed. It is with policy for the organizational sector that we are concerned in this chapter.

---

[1]Robert A. Solo, *Economic Organizations and Social Systems* (Indianoplis: The Bobbs-Merrill Co., Inc., 1967).

Anti-Antitrust

The American state had only one coherent and purposeful economic policy during the long epoch of ideological liberalism (through to the 1930s). This had to do with prosecuting monopolies and conspiracies in restraint of trade along with a certain number of anticompetitive practices under the antitrust laws. These laws and this policy were of no relevance for the decentralized, price-directed sector. For the decentralized, price-segmented sector, they were effective, with hundreds of successful prosecutions of arrangements between individual firms to eliminate or lessen competition. Their application can be credited with preventing the cartels which generally prevailed in pre-World War II Europe from developing in the American economy.

What of the organizational sector, where the sheer arbitrary power (in the eyes of the economists, the power of monopoly) to control price was at issue? There the court, presumably concerned with the untoward effects of dismemberment on productivity and technology, rejected antitrust demand that the corporate giants be "broken up." The "good trusts" were absolved from the antitrust rule until war and depression brought the epoch of liberalism to a close.

Across the threshold of a new era, the Court, accepting the necessity of a positive state able to act on its own responsibility with accountability due not to the courts but to the electorate, removed those reins that it had for long held all public agencies tightly in check. Beginning in the late 1930s, the antitrust agencies were free to attack; and repeatedly they did attack the monopoly power of the large corporations successfully; with the acquiescence of the courts, producing a long string of victories against monopoly.

What did this achieve? For the lawyer, for the Attorney General, the measure of achievement is in the number of cases won, the scalps in the belt, the niches on the gun. For the lawyer there is no looking back, or ahead. Suffice that the crime was punished. Suffice that justice was done. Nor are the courts institutionally equipped or in any way geared to evaluate impacts and take consequences into account. And that is the fatal flaw in the use of the courts, when the objective is not to chastise evildoers and punish sin, but is rather to raise the level of economic or social performance. And surely there can be no other purpose to the antitrust laws or to any law or measure that favors or forbids a particular kind of business entity or market system. And so I asked the question that the court never asks, and that I thought had not been asked before. What happened then? After the glorious antitrust victories, what happened then, to prices, to wages, to profits and dividends, to production, to employment, to productivity, to the rate of invention and innovation hence to technology, and product variety, to the strength of industry in international competition, in a word to whatever might reveal the impact of the "victory" on the level of economic performance.[2] I was to discover that a distinguished researcher had asked the selfsame question some sixteen years earlier, with respect

---

[2]Robert A. Solo, *The Political Authority and the Market System* (Cincinnati: South-Western Publishing Co., 1974), especially Chapters 11, 12, 13.

to a quite different set of cases.[3] The conclusions of our independent studies turned out to be the same. By the measures of performance, the antitrust victories yielded no benefits. On the contrary. Every strong antitrust action in the organizational sector was positively detrimental.

Never were the sluggards, the laggards, the bad performers, the continual losers that dragged down the economy in those failing industries that cried out for curative change, brought under attack. The star performers, the aggressive, innovative, high achievers only bore the brunt of the antitrust onus and were sometimes destroyed by it.

One sure guarantee of disaster would be to follow the prescription of some antitrust liberals to go still further, treating an induced malady by stronger doses of the same poison, so fragmenting corporate industry that it would operate according to the canons of pure competition. Nor is there the slightest possibility of this occurring.

As ideological design and as instrumentality for upgrading performance in the organizational sector or for in any way assuring that the public interest is served through the activities of that sector, antitrust policy is worthless; worse than worthless; it should be abandoned.[4]

This certainly is not to say that there should be no collective concern with price, productivity, income distribution, and other appropriate measures of corporate performance or that positive action should not be taken in the face of failures of performance, technical lag and the loss of international markets, or the misuse of arbitrary powers. It is to say that given the need for positive action, another policy design and a different instrumentality of control is called for.

Dual Management for the Organizational Sector

Consider then this sector, composed of industrial sets that are each a unique and complex communal matrix and where each of the relatively few major constituent entities is enormous in size, unique in character, complex in organization, with numerous satellites geared into its operation. Let it be agreed that as a form of economic organization, this sector has some great social advantages, in combining variety and flexibility with economies of scale and benefits of planning, and yet

---

[3]Simon Whitney, *Antitrust Policies* (New York: Twentieth Century Fund, 1958).

[4]When I published this position in 1974, I was quite alone in the profession, truly the proverbial voice in the wilderness. Now, even as I prepare the final revisions of this book in 1981 I read:

"ANTITRUST GROWS UNPOPULAR. Opposition to the nation's 90-year-old antitrust policies is beginning to sweep the country, and it is coming not from corporate executives but from economists, who say these policies are not serving the economy well. There is a broad consensus of economists— including some leading liberals—who now believe the decline in U.S. competitiveness at home and abroad is partly the result of outdated antitrust enforcement practices. They say the government's views about what constitutes market power are far too restrictive and are calling for major policy revisions to give business a freer hand.

". . . Such harsh critics as liberal economist Lester C. Thurow of the Massachusetts Institute of Technology are even urging that the government abandon almost its entire system of antitrust laws and enforcement mechanisms. . . ." Reprinted from the January 12, 1981, issue of *Business Week,* p. 90, by special permission, © 1981 by McGraw-Hill, Inc., New York, New York 10020. All rights reserved. See also "Antitrust: Big Business Breathes Easier" *New York Times,* Section 3. p. 1.

allowing the individual considerable freedom in a choice of association. But, on the other hand:

1. Demonstrably, the internal drives and motivations that determine corporate behavior are highly equivocal. There is no necessary correlation between insider's gain and corporate benefit, nor between managerial motivation, corporate policy and that which society values, for example, low prices, high wages, career opportunity, nondiscriminatory recruitment and promotion, the conservation of critical resources, invention, and innovation leading to increased productivity or product variety, sustained technological development and stable economic growth.

2. Nor need external forces, for example, those of competition, so constrain and direct corporate behavior to assure that policy and action conforms to the public interest.

3. Nor does there appear to be any necessary mechanism for the spontaneous elimination and replacement of poor performers and especially when poor performance is indigenous to the industrial set, nor need there be any spontaneous rejuvenation of the failing firm and sluggard industry. These corporate entities and the industrial sets of which they are a part have great defensive and inertial powers, with decline and deterioration continuing for decades, even generations.

4. The collapse of an industrial set, or even of one of major constituent entities may have catastrophic, irreparable consequences, spreading waves of disaster and dragging down a host of related structures.

Accepting all this, accepting the potentials for exploitation, misadventure, failure, and catastrophe; accepting the lack of any spontaneous rejuvenator or self-generating correctives, and accepting the residual responsibility of the state for economic performance, how is the positive state to organize itself to fullfil its responsibility with respect to the corporate sector?

There must come to be created a system of dual management as the nexus that links the positive state to each industrial set of the corporate sector; with one level of (private) management having responsibility for operations with corporate answerability, and the other level of (public) management with responsibilities for the encompassing industrial system and answerability to the public via the political system. Either we will create such a system purposefully and rationally or we will be driven towards it along the path of crisis and despair. Our economic destiny will depend in good part on the quality and character of what emerges.

Suppose such a system, with management corps of public and of corporate professionals, their competences developed along parallel lines, but lines that do not intersect, with career crossovers discouraged or forbidden at every level so that the former are not captivated or captured by prospects with and promises of the latter. On the public side each of the industry-focussed management corp (united perhaps in a Department of Industries) would be systematically exposed to a variety of work experiences and otherwise trained to a deep and intimate knowledge of the technologies, both in this country and abroad, of their industry and of the organization, operations, policies, internal-relations, performance and problems of the key corporate entities of their industrial set, with such learning always from the perspective of social purpose, collective values and the power structure and decision-processes of the political system.

A public management corp operating within prescribed constraints, would be accountable to Congress and to the policy-echelons of the executive for the performance of its industry. It would require considerable autonomy and discretion in the exercise of its real but limited leverage on the corporate entities of its industrial set. Its autonomy would be based in part on its possession of a body of knowledge and a competence that is unique and invaluable, in part on the public support that it, like other agencies, would cultivate.

The public management agency would act as an intermediary between and in proxy for such functional agencies as EPA, OSHA, the Department of Energy, and the Department of Transportation, facilitating the transmission of social imperatives to corporate management and transmitting the knowledge of operating constraints, of industry limits, and preferred alternatives to the functional agencies.

The relationships between corporate and public management would sometimes be conflictual—they would serve different clients and reflect a different set of interests. But for the most part their relationship should be symbiotic. Both would have a critical interest in the systemic values, for example, the stability, prosperity, technological advance, and sustained growth of the industry. The reputation of the public manager, his success, his capacity to satisfy public expectations and to achieve social goals, requires and depends upon the existence of efficient corporate operations, and on an innovative, effective, receptive corporation management. And the intelligent corporation manager will also benefit inasmuch as his point of access to and interface with the power structure and policymaking processes of the state is deeply knowledgeable concerning the technology, the internal circumstances, the intrinsic potentials, and the critical problems of the industry.

What are the tasks in the public management of the corporate sector?

Public Management and Corporate Enterprise

Some of the tasks appropriate to public management in the organizational sector will be developed here in a series of scenarios.

There is, first of all and continuously, the need for it to *monitor,* to study in depth with full access to information under conditions of high confidentiality, the circumstances and the operations of each corporate entity in its industrial set. Monitoring is the essential tool in learning, in creation of the relevant competence, and in creating the basis for sophisticated judgment and rational policy.

Eventually inescapable is the task of wage-price control for the organizational sector; and the agency of public management would be the public participant in the formation of corporate and trade union wage-price policy. Taking general social objectives and industrial realities into account, it would have the power to approve or to deny corporate demands for price increases.

Suppose this situation. The agency of public management is in a position to approve or deny a particular price increase that Ford can live with, that will net General Motors a tidy profit, but that will bankrupt Chrysler, Should the failure of Chrysler be allowed, declaring good riddance to a company that has been a drag on the industry and a burden to the consumer, with efforts of the public management focused all out in assuring that the other American automobile producers will rapidly take up the slack of Chrysler's decline? Or, in the light of what is considered to be that automaker's growth and development potential, and taking into account the industrial and financial disruption that would be occasioned by its failure, should a larger price increase for the sake of Chrysler be allowed? Or without allowing that price increase, should some other form of assistance, in loans or subsidies, be mobilized by the agency of public management and made available on terms to the automaker.

This problem of what to do when great corporate entity verges on bankruptcy and collapse transcends the matter of price-wage control. It has occurred, it is occurring, and it will occur with increasing frequency in the future. And if, in recognition of the danger of spreading waves of disaster and irreparable damage to the economy, and in the knowledge that there is no mechanism of spontaneous rejuvenation, reparation, replacement or cure, aid is offered at the public's cost, on what terms should it be given? Or rather what should be done to insure that the crisis will not recur, that the failure will not merely be postponed, that the demands upon the public purse and the consumer's pocketbook will not be repeated, that the weaknesses and causes of decline, whatever they are, will be overcome? Should a top-to-bottom purge of management be required? Should the board of directors be reformed, with its members, selected with public approval, to include trade union and public representation? Should there be a sharp reduction in executive salaries and the elimination of executive perks? Is a change in financial practice, in recruitment, in merchandising, in R&D investment, called for? These are in fact the stuff of the agreement that Chrysler has made with the United States Treasury, as a precondition for the government guaranteed loan. That agreement, however, is now purely a paper arrangement, something to safeguard negotiators from later reprobation ("we did our best"), and as a public relations gesture. It cannot now be more than that because there does not now exist in the American state any locus of competence and authority with the deep and intimate knowledge of the technology and circumstances at issue, such as would permit an evaluation of the qualities of a specific management, or the quality of those proposed as replacement, or to identify weakness and the sources of failure, or to activate technological rehabilitation or organizational restructuring, or for the long haul to be able to monitor the implementation of corrective and rehabilitative arrangements. With an agency of public management, that locus of competence and authority would exist. That is the difference.

A Japanese Option

Traveling briefly in Japan I learned in bits and pieces and without much authentication something of Japanese business practice. I was fascinated when I was told that as much as half the income of a Japanese comes in the form of an annual bonus;

a practice which must be enormously advantageous to the Japanese corporation. First because it identifies every worker's welfare with corporate performance, building a matchless material basis for cooperative endeavor (teamwork) and providing a work incentive in relation to which touted employee stock ownership schemes seem trivial. Secondly, having through collective bargaining, agreed upon a system for income sharing, there is no need or pressure for an annual or periodic wage bargain where wages are ritualistically raised by an annual or periodic percent increase which produces and is canceled out by an inflationary price increase, a practice that cannot be reconciled with any viable system of wage-price control. Finally, the corporation would possess a newfound flexibility and staying power. In the face of declining demand and reduced corporate income, bonus payments to labor and management, hence costs, would go down correspondingly. The survival of the entity would not, in anything approaching the same degree as now, be threatened, nor would the level of employment. The Chrysler Corporation, under those circumstances would not have been pushed to the edge nor forced massively to disemploy its workforce. One wonders whether, in the Chrysler case, the union might not have been persuaded and management required to accept such an arrangement providing precisely for the distribution of all income, net of obligatory costs, with the union offered employment benefits, where *base* wage and salaries would be reduced throughout (say from 10 to 70 percent), drastically at the high salary levels of upper echelon management, least at the low end of the wage scale, conversely with a larger share of profits accruing as a bonus for the upper echelons, and a smaller one to the routine workers at the lower income scale.

Mergers and the Structure of the Economy

To say that the attempt to act upon the organizational sector through the judiciary under the laws of antitrust, ought to be abandoned, is not to suggest that there ought to be no concern for competition, or that the structure of industry or of the individual corporation ought not be subject to scrutiny, and, if found lacking, to be changed. With regard to such, we have only one constraint to propose. For firms and for industries that meet the tests of performance, that produce efficiently, that generate high wages and profits and sell at low prices, and contribute to the advance of technology; follow this simple rule. Don't kill the goose that lays the golden eggs. Too often, it is that goose precisely that attracts our butcher's knife. For the rest, let it be remembered that there is no inherent, natural right to any given industrial arrangement. All economic institutions, all forms of economic organization, are instrumental, and justifiable only in terms of their produce, their consequences, the benefits that they yield. There is no inherent, natural right to incorporate. There is no inherent, natural right for corporations to merge. It is something allowed. It can be disallowed. If its social benefits do not outweigh its detriments, then it should be disallowed.

The Clayton Act forbade mergers between corporate competitors.[5] Business

---

[5]Section 7 forbids one corporation from acquiring the shares of a competing corporation or from buying the stock of two or more corporations that were competitors where such action might substantially lessen competition or tend towards monopoly.

found and the courts allowed a loophole to that barrier.[6] From 1940 to 1947, some 2,500 firms, constituting 5 percent of the assets of American manufacturing and mining industry, disappeared through merger. The loophole was eliminated by the Cellar Antimerger Act of 1950. Mergers were thenceforth vigorously prosecuted, with an uninterrupted stream of governmental victories. Withall, the rate of merger accelerated and at an unparalleled rate, for example, from 219 mergers in 1950 to 5,600 in 1969.[7] Especially the wave of new mergers was concentrated among very large corporations so that between 1948 and 1968 the share of total U.S. industrial assets possessed by the 200 largest corporations, increased from 48 percent to 60 percent.

Robert B. Reich, at the time of writing the director of policy planning at the Federal Trade Commission explains the fact that:

> The United States has now the highest percentage of obsolete plants, the lowest percentage of capital investment, the lowest growth in productivity and savings of any major industrial society.

by reference to the "deeper roots" of the crisis:

> Simply put, the structure of our economy—its underlying organization, the incentives it offers—has discouraged long-term growth in favor of short-term paper profits. An ever larger portion of our economy is focused on rearranging industrial assets rather than on increasing their size. Instead of enlarging the economic pie, we are busy reassigning the slices.
>
> Look around you, and you can see the rearrangers hard at work, prospering. They are the accountants who manipulate tax laws and depreciation rules to produce glowing—or at least presentable—annual reports. They are the financiers who think up new varieties of debentures or new mutual funds. They are the consultants who plot acquisition campaigns and the lobbyists skilled at obtaining government subsidies. They are the corporate executives, trained in law and finance, who hire all of the above, and the lawyers whose briefcases bulge with statutes, opinions, depositions, interrogatories, motions, and prospecti necessary to carry out their strategies.
>
> Whom you hear less and less of are the pie-enlargers—the engineers and inventors who create better products at less cost, and the workers and entrepreneurs who translate those ideas into new factories, new jobs, and ultimately into goods and services that people want to buy. By any number of measurements, including the total amount of money, effort, and media attention devoted to each, the ratio of asset-rearrangers to asset-enlargers in our economy is running at about two to one.
>
> The most obvious example is the continuing rage on mergers. In the last three years some $100 billion of corporate cash resources have been used to acquire existing corporate assets through tender offers. This money otherwise could have been spent on new factories and other productive uses. . . . Instead of generating

---

[6]In the *Thatcher* and *Swift* cases (1926), the Supreme Court decided that since a company acquired the controlling shares of a competitor and used its control to procure its competitor's assets, it automatically removed itself from prosecution under the Clayton Act.

[7]For this and other data presented in this section, refer to Solo, *ibid.,* Chapter 13.

future economic expansion, the money circulates among companies like stakes in a floating dice game.

The pace of this game has been accelerating. In 1978, 2,106 acquisitions were announced, valued at $34 billion, a 54 percent increase over the $22 billion reported in 1977. In 1979, the figures jumped to 2,128 acquisitions valued at $43.5 billion, almost double the 1977 figure.[8]

The successful antitrust prosecutions of mergers had this important consequence. From 1948 until 1955, before its full impact was felt, some 62 percent of all mergers were horizontal or vertical (bringing together firms that produced the same product possibly for sale in the same market, that is, horizontal mergers; or firms whose outputs were linked in the integral raw materials-to-intermediate product—to end product chain, that is, vertical mergers). Whereas by 1968, 90 percent of all mergers were conglomerates; bringing under a single corporate ownership, operations with nothing technologically or functionally in common. Unlike vertical or horizontal mergers, conglomerates cannot possibly be understood as rationalizing production and reducing the costs of production, nor can they be understood as possibly insuring a stable, low cost supply of raw materials or intermediary products and services, nor can they be understood possibly as insuring a secure outlet for the production of raw materials or of intermediary products and services, nor can they be understood as a means of possibly more fully capitalizing on established distributional outlets and reducing merchandising costs, nor can they be understood possibly as a means of countervailing against the high-pricing practices of suppliers or of eliminating the costs of unnecessary middlemen. It is not, and this is the fact to remember, possible to justify conglomerate mergers on grounds that they yield some benefit, through a contribution to efficiency in any form. Nor is it possible to attack conglomerates as anticompetitive. If Swift should acquire Armour, then concentration would increase in the meatpacking industry, and off would go to the antitrust alarms. But what if Greyhound Bus acquired Armour Meats? Competition measured by the numbers and strength of the competitors in each of the two markets would not have changed. The danger and the distortion that inheres in conglomeration escapes the antitrust criterion and the net of its law entirely.

If conglomerate merger has, and can have no organizational, no technological, no marketing rationale, then what can account for this extraordinary movement, profoundly impacting upon the industrial structure?

It would be good to have a definitive answer to that question. In part it could be accounted for by the megalomania of corporate empire builders; in part because, through merger, by allowing accumulated profits to be unloaded as capital gains, by the shift of book losses, and otherwise, taxes can be evaded; but for the most part, I am convinced, the reason for conglomeration rests in the interests of and benefits accruing to financial insiders and stock manipulators.

A strange phenomenon, the stock market. One need do no more than reflect on its daily and radical gyrations to know how capricious and irrational an instrument

---

[8]Robert B. Reich, "Pie-Slicers vs Pie Enlargers," *The Washington Monthy.* (September, 1980), pp. 13–19.

it has to be in the allocation of investable resources, though its function in channelizing funds into industry is entirely peripheral to the back-and-forth trading of existing securities.

An army of brokers and "analysts," ignorant of and indifferent to the technological and organizational realities of the industrial economy, earn their living by whipping up and capitalizing upon the hopes and fears of a multitude that knows nothing and can know nothing of the corporate universe upon whom their decisions bear. The securities market is, in effect, a great floating crap game operated and masterminded by the con men and bunko artists of our time. Its rapid and random price fluctuations produces fluctuations, as rapid and random in the magnitude and the distribution of the community's wealth, hence in the levels of consumer expenditure with all the consequences thereof; it is, in short, inherently destabilizing, dangerous, wasteful. Its supergamblers and manipulators used the opportunity to conglomerate as an instrument for stock promotion, grinding out the profits through their security mills. By the time the market turned sour on their offerings, they had already discovered how to capitalize on their position and use their expertise in market manipulation to "takeover" the complex apparatus of the producing economy, replacing in the niches of corporate command that breed of management who had worked in the business, knew the business, had built the business, with the new host of financial manipulators, stock promotors, inside wheeler dealers, takeover artists, superaccountants without deep knowledge of or interest in the technologies of the heterogenious tangle of enterprises in their hands, hence totally incapable of evaluating new technology or assessing the distant potentials of significant innovation. In treating the operations under their control, their acquisitions, as sets of assets merely, cards in the hand to be shuffled in and out of the pack and dealt out on the gaming table, they have transformed American industry into a jungle of organizational monstrosities. Their ignorance and indifference is a major blockage to the introduction or development of new technology and significant innovation; that and the heavy burden that labyrinthian conglomeration places upon any possibility of rational management, accounts in good part for the precipitous decline, of a rapidity quite without precedent, in American technological *cum* industrial preeminence.

Again we return to the fact, and to the question. Corporate merger is not an inherent right. It is something we have allowed. It is something we could disallow. Ought corporate merger be forbidden?

If one has the courage to ask the question of what would be gained and what would be lost, the answer by any reckoning of social benefit against social cost is clear and unequivocal. By the measures of management effectiveness, business stability, operating efficiency, the advance of technology and the increase of productivity, competition, growth in the GNP, equity in income distribution, *nothing* would be lost by forbidding all corporate mergers; and by those same measures of social benefit, a great deal could be gained. Corporate mergers should be forbidden.

If corporations wish to diversify or to extend their operations and activities, let them. Nothing to stop them. Save that they would have to do it by creating new operations and competing to establish themselves in new markets. All the better for dynamics of capitalism.

Perhaps there are exceptions. There may be cases where merger would add to efficient operations, or could be justified as yielding other positive social benefits. If so, let the companies make their case to the agent of public management, and give to that agent the power to grant waivers.

There is the further matter of disentangling these conglomerated monstrosities, and restoring into industry a rational order of organization. For this there is a precedent. During the 1920s in a manner analogous to the recent wave of conglomerations, there were formed vast utility empires brought together through holding companies, holding controlling interest in the holding companies that held controlling interest in the holding companies that held controlling interest in the holding companies . . . as many as seven tiers deep, all without territorial, technological, managerial, organizational linkage and rationale, serving to evade the force of regulation and to siphon profits and focus power into the hands of a tiny set of insiders. With the Great Depression, those "empires" collapsed like houses of cards. It became the first task of the new Securities and Exchange Commission to restructure the electrical utility industry into viable sets grouped according to locational proximity, technological advantage, and managerial convenience. To strip down and restructure conglomerates and conglomerated industries in distress is another task for public management.

Financing the Transformation of Technology

There can be no satisfaction of expectations of betterment without an increase in productivity (understood as the relationship between the quantity produced and the amount of work needed to produce it, or more generally in the ratio between the satisfaction of needs and the sacrifices made). And there can be a stable and significant rise in productivity only when and inasmuch as technology advances. The core of growth and the absolute prerequisite to economic betterment is technological advance.

Alas, in no other country in the world has the decline in technological preeminence been so rapid as in the United States during the last two decades, a decline concentrated in the organizational sector. Something of this state of affairs is shown in Table 1, page 108, with data from 1960–1975. Subsequently to 1975, comparative conditions for the United States have worsened. Two probable causes for this are, (1) the great drain of technologically-oriented, science-trained research brainpower into the Pentagon maw, and (2) the just examined conglomeration of industrial enterprise.

The economy outpaced, faced even with years of absolute decline in productivity, and the American State offers only tax gadgetry and political rhetoric; for those in charge are without the competence to conceive of or control, or deal constructively with the system of technological advance. Here, clearly, are critical tasks for positive action by a competent public management. The problems and options of the state in policy for and action related to the systems of science and of technological advance will be discussed in a later chapter. Here we will consider only a facet of this, namely, policy for financing by the state of critical transforma-

TABLE 1-Productivity Growth of OECD Nations

Nation	Growth Rates of Gross Domestic Product Per Person Employed		Growth Rates of Productivity by Sector, 1955–1968			Manufacturing Output Per Man-Hour Worked	
	1960–1973	1969–1975 [a]	Agricultural Industry Services			1960–1973	1973–1975
Canada	2.4	2.8	4.8	3.8	−0.1	4.3	−0.8
United States	2.1	2.6	5.4	2.9	1.7	3.3	−2.4
Japan	9.2	9.6	NA	NA	NA	10.5	6.2
France	5.2	5.2	6.1	5.3	3.4	6.0	3.6
Germany	5.4	4.4	6.1	5.0	2.5	5.8	4.0
Italy	5.7	5.3	7.8	5.8	3.7	6.4	NA
United Kingdom	2.8	3.1	5.8	2.9	1.4	4.0	0.1

NA=not applicable.
[a] Estimated.

SOURCE: *Expenditure Trends in OECD Countries, 1960–1980,* Table 5 (Paris: OECD, 1972); *The Growth of Output, 1960–1980,* Table 7 (Paris: OECD, 1970) "Report by OECD's Manpower and Social Affairs Committee," *OECD Observer,* March-April 1976, p. 10.

tions of technology in the organizational sector. Such financing might be urgently needed in the public interest, providing there is a public management competent to evaluate and assess the benefits of such transformation and to set conditions guaranteeing that such benefits will accrue to the consumer as lower prices.

Before World War II American industry and technology were in every way supreme. During the war the capital equipment and industrial infrastructure of erstwhile competitors, particularly of Germany and Japan, virtually were obliterated, but those of the United States emerged unscathed and, indeed, greatly enhanced. Yet, in only a few decades, the technology of those competitors has, in important instances, overtaken and outdistanced that of the United States, particularly in those high technology areas (like steel) characterized by heavy investment in producer durables. The United States seemingly is replicating Great Britain's Nineteenth-Century industrial decline from the heights of technological supremacy, recalling Thorstein Veblen's forewarnings about the dangers of being ahead.[9]

We will hypothesize a case, speculative in character but approximating, we believe, the industrial realities and intended to illustrate another role of public management. Suppose a steel industry in two economies, call them Japan and the United States. The management of each is equally skilled, foresightful, and self-interested; variations in the skill, energy, and wages of labor can be disregarded. Investible funds are mobile, and private investment in the transformation of industry

---

[9]Thorstein Veblen, *Imperial Germany and the Industrial Revolution* (New York: Macmillan, Inc., 1915).

in either country can draw upon the savings of either country.[10] The structure of producer durables in the United States is intact, but in Japan it has virtually been destroyed by the depredation of war. Suppose that the intact technology of the United States produces steel at an average cost of $100 a ton, including a return on prior investment of 8 percent. Suppose that a new technology is in the offing that can produce steel at an average cost of $50 a ton, including a 12 percent return on the investment required to install that new technology. Thus the annual reduction in production costs would be far and away greater than the annual cost of installing the new technology. The intent here is to postulate an extreme case where, on rational grounds, taking net income or the net increase in the real value of outputs per unit of input as the criterion, the installation of the new technology will be, as the economists say, "pareto optimal," all plus and no minus, hence absolutely in the public interest. The question we would ask is, given this opportunity, whether Japan, or the United States, or both will install the new technology?

Japan's choice is inevitable. If it is to rebuild its industry at all, it would do so by installing the new and advanced technology. The cost of producing steel in Japan, relative to costs of the prior technology, would be reduced correspondingly. What of the United States? With the reduction in cost being so greatly in excess of the discounted value of the cost of replacing the existing installation, *rational* choice should be equally unequivocal. The social interest would require that the old be scrapped and replaced. In so doing the United States would have an advantage over Japan, since the junk value, and/or the possibility of depreciation without replacement of elements of the old capital structure would reduce the costs of the technological transformation in the United States as compared to the cost of installing the new technology in Japan.

What would happen according to the theory, and in the circumstances of pure competition with its decentralized, price-directed markets? Or what would happen if the industry was monopolized and monopolists acted as neoclassical economists believe they do? Or what would happen under socialism with a planned economy, centralized and politically directed? In the decentralized, price-directed markets of

---

[10]In fact, wisely and under a competent public management, Japan disallowed the overseas investment of its savings unless it could be established that such investment was related to and would benefit the system of production in Japan. In the United States, on the contrary, not only were financial interests and corporations given a free hand in this regard, but through tax benefits, investment abroad has been subsidized relative to investment of American savings domestically. This accelerated United States corporate investment overseas and the corresponding extension of the foreign operations of United States corporate enterprise, with two consequences for the American economy. Inasmuch as it was a flight from the power of organized labor to regions of the world where labor can be easily exploited, it eroded the bargaining position and distributional share of United States labor and produced islands of industrial depression in the United States. Its more critical effect was in drawing off the cream of United States managerial, entrepreneurial, and innovational skills and talent, thereby diminishing that which produces technological advance and industrial innovation in the United States, as well as denying the American economy the associated benefits (external economies) of such investment. The importance of this diversion is indicated by the fact that for the years 1971–1975, investment in plant and equipment abroad by affiliates of United States corporations (totaling $79 billions) was 41 per cent of all equivalent plant and equipment expenditure for the entire United States private economy. Nearly twenty years ago I forewarned of this trap and pleaded for a change in the policy of subsidizing overseas investment. Robert A. Solo, "Economics of the International Base Company," *The National Tax Journal,* Vol. 14 (March, 1961), pp. 70–80.

pure competition, innovators would enter the industry and introduce the new technology. As the innovation spreads and the industry was transformed in the image of the new technology, competition would force prices down to an equilibrium at the lower average cost level. Consumers would benefit and for a while innovators would reap a windfall gain. On the other hand, equity ownership in those operations rendered obsolete would suffer losses. What Alfred Marshall would have called their quasi rents would be eliminated. Both the rational monopolist and the socialist planner would seize the opportunity offered by the new technology. Both would immediately transform operations, bearing the costs and appropriating the more than compensatory benefits. The difference between them would be only in the manner of distributing those benefits and costs. But in the peculiar circumstances of our organizational sector, given the opportunity to install a new technology that brings savings greater than the costs of transformation, including the opportunity costs of using the old technology with a zero return on investment, transformation will be prevented or delayed by the existence of an intact capital structure. This will be so no matter by how much savings in costs overbalance the costs of transformation, *given* the pricing conditions characteristic of large-scale enterprise in the organizational sector.

The argument requires a number of assumptions, namely: (1) the entry of new firms into industries such as steel is difficult and rare. Hence technological transformation depends on those already in the industry. (2) Management anticipates that the political authority will protect the domestic market against foreign producers when the latter offer their outputs at prices below average domestic costs. (3) Price in the American market will find its equilibrium at average costs for a prevailing technology, including in costs the conventionally acceptable return on the investment required to install the technology, in the sense that this would be the only price that can for long be justified before the bar of public opinion, kept safe from public intervention, without tempting producers to shade prices or trade unions to accelerate the upward thrust of their wage demands. The consequent pricing behavior would be analogous to that associated with regulated public utilities where rates are held to the level of average costs, including a fair return on investment. These assumptions are, I suggest, in line with observable organizational realities.

Suppose then as the conventional outlook, encouraged as a stabilizing element and one that produces common policy responses throughout the industry, that management does anticipate that future prices will settle at that level of costs, including in costs a return on investment made in installing the prevailing technology *whatever it might be*. What would the rational response of management be to our hypothesized opportunity of adopting a new technology that would greatly reduce production costs and, at the same time, require massive new intestment?

Management would have three options in financing that transformation of industry. It could reduce or eliminate dividends, accumulate cash and through this process of reinvesting corporate income use that cash to install the new technology. Such a reduction or elimination of dividends. would rouse the shareholder's wrath, and, at the very least, would lead to a drop in the traded price of shares. Low priced shares, with great accumulated cash reserves, would tempt the conglomerators, the financial wheeler-dealers to take over the company in order to siphon off those cash reserves. Or the corporation could try to transform through normal replacement, using that share of income set aside for maintenance and depreciation to acquire different equipment rather than replicating the old. But this is a very long, slow process. It is, moreover, likely to be impossible thus to transform a production *system,* through the piecemeal acquisition of items that must be fitted into an existing system. Or the corporation could borrow the necessary funds through the sale of bonds or from the banks, or raise them by the sale of equity shares.

Suppose the industry, one corporation perforce following the other, does undertake to transform its operating structure by installing the new technology; and does so through massive borrowing through the sale of (20 percent interest) bonds. And, as management anticipated (and following the conventionalized practice) prices are stabilized at the new lower level of production costs plus (or including) the 20 percent annual interest rate on the investment required to install the new system of production. Who benefits? Who suffers? Consumers enjoy lower prices; workers probably receive higher wages; certain investors are better off because of the incremental investment opportunity. But what of established ownership whose prior investment had financed the technology which was replaced and to whom a stream of dividend and interest payments previously had been forthcoming? They must lose. The technology whose installation they had financed and the capital structure to which, on that account, they might lay claim, has gone into limbo. The real values of their ownership have been reduced to nothing. Prices would drop to average costs at the prevailing technology, including an investment return only for those who had financed its installation. Or if returns are shared by the new and the old equity holders, then both would lose, and the allowed return would not suffice to support any influx of new investment for extending and accelerating the technological transformation. Under the postulated conditions, the prior investors' losses would be equivalent to those which would occur under pure competition.

Joseph Schumpeter called this elimination of equities attaching to a displaced technology the "gales of creative destruction." The difference is that producers in pure competition cannot resist those gales of creative destruction. In the organizational sector, they can resist them. The former have no defense against the hurricane of change. The decision to transform is not made by them but by others, by infiltrating innovators to whom great new prizes go. But in a large part of modern enterprise, where entry is rare and its significance is marginal (the great companies that control the steel industries of the world have not changed in generations), it is the existing community of producers that makes or refuses to make the decision to transform technology. It permits or it excludes the influx of new investment. It has and it exercises power to resist technological change. Unlike the monopoly of the economist's conception, it cannot capture for ownership the whole new increment of value attributable to technological advance, but unlike pure competition it can resist that advance. Under circumstances where prices can be expected to follow average costs at the prevailing technology, existing ownership must suffer from the transformation to a more advanced technology, no matter how great the net saving in costs and no matter how great the net gains in GNP. The community of producers can resist, and, in the interest of ownership, management will resist, the transformation of an established capital-entrenched technology whenever a significant influx of new investment is required to cover the costs of transformation.

In these terms, in our hypothetical example, the acceptance of a new steel technology in Japan and its rejection in the United States follows as the consequence of rational business choice. In Japan, where the capital structure had been obliterated, the option of avoiding an influx of external investment by perpetuating the old technology does not exist; in the United States that option remains. In these terms it is possible to explain why Japanese and German steel technology has raced ahead relative to that of the United States, while in those postwar industries where the United States also started from scratch, such as electronics and computers, American technology remains supreme.

It is not only the ownership interest that enters into corporate decisions; there are other incentives and pressures for technological transformation that may countermand that interest. Nevertheless, if our assumptions and their consequences are, in fact, characteristic, a built-in bias against technological advance is there.

The problem can be stated simply. In this form of organization the system of pricing externalizes the benefits and internalizes the costs of technological change; the costs must be borne by those who make the decisions, and the benefits accrue to others. No matter how great the gains to consumers, workers, and new investors, the quasi rents of prior investors and present owners will be jeopardized. Nor is management culpable in seeking to fend off windfall disaster for the ownership interest. If prior ownership and a management that acts in its interest are not motivated to transform technology because they cannot benefit, is it not admissible that the public-at-large should pay for the installation of that technology as long as it is fully assured that that public-at-large will receive the benefits thereof?

Under these circumstances it would be the task of public management to identify, evaluate, insist upon, and also if necessary, stand ready to finance economically desirable technological transformations *on the condition* that consequent reductions in costs would be wholly reflected in price reductions, and/or that consequent improvements in quality should not be reflected in any price increase; requiring in other words that even though the proportion reserved to the old equity ownership might be preserved, the incremental gains made as a consequence of public financing should accrue to the consuming public and not to equity ownership.

The Regulation of Public Utilities

Among the states and at the federal level, for upwards of a century, there have been commissions with the task of regulating rates in those industries, a subset of the organizational sector, designated as public utilities, particularly corporations supplying electricity and gas, telephone service, truck, railroad and air transport services. At most this regulation has served to constrain price increases, under the criterion that prices should not exceed operating costs plus a "fair return" on investment, with the calculus of fair return specifying the value of the "rate base" (the value of property or investment) and a conventional percentage to be applied as "fair." Curiously at the federal level, reflecting that resurrected yearning to return to some golden age of laisser faire, the airlines and land transport have been substantially deregulated, even at a time when circumstances press every Administration towards a general wage/price control for the organizational sector.

In the conventional long-standing approach to rate regulation, there is a fundamental contradiction. It is the objective of regulation to adjust rates to cover operating costs *as given* plus a fair return and no more than a fair return to investors, with fair return taken as the equivalent of normal profits to equity ownership. As a system which (at its most effective) would guarantee a fair return on investment, raising rates when return is less then fair, reducing them when the criterion of fair return was exceeded; it eliminates all incentive to reduce operating costs.

No matter how fair, and more than fair this regulated return might be, it does not perform the economic function of profit in a competitive market. It approximates rather the cost-plus-fee military-industrial contract, save it is consumer and not the state that pays the bill. Profit in the competitive market builds in an incentive to lower costs through operating efficiency and technological innovation. Under the regulated fair return, as under the cost-plus contract, no built-in motivation for efficient, low cost, high productivity operations exists.

Public utility regulation, moreover, as a system that calculates the allowable return by reference to the magnitude of investment, provides a positive incentive to overinvest in order to increase the size (value) of the rate base and correspondingly the allowed return. This indeed may account for the massive investment in nuclear facilities, so immensely expensive, with operating costs higher than before.

The regulatory process, primarily now in the control of state commissions, absolutely requires that cost efficiency norms to be imposed as a control upon regulated companies. If the public interest in efficient, high productivity (hence, low cost, low rate) operations is to be protected, then utility management must be made accountable for costs and quality of outputs; and regulators must in turn have the norms against which to evaluate performance. The rates permitted and the returns allowed should be conditional on managerial efficiency, above all with managerial remuneration rather than shareholder dividends, variable and controlled by regulation with reference to the record of comparative performance.

It is also necessary that commissions control the magnitude and direction of investment by the regulated companies, especially at this time of pressure to transform utility operations to nuclear, solar, and other energy bases, through an evaluation of alternatives that is fully informed, technologically competent, and made by reference to a table of social values. Beyond that the commissions need to be able to replace corporate management and to restructure utility operations where norms of cost efficiency are not met. It is unlikely that the state commission can themselves develop the requisite judgmental norms or acquire the competence needed for critical technological *cum* social evaluations and planning. But such evaluations and guidance could and should be offered to them by a federal agency of public management.

A POLICY FOR INTERNATIONAL TRADE AND EXCHANGE

This chapter will propose certain trade policy options for the positive state. But first, by way of background we will venture a summary view of what has come to pass with regard to institutional arrangements and the problems and circumstances of international trade.

Breakdown of the Classical Rules

Great Britain dominated both thought and practice in the organization of international trade through the Nineteenth Century. Under its imperial aegis, a set of rules evolved for self-regulation by the trading partners. These were accepted by statesmen almost as a code of national honor, by bankers as honest practice, and by economists as rational policy.

It was taken to be the obligation of each nation to maintain the value of its currency in fixed relation to the other currencies of the world. This was to be done by the willingness of the treasury or central bank to buy any offering of its own currency for gold or for some other currency that the foreigner would accept in lieu of gold, at a fixed rate of exchange. The nation's treasury or central bank got its fund of gold and foreign currencies from that received by its nationals in payment for the goods and services they exported abroad. In turn, the demand upon the central bank or treasury for foreign currencies and gold would arise from the need of its nationals to pay for the goods and services they imported from abroad. When the values of imports exceeded the value of exports, then the gold/foreign currency outflow would exceed its inflow, and reserves of "foreign exchange" would be depleted. In order to protect its reserves and hence to protect the value of its currency, the state must reverse this flow. It did this following the accepted rule, by raising domestic interest rates and tightening credit. In consequence, it was supposed, the high interest rates would attract funds from abroad, thereby, in the short run, replenishing the reserves of "foreign exchange." In the longer run the higher rates of interest and tightened credit, in cutting down on domestic investment and hence consumer income, would deflate the domestic price level. Lower domestic prices would reduce imports, for now consumers would now prefer their own lower-priced products, and would increase exports since the foreigner would now be attracted by the opportunity of buying more for less.

If this didn't work, if in spite of everything the balance of trade continued to be unfavorable, then the state must devalue its currency. Devaluation, like the aforementioned deflation, would reduce domestic in contrast to foreign price levels.

In those earlier days, currency devaluations were much resisted by economists because they introduced debilitating uncertainties into international trade and contract; by statesmen because devaluation was taken to be a sign of national weakness; and by bankers who feared that foreigners, with no more confidence in the integrity of their national currency, would bank their funds and invest their savings through financial institutions elsewhere.

The classical rule safeguarded the parameters of international trade and investment by placing the full burden of adjustment on the domestic economies of the trading partners.

It all seemed to work well enough in the Nineteenth Century through the first decade of the Twentieth Century; but in the 1920s and 1930s, with the long years of economic stagnation for some, followed by the catastrophe of world depression, it became evident that in an economy dominated by modern corporate enterprise, deflationary measures did not so much reduce price levels as create mass unemployment. The focus of public concern shifted away from preserving stable parameters for international trade and investment to the amelioration of the domestic crisis. What had once been an almost sacred commitment to fixed and stable currency ratios, disappeared. One country after another cut loose from that obligation to be free to use all their monetary and fiscal power to reemploy labor and to raise the levels of industrial production.

After World War II the Western Powers attempted to reintroduce stable relations between their currencies but on a looser, more permissive basis. An international bank was established with reserves contributed by the consortium of nations and with the authority to make loans to cover the trade deficits of member countries, thereby giving those countries time and leeway in regaining a trade balance. The dollar became the standard to which the values of all the worlds currencies were pegged. And great stocks of dollars were accumulated in banks and financial institutions of the world, not as an instrument of active exchange in the process of international trade, but as a constant reserve of foreign exchange. Thereby dollars created by the fiat of the American treasury migrated abroad, giving Americans a power to procure goods and services and to buy up the control of business enterprises abroad *not* offset by the foreign procurement of American imports, but with those dollars simply swelling the foreign exchange reserves of banks and financial institutions. This was the phenomenon of the "eurodollar."

Meantime, partly as a consequence of our prodigious military spending in foreign wars and in maintaining armies and military bases all over the world, and of the sharp and continuing decline in the relative preeminence of American technology and productivity, the balance of trade turned against the United States. Year after year, Americans have procured more from other countries than they sold abroad. The glut of dollars increased, and there began a series of revaluations; reducing the value of the dollar in contrast to other currencies and especially to the Japanese yen and the West German mark. A weak dollar, its present value uncertain, could no longer serve as the universal monetary reserve. Hence, the stocks of eurodollars began to chase after gold, after marks, after yen.

The response of government was to institute a system of floating exchanges where, with no governmental intervention, all was left to the traders on the blessed "free markets," such as New York, London, Zurich, and Tokyo. The currency values, it was supposed, would find their natural level. Thereafter, trade transactions would tend to stabilize exchange rates around these points of equilibrium.

Meantime another complication arose. With OPEC and the revolution in petroleum prices, oil producing countries have accumulated enormous dollar and other balances without the capacity to import and consume the quantities of goods and services to which their dollar claims entitle them.

In the logic of trade, exchange rates should equilibrate procurement values among the trading partners so that under conditions of equilibrium a dollar or a yen or a mark would have the same purchasing power in United States, or in Japan, or in Germany. Fluctuating exchange would be the means of equating comparative national price levels and production costs. It hasn't happened. Currency exchange rates, hence, trade, has been endlessly destablized but comparative national price levels and factor-costs have not been equilibrated thereby. On the contrary, the movement of exchange rates has even augmented the discrepancy between the purchase price of goods, services and production factors offered for sale in the domestic markets of trading countries.

If for example we compare the movement of price levels (inflation rates) in the United States and Japan, the changes in the dollar/yen rate of exchange between the years 1970 to 1978, we discover that with the pace of inflation more accelerated in Japan in those years than in the United States, Japanese prices rose much more rapidly than did American prices. Hence, to equilibrate the two price levels, compared to the dollar, the yen should have lost value (one dollar should have purchased more yen) in currency exchanges. Exactly the opposite happened. During those years the exchange value of the yen actually doubled in relation to the dollar (a dollar could purchase only half the yen as before). And as every American traveler knows, a dollar buys far more at home than it does when spent in Europe or in Japan.

The reason that free floating exchanges have not brought country to country procurement values into line, is that the free currency market does not equate procurement values but finds its equilibrium rather in the supply of and demand for the huge stocks of diverse currencies and of gold in private hands, with the size of these currency and gold stocks a matter of historical happenstance, and with demand for them a function of shifting preference, fears and speculative fever beyond any logical accounting.

Thus with rates infinitely destabilized and swiftly changing, producing great discrepancies between exchange rates and procurement values, and with enormous dollar and other currency balances in private hands casting a dark shadow of uncertainty over the future of economic event, it would seem there has ceased to be any rational system of international trade and investment whatsoever. What is most remarkable is that international trade and investment continue nevertheless, largely through ad hoc arrangements of public and corporate organizations that transcend the nonsystem of exchange rates.

We will propose options that have as their objective to reestablish a viable system for international trade and investment by (1) developing rules and an approach that would permit trade to be brought quickly and surely into balance with no adverse effects on the domestic economies of the trading partners, and (2) by defusing the enormous floating dollar balances of their potential danger for the operation of the national and international economies while enabling an appropriate liquidation of those balances through the procurement of goods and services, by their possessors.

Public Sector Procurement as a Policy Variable

It is said that after World War I, the then British Prime Minister Lloyd George advocated a hard peace, demanding heavy reparations from Germany, until his expert advisors, economists of course, with John Maynard Keynes among the foremost, gave him a lesson in liberalism, pointing out that a great war debt could be liquidated only by a transitory dumping of German goods on British and world markets (selling massively and cheaply, without buying anything back in exchange), in order for the Germans to acquire the pound sterling they would need to make payments. This would disrupt and even destroy viable organizations and established trade relations; trade relationships that were but the outward manifestation of an underlying balance of ongoing processes, of complex delicately integrated networks of skills, commitments, expectations, created through generations that, once disrupted need not be resurrectable. When the Prime Minister considered the effect that dumping German coal on British markets would have on his own Welsh mining constituencies, he changed his mind, became an advocate of a soft peace with the elimination of reparations entirely. This change in policy would make good sense in the reckoning of British interests, if the transactions *had* to take place through market sales in the private sectors. Then the transitory availability of cheap German imports would not have been worth the disruption of the market economy. What the argument failed to recognize was the possibility of organizing additional consumption on public account, planned and organized under the aegis of the state to meet collective need, without affecting market relationships. If procurement by the state on public account for collective needs had been considered a viable alternative, Lloyd George might have come to a very different conclusion. Through reparations, he might have, as a matter of public investment, imported German equipment and engineering talent to make those

Welsh coal mines safe and productive, thereby avoiding the disastrous years for British coal that lay ahead.

Following World War II, Americans, moved by compassion and motivated by anticommunism, exported billions in aid to refurbish the economies of old friend and old foe alike. It was state-to-state transaction without peacetime precedent; more unprecedented still, no repayment was asked for. Why was this Marshall Plan a gigantic giveaway? The economists' rationale was the same as the liberalist argument that had convinced Lloyd George. It was alleged that Europe and Japan could not repay such an enormous sum without damage to the American economy, assuming that in order to raise the dollars needed for repayment they would either have to exclude U.S. imports or flood the U.S. market with European and Japanese exports sold at desperation prices. Either way American industry would be gravely injured and would demand, by way of retaliation or protection, that tariffs and quotas be raised against European and Japanese imports. World trade would spiral downward, and, since the Europeans and Japanese would, in consequence, be unable to raise the surpluses required for repayment, repayment would be kept forever out of sight.

All that seems incongruous now, in the light of the great trade deficits the United States has been running every year in its trade balance with Europe and Japan. But, at the time, it was a possible scenario, and made a reasonable argument for a giveaway policy *if* it was assumed that transactions were limited to market sales and purchases in the private sector. It made no sense at all in the calculation of American benefits, if the consumption of imported goods in the public sector under the aegis of the state, was recognized as an alternative way of taking repayment.

If there was a state-to-state giving, why shouldn't there be a state-to-state repaying? If the European governments directed the use of the American resources under the Marshall Plan, then why couldn't the American state direct the use of the resources returned on Marshall account? It is precisely because the transaction from its incipiency was state-to-state, exogenous to the market, that it could not, without possible disruption, be accommodated to the processes of the market.

The Marshall Plan need not have been a giveaway. And the American people would have benefited if the American state had arranged for repayment via the American state. That repayment could have been used either to offset deficits incurred through trade (as was the case) or, alternatively, used to procure and consume imports on public account, to be utilized in the public sector, outside the web of market transactions.

The point is this. Under the circumstances of the positive state there are virtually boundless collective needs (in upgrading the systems of the infrastructure, health care, education, the quality of life, environment, and defense) that can be satisfied by imports over and above the allowable level of domestic procurement, with no disruption of market relationships in the domestic economy.

The relatively recent installation of a world system of free floating exchanges has not provided a stable basis for the conduct of trade. On the contrary, it has introduced monetary and trade uncertainty and instability that spills over into the conduct of internal economic affairs and the formation of domestic policy. Nor has it produced a rational equilibration of price levels and factor costs between trading nations. On the contrary, it has led to grotesque discrepancies. Indeed, measured against the ostensible objectives of the system, it has been a total failure. A return of exchange rate regulation under the aegis of the central banks of the trading nations is surely inevitable. Nor is it desirable that this should mean going back to the old rules of the game. This time the potential for public consumption under public control should be introduced as a variable in the formation of international trade policies of the positive state.

New Ground Rules for the Organization of International Trade

In light of the above, we would propose the following as ground rules in a new system for the organization of international trade.

1. Though a consortium of the trading nations (the institutional basis for such coordinated action is now available) rates of exchange would be set by reference to comparative price levels and factor costs. These rates would be supported by central banks and, following prior practice, all foreign exchange transactions would be through the agency of the central banks.

2. The obligation to adjust any imbalance of trade should fall, directly, immediately, and under international pressure and sanction on the recipient of the trade surplus. Adjustment should be the task of the nation or nations having a favorable balance of trade rather than on those who are losing reserves. It is far easier for the actor and less disruptive for the world economy if the adjustment is through the disposition of a surplus than in the making up of a deficit. It would be considered as in violation of the code that any nation accumulate reserves beyond a predetermined margin of safety. Thus no central bank would be allowed (would allow itself to) accumulate foreign exchange beyond that margin of safety. Hence, the countries with a favorable trade balance would be obliged to reduce that trade balance to the end of achieving a general trade equilibrium, rather than, as hitherto, the burden of adjustment being upon those losing foreign exchange. Again the logic of this role reversal is that it is infinitely easier to reduce a trade surplus than it is to overcome a trade deficit without detrimental effect upon the domestic economy.

3. In acting upon its trade surplus, the recipient of the favorable trade balance would have these options:

    a. It could act to reorient domestic industry from the production and marketing of exports to the production and marketing of goods and services for domestic use, possibly by taxing exports and subsidizing the consumption of domestically produced or imported goods and services (the reverse of habitual practice).

    b. It could accelerate the growth of GNP by raising the level of aggregate spending in Keynesian fashion. This would mean that more would be spent for goods and services, whether domestically produced or imported. On that account imports would presumably increase. If the effect of greater spending was also to raise the price of the factors of production and of the home-produced goods and services, exports would be discouraged. Both options (a) and (b) would put the burden of adjustment on the internal operations of the market economy.

    c. Or the state could directly import goods and services for consumption on public account in the public sector or under public aegis, thereby more fully satisfying collective needs and social goals, without being in any way obliged to reduce public demands on domestic production. This last of the three options would be the most certain, the most expeditious, and the least disruptive of established industrial and commercial relationships. It is indeed the one option that offers the opportunity for positive gain without any threat of economic disruption. Using the foreign exchange accumulated in its central bank vaults, the country enjoying a trade surplus can always import goods from abroad on public account to satisfy more fully the vast and unfulfilled needs that characterize the public sector of every modern economy, for the public's benefit with no adverse effect on business relationships in the market economy.

    4. Periodically, the international trade consortium would reexamine the whole matrix of currency exchange rates, and adjust rates as has become appropriate.

The Use of Counterpart Funds

Our emphasis is on the option of procuring imports for public sector consumption as a means of achieving balance in international trade. Here, we will further explore the potentiality of such public procurement in the settlement of international accounts. Consider counterpart funds.

Over the years the American government has shipped quantities of grain to India selling it to the Indians at low prices and taking payment in inconvertible rupees which must be spent in India for Indian goods and services. When senator Moynihan was Amabssador to India under the Johnson Administration, he made a stir by suggesting that since the State Department had found no use for the many billions of dollars of counterpart funds in its charge, those funds should be made a free gift to the Indian government. Idle counterpart funds exist in many countries.

Billions of dollars in counterpart funds that the State Department cannot make good use of! That strange failure flows from the self-same antistate bias and institutionalized blindness that prevents us from using the systematic procurement of imports for public sector consumption to bring international trade into balance. Counterpart funds are like the Marshall Plan funds; both were instances of state-to-state giving, that should be offset through state-to-state repayment, outside of the system of market exchange. The State Department is in no way competent to organize the systematic procurement of goods and services for public sector consumption in the United States. That should be a function of those agencies that carry out the responsibilities of the positive state, for example, with responsibility for the national system of transportation, communication, energy, health care, education.

These agencies should be given the opportunity of using the resources that counterpart funds represent to help in satisfying their almost boundless responsibilities. A competent and aggressive Department of Transportation, without any reduction in the level of domestic procurement as allowed by Congress, could *in addition* utilize all our counterpart funds in India to organize an industrial operation there that would produce the rolling stock required to refurbish at a level of real comfort and luxury, the American passenger railroads, operating after the public takeover of the deteriorated residual of private industry's failure, now as AMTRACK; or to produce a reserve of rolling stock needed to enable the massive shipments of coal required to deal with oncoming energy needs. Nor would the establishment in India of such an industrial activity be to India's disadvantage.

Earning Foreign Exchange

The International Monetary Fund was in part designed to supply foreign exchange to its members out of a pooled reserve as a means of allowing them the time they might need to correct a trade imbalance. What of the situation when trade imbalance is deep and persisting, uncorrectable by the conventional methods, and when no one knows how the country might find its way out of a morass?

Great Britain is a case in point, with a persisting need to find outlets for its underutilized capacities and particular skills, as a means of earning foreign exchange. Rather than a loan from a consortium of states, that same consortium of states might, as an alternative, offer to buy what that country is peculiarly equipped to offer to that consortium of states to satisfy collective need in their public sectors.

At the end of World War II, there did occur a nearly unique instance of the planned use of counterpart funds to procure services for consumption in the public sector. Senator William Fulbright, himself a Rhodes Scholar, knew how very valuable it could be for an American to study abroad in the great universities of Europe. Through his efforts, Congress passed the famous Fulbright-Hayes Act which used counterpart funds, gained in exchange for certain structures and equipment made available to our World War II allies, to finance educational opportunities for Americans in Europe. The Fulbright-Hayes program was one of the great and unequivocal successes of American postwar policy. It gave a new and wider perspective to generations of Americans and contributed in good part to the postwar preeminence of American science and letters. Those counterpart funds that financed the Fulbright-Hayes program in Great Britain are exhausted. The great universities and science establishments of Great Britain have ceased to be a place for the congregation of American students and scholars. Thus for example, instead of a loan, might not that same consortium purchase opportunities for graduate study and scientific training to be made available to their oncoming generations, which the great educational establishment of Great Britain is still splendidly equipped to provide?

Public Procurement for Private Consumption

There is thus a need in the sphere of international trade and development, for the systematic procurement, organized by the public management of the positive state, of imported goods and services for consumption in the public sector. There is also the need for the systematic procurement of imported goods and services for consumption *in the private sector,* organized and planned by the positive state. Indeed there is no other way than through the public procurement of imports for consumption, both in the public and private sectors, to achieve the full scale development of trade relationships with the Soviet Union, China, and other socialist countries.

Consider, for example, the development of trade relations with the Soviet Union which, along with the prospect of political detente and reciprocal disarmament, began so hopefully a few years ago, and is now (at the time of this writing) in a period of miserable and tragic decline.

At long last trade between the two countries was to be inaugurated! The Russians wanted to procure great and continuing quantities of our grain and for good reason. Our agriculture compared to theirs is extremely efficient, and, in terms of the climatic and other growing conditions, highly advantaged. We are in a position, moreover, to expand our normally restricted grain production, probably at declining costs, to accommodate their needs. The Soviet Union, with the largest reserves in the world, offered petroleum and natural gas in exchange.

It was a perfect match—American grain for Russian oil. It should have pleased everyone. It should have pleased our doves, for it meant the development of a mutually beneficial interdependence as a basis for political detente and escape from the shadow of nuclear holecaust. It should have pleased our hawks, for it meant that those Russkies would be depleting their strategic reserves of energy and we, therefore, would be able to preserve a margin of safety by slowing down the depletion of ours. It should have made our producers and consumers and politicians positively ecstatic, for it would contribute significantly to the solution, in the short term at least, of our energy crisis, break the OPEC stranglehold, reduce energy costs and hence increase our real GNP and hold down prices, and reduce trade deficits with the consequent plunging value of the dollar.

In the first instance, the American state extended to the Russians the credit they needed to buy American wheat. Then, in a kowtow to the idols of free enterprise, our government required that everything be handled thenceforth through private dealers. Subsequently it was said that the Russians bought the wheat more cheaply than they should have, with their low-cost purchases forcing up the price that American consumers subsequently were obliged to pay for bread. This was probably the case, and inevitable, since the Russians were in a position to take into account the effect of their purchases on world wheat prices, whereas the private dealers who handled the transaction from our side were neither able nor inclined to do so. The advantage of a monopsony buyer, needs to be offset by that of the monopolistic seller: a reasonable bargain requires bargainers of equal strength; with a state on the one side there must be a state on the other. In any case the Russians got their wheat. And the American state had a credit with which Russian oil and natural gas could have been purchased.

But how in the absence of any procurement by the state was this credit to be actualized in the procurement of petroleum and natural gas from the Russians, to our own great and obvious advantage? Could that public credit be sold to American consumers so that they could buy oil and natural gas from the Russians? It could not. The gateway to the private market in imported petroleum and natural gas is controlled by a few great oil companies. They control the importation, refining, and distribution of all foreign crude, which they procure from their own oil drillings in their own oil fields or in those of client states. What interest have they in acting for the American state to procure oil from the Russians so that the American consumer and the American economy can benefit by this repayment of the Russian debt? None at all, assuredly. For decades the Russians have been offering crude oil at bargain prices, but none has reached our shores. Russian oil for them is anathema; it undercuts their profits and that of their client states. More, it threatens their whole apparatus of production and distribution, from drilling rig to filling station. What does it matter to them that the importation of Soviet oil and natural gas would ameliorate the energy crises, would lower American energy costs, and, by cutting imports of OPEC oil, would reduce the American trade deficits? None of that is their business. Energy crises or not, financial debacle or no, the oil companies are being paid and paid a high price, and are making big profits on the oil they bring in from Arabia, Indonesia, and Venezuela. They have in the material sense absolutely no incentive to procure, nor any interest in the importation of Russian oil or natural gas in any form; all their interest is against its procurement—and they control the gateway to the American market. In consequence no Russian oil or natural gas has reached our shores. The eminently advantageous exchange has not been consummated. Nor will such exchanges take place, except through an agency of the American state that sells the grain and procures and organizes the disposition of Soviet oil and natural gas, through arrangements that are both bilateral and multilateral, for example, sale of grain to Russia in exchange for Soviet crude to Japan or Germany in return for dollars accumulated through Japanese or German trade with the United States. Nor given the record, the outlook, and the political muscle of those great oil companies, is it likely that they would cooperate on this score with an agency of the state. Quite the contrary. To consummate this eminently advantageous exchange, and this fact dare not be blinked, would require that an agency of the state of the highest technical competence organize the procurement, importation, refining and distribution of fuels from the Soviet Union and China, in competition with corporate enterprise.

Competition is a virtue if and inasmuch as it forces individuals, corporations or government agencies to behave in a manner commensurate with the public interest. Competition in particular markets, though intense, need not produce such behavior. Nowhere is this more evident than in the oil industry where the most intense competition will not, for example, lead to the procurement of Soviet crude in place of that from OPEC, nor to an exploration vectored to the discovery of the most strategically-significant reserves, nor to an optimal depletion rate, nor to a conservation geared to public need. Only a state agency, able to compete technically with its corporate counterparts, could fill some of these lacunae of public need.

The Insulation of International Currency Balances

We have lived with the phenomenon of internationally footloose money balances for a long time, and have suffered their disruptive effects. These balances are now of an unprecedented size, and their sheer magnitude may bring dangers of a new order. What then are the dangers implicit in footloose monetary balances.

Think of the Arab oil potentate with a huge dollar account in American banks. He becomes pessimistic with respect to the future course of economic events in the United States, and so he writes a check on his American account with the intention of depositing his funds in a German bank. For that purpose he must buy German marks. The influx of dollars into the currency market, does not change the quantity of procurable marks, but only their price relative to the dollar. The value of the mark goes up, and the dollar down, for reasons that have nothing to do with the real procurement values in the two countries or with the flow of trade. Currency exchange rates are destabilized and trade suffers. And the Arab may now invest his funds in Germany in ways that society could consider as deterimental for economic organization, for example, the taking over of business corporations; or detrimental for social relationships, for example, the purchase of farm land.

The same disruptive effects would arise if, rather than through the currency speculation of the oil potentate, the shift of funds was at the behest of an international corporation or of any individual American or Frenchman or Britisher or Japanese or German, or whoever possesses a significant claim on internationally footloose currency. The following, institutionalized under pressure and sanction, as international practice would serve to maintain effective surveillance of such funds, to insulate currency exchange rates from the effects of their shifts and movements, and to control the uses to which they are put inasmuch as these may be considered detrimental.

All balances deriving from international transactions and held on foreign account, (such balances may as well be held by nationals as by foreigners) should be set apart as an essentially separate but related currency (in the American case, say, F-dollars in relation to dollars), and held in separately designated and specifically regulated banks, agencies or accounts. The special currency could be converted into regular currency usable for domestic transactions under specified conditions. Thus, for example, F-dollars could be immediately converted into dollars to purchase goods and services in the United States for export or to settle debts incurred through such transactions. Only then would they effect currency exchange rates through an impact on trade flows. Other uses of these funds could be regulated as seemed appropriate.

10

A POLICY FOR SCIENCE AND TECHNOLOGY

For a variety of reasons, and particularly because these are the prime ingredients of power and productivity, the positive state is deeply involved with science, with research and development, and with technology, though it cannot be said that it has in the United States, a "policy" with respect to any of them. Our purpose in this chapter is to propose options for such a policy. But first a word on the meaning of the terms, and the nature of the phenomena.

I. Science, Research and Development (R&D), and Technology

Academic Science

When one speaks of Science, it is generally academic science that is meant. What are the key characteristics of this traditional science of the universities, which was the original science, and is sometimes called pure, or basic, or fundamental?

It is first a body of information about observable or otherwise experienced phenomena, organized as integral sets or clusters of statements around problem foci, accumulated, preserved and perpetuated through the institutions and instrumentalities of the archive.

It is second a number of coexisting paradigms, each one delineating and imposing boundaries upon a particular discourse, for example, physics, or within the boundaries of physics, the more proscribed boundaries of, say, solid state physics, each one with its particular analytic approach, its distinctive conceptual structures, leading imageries, axioms, theories, evaluational norms, research techniques, and experimental models. The paradigm of a science is the thinking caps worn by its practitioners and passed on from one generation to the next.

It is finally an open system (or systems) of speculation and search with built-in incentives for the aggressive, universal, and free communication of hypotheses and of the results of research, institutionalized for the testing, evaluation, and selection or rejection of information by reference to its criteria of credibility and significance (significance always in relation to the norms of the paradigm and the interests of the group), and for generalizing upon and synthesizing the information research produces, and for cycling it back into the processes of education

Other social systems overlap or tie into that of academic science; thus the political system on which it depends for financial support; the system of technological adaptation and advance through the linkage of R&D, and especially the system of education. For if the educational system teaches, it is academic science that develops and feeds in that which is taught. It is through the practice of academic science that a mastery is acquired over the paradigms of science; and some students will carry the acquired analytic approach and problem-solving apparatus to practice science of another order. For there is another, very different system of scientific endeavor.

Research and Development (R&D)

At least until the mid-Nineteenth Century, academic science was Science; there was no other. It was a closed system in the sense that it operated by reference to its own intrinsic purposes with its activities to be justified by the intrinsic values of the information (the knowledge) it produced. In the mid-Nineteenth Century, starting in Germany at the behest of the German state, scientists were professionally engaged and systematically organized, under the ultimate direction of those outside of any system of science, to produce information relevant to the interests of industrial and military technologies, with their activities integrated into the industrial and military development of such technologies. Thus was created "research and development" (R&D) which has become of critical importance in our time.

There are fundamental differences between R&D and academic science. The problems and the purposes of academic scientists are chosen by those scientists on the basis of that which interests them, or at least chosen through processes and norms internal to the institution of academia. Whereas R&D is geared to the solution of problems of technology as determined by those who operate and direct industrial and military activities, or, if problems and directions of research are chosen by scientists, they must be chosen necessarily with an eye to the interests of industrial and military (or other) clients. In academic science the self-interest of the individual scientist is indissolubly and tightly bound into the energetic, widespread and unconstrained communication of the information that that scientist through research produces. Whereas there is no built-in incentive for the R&D scientist to communicate the information produced through R&D. On the contrary, there are barriers and constraints against any such general communication.

Academic science operates as a discourse organized systematically to test, evaluate, select, or reject the information produced through research, and to generalize upon and to synthesize that information, and to propagate it through education, and to enable its general and continuous availability through the archive. For the information produced through R&D there is normally none of this. The information that R&D produces is communicated, if it is communicated at all beyond the operations of the organization that produced it, as an incident to the dissemination of technology.

Since World War II, the scope and magnitude of all scientific activity has increased enormously. In the United States, the bulk of this increase has been of R&D, and the largest part of this R&D has developed under the aegis of the state, mostly in relation to military problems and purposes.[1] Nor is the role of the state and its problems of policy the same for corporate R&D in industry, as for public sector R&D, or the same for all forms of public sector R&D when its orientation differs, for example, as between military, space, medical, agricultural, transportation, communication, energy objectives.

Technology

By technology is meant any organized, replicable, transmittable capacity for some (for any) purposeful activity. Certainly there are technologies of many sorts, technologies of science, and of art, and of war, and of child rearing, and so forth. Our interest is in and our use of the term will be confined here to technologies related to the production and distribution of valued goods and services whether consumed under the aegis of the state or sold through the market. By "advance" of technology is meant the development of (organized, replicable, transmittable) capacities to produce (or distribute) more (or more valued) outputs with the same endowment (inputs) of labor and or other resources, or to produce (or distribute) an equally valued product with a less valued set of labor and other resource inputs. In a word, the measure of technological advance is the increase of productivity.

Science *may* provide the learning relevant to (and necessary for certain avenues of) technological advance. Through R&D, scientists are professionally and directly engaged in efforts to advance technology. It must be insisted, however, that neither science nor R&D are necessarily required for technology to advance; that the mastery of the paradigms of science is not the only kind of learning nor is R&D the only information source relevant to and important for technological advance. The enormous strides of the great industrial revolution took place with no R&D linkage between science and technology. That revolution of the Eighteenth and Nineteenth Centuries was based in the ingenuity and inventiveness of craftsmen and entrepreneurs who acquired a mastery of technology on the job as part of the job (they learned by doing), and who experimented and innovated within the confines of their

---

[1]*See* Robert A. Solo, "Gearing Military R&D to Economic Growth," *Harvard Business Review* (November-December, 1962) and J. Herbert Hollomon, "America's Technological Dilemma," *Technology Review* (July-August, 1971).

farm, shop, or factory, while using the prerogatives, undertaking the risks, and anticipating the gains of ownership.

II. The Market Sectors

For each of three coexisting and overlapping systems of technological advance in the American market economy, the role of the state, and its problems of policy, will differ. These three systems of technological advance correspond to the three sectors of the economy, which I will designate as the organizational, the decentralized market-segmented, and the decentralized price-directed. The organizational sector is characterized by a scale and complexity of operations that prevents any individual from comprehending and mastering an integral technology through on-the-job observations and experience. Technology there is not something that can be learned by doing. The relevant contrast and comparison is as between the farmer in the decentralized price-directed sector and the assembly line worker in the organizational sector with respect to the opportunity to learn, to experiment, to innovate on the job as part of the job. To comprehend the technologies of the giant organization, one must stand outside operations to analyze the system and its elements. Hence that knowledge of technology required in order creatively to advance technology in the organizational sector must be taught through formal processes of education and training. This becomes, at least at the initial stage, a task for the university. Nor in the corporate sector, can the individual who occupies a niche in an organizational plan, experiment or innovate without upsetting that plan. Perforce the organization relies, and must rely on a small science-trained R&D elite, specialized professionals, outside of operations, to act as the organization's agency of learning, experimentation, and innovation.

Virtually no scientists or trained engineers are employed in the small operations of the decentralized market-segmented sector. Nor, excluding that of satellites of the large corporations, is there any R&D. There are inventions and technological advances nevertheless. The man-sized operations and imperfect markets of this sector are the natural breeding ground and proper domain of the itinerant inventor and the inventive entrepreneur; and it is here that the venerable institution of the patent plays a central role. In the proprietary operations of such industries as construction or retailing, with activity and organization expressing the volition of the individual who owns, the technological mastery prerequisite to invention can be and normally is acquired not through formal education but through observation and experience on the job as part of the job. So, too, experimentation (trying it out) obtains as a matter of the entrepreneur's interest and curiosity, and innovation (putting it into production) is a consequence of the selfsame entrepreneurial choice.

For American agriculture, still decentralized and price directed, approximating the ideological norm of pure competition, patents have little meaning, nor is there any spontaneous investment by farmers in R&D. The system of technological advance has been virtually a function of corporate suppliers and of public intervention, with the state operating regional experiment stations, with an extension service to evaluate and communicate information to the farm and to promote innovation there, with the state financing such major transformation of agricultural technology as that of rural electrification, and with the state by maintaining price supports providing farmers with the income security needed for private long-term investment where the return on innovation depends of the price received for future yields.

III. Information

The stuff of science is information. What research produces is information; information that is sometimes interesting, is sometimes useful, is sometimes relevant to the development of one technology or another. What then should be the appropriate rule for the communication of such information?

There are in fact, three distinctive rules: (1) The Rule of the Public Good, (2) The Rule of Comparative Advantage, (3) The Rule of the Market. Each of these prevail in a different universe of activity, each operates by reference to a different criterion of value.

The Rule of the Public Good

Of all society's resources, information has this unique quality. It is not exhaustable through use. Given a useful bit of information, that an additional person, or another million, or an infinite number of people come to possess and to utilize that information, adds not a whit to cost. The marginal cost of expanded possession and a multiplied use of the information resource is zero; a remarkable, almost magical quality. In the dissemination of useful information, there is always a net addition to the public good so long as its value to those who use it is greater than the cost of communicating it to them. If knowing and using an item of information will improve health and increase longevity, then the more who know and use it, the more that lives will be prolonged and less will be the suffering inflicted by illness. If knowing and using an item of information increases productivity and the real values of production, then the more who know and use it, the greater will be the real value of output. And for all these benefits there is no compensating costs, except in that of communicating. Hence, as a general rule, the public good is served by the freest, fullest dissemination of the information research produces. The more who know, and the more they know—the better. That is the rule of the public good.

Academic science is at present the only institutionalized activity that is organized for the full and free dissemination of the information that research produces, with the incentive to spread the knowledge and use of such information built into the self-interest of those who produce and possess it. Only there does the rule of the public good spontaneously prevail.

The Rule of Comparative Advantage

The research-related objective need not be to add to the totality of social values, or to serve the public good. The objective may be to enable A (individual, business enterprise, group, army, nation) to conquer, or destroy, or outcompete, or eliminate, or dominate B. Here *comparative advantage* is the criterion of value. Where comparative advantage is the objective, it is just as important to keep B weak as to have

A strong. Given an item of useful information, it is as important that it be denied to *B* as that it be available to *A*. Therefore, in the interest of comparative advantage, *A* will deny access to any possibly useful information in its possession, to *B* its rival, enemy, competitor, or to any of those who might become the rival, enemy, or competitor of *A,* or to any others through whom such information might be leaked or otherwise revealed to actual or potential rivals, competitors, enemies. Hence, under this rule, the dissemination of useful information will be minimized. The fewer who know, and the less they know—the better. That is the rule of comparative advantage.

The rule of comparative advantage absolutely prevails for military intelligence, and wherever the information produced through research is controlled by military intelligence or those who think in its terms.

The Rule of the Market

Actors in the market, we presume, have a dual motivation: (1) to maximize their net income through exchange, (2) to maintain or increase their comparative advantage *vis a vis* actual or potential rivals and competitors. Information produced through R&D may be revealed if it pays the possessor to reveal it. If patented, it maybe licensed. If it is embodied in a product it may be aggressively promoted—but always for a price. Such information will be withheld; its dissemination will be limited so as to gain through higher prices. And, in the interest of comparative advantage, all access to information will be denied where it cannot be sold for a price, or for a price sufficient to offset the possible loss of comparative advantage. Information will be disseminated through the market, and sometimes aggressively, but such dissemination will never approach the boundary of the public good.

The question we will broach for social policy, is how better to reconcile the interest in general dissemination, that is, the rule of the public good, with those activities where the rule of the market or the imperative of military intelligence prevail.

Proprietary Subsciences in the Corporate Sector

Corporate research produces information, not invention. Some of that information will be useful in devising patentable devices or in leading to the patenting of selected chemical compounds. Leave aside the problem of patent policy at this juncture, consider rather the information base, the working tool, the vast, private, hidden archives produced over decades at a cost that runs to billions of dollars, by the great chemical, pharmaceutical, and electronics companies.

I became aware of these hidden archives on a visit, in 1963, to the R&D operations of a medium sized pharmaceutical company. The heart of that company's research effort was its file of chemical compounds. It was not to the general scientific literature, but to this file that its researchers turned first in their work, and it was on this file that they primarily depended. It contained the results of the careful analysis and clinical testing for a wide range of animal and sometimes human reactions to 17,000 different compounds ingeniously arranged and coded by chemical structure rather than chemical terminology, then on IBM punch cards, now surely long since computerized. Considering that at that time it cost $2,000 simply to prepare a compound for such testing, it becomes evident that the information contained in those files represented an enormous expenditure of funds and of research efforts. And these rapidly accumulating and very expensive masses of data were held in strict secrecy, available only to a few scientists in a single company. Data that might have supported the research efforts of ten thousand, served only the needs of ten.

These stores of proprietary information are subsciences in effect, to which none but the team of company research workers have any access. Such information might be of great value to general science and technology, hence for the social ends which science and technology serves, if it could be made available; nor would any sacrifice of resources be required, that is, there would be no real cost in achieving those values through the release of these proprietary information stores.

One cannot now know the potential and unexploited value of these information stores, because they have been hidden and held outside the reach of any objective evaluation. Nor has their disposition ever been a political issue, simply because their existence is outside the scope of public awareness. That very lack of awareness is a part of the price we have paid for being without any competent and effective agency of public management for the corporate sector.

And yet, since they are demonstrably a key instrument in the success of major corporations, there is surely reason to suppose that those information stores may be a wasting resource of great and unexploited potential, dwarfing in importance such things as patent policy which have for so long been a liberal preoccupation and a focus of political controversy.

But how to obtain or require the release of such information without destroying the incentive to produce and accumulate it? Or assuming that a price must be paid to compensate those who produced it, how should such information be made available without a loss of comparative advantage to American industry *vis a vis* that of countries that did not share in the cost of producing or procuring it?

I would propose the following policy sequence:

1. Let the relevant agencies of public management organize on a confidential basis, in-depth studies and evaluations of the corporate (R&D) archives for each of the industrial sets to which their powers and responsibilities relate, in order to determine the character, and to evaluate the worth of those proprietary archives. Such an evaluation would take into account: (a) where and by whom, outside of the owning corporation, on another level beside the industrial set of which the corporation is a part, that information might be used; (b) the degree to which information is replicated among the different corporate archives and to which it is already available in the public archive; and (c) whether and for how long the information of the archive remains the exclusive possession of the corporation that produced it, and how rapidly it is reproduced or otherwise finds its way into the public domain.

   It may turn out in particular cases, or in corporate R&D archives throughout industry that there is little of significance or of general value, or that is not otherwise obtainable. Our hypothesis should then be rejected, with nothing more to be done. But what if the archives were found rich in unexploited values, with a potential for contributing significantly to the advance of science and technology?

2. Then the agencies of public management would negotiate for the procurement of the nonpatented material of the R&D archives of the corporations within their industrial sets. Voluntarily or under powers of eminent domain, these information stores would be purchased, providing, for example, that the state would procure information (say) six years after the date that it had been acquired through the corporation's research and development. Thus the company would have a full six years of sole possession, and the longer protection of items patented on the basis of such information. Since the accumulations of the past would be of less significance in its competitive position, the current effectiveness and magnitude of its R&D would be more critical than ever to its competitive success and comparative advantage. And that in return for their contribution to the information now procured by the state, the corporation would receive a lump sum payment reflecting the value relative to that of its rivals of the accumulated archive currently in its possession. Thereafter, it would be paid annually for each sixth year increment to its archive accruing to the state under the agreement, with that payment presumably based on the magnitude (as a percent of) its annual R&D expenditure.

    The general effect of this should be to increase the magnitude and intensity of industrial research and development, (a) since the corporation would have a significant proportion of its research costs offset by the state purchase, enabling it to put more resources into current efforts, (b) since current R&D outputs would be competitively more significant than before, and (c) since it would now be motivated to utilize more fully and immediately the production potential of its current research outputs, before that information is released under the agreement.

    The agency of public management would be then in possession of the archival (R&D) material procured from key, selected, or from all of the corporate entities of its industrial set; and that material has been integrated into a single archive. How and to whom should that information be made available?

    To avoid a free ridership for foreign competition, rather than making it generally available, the agency of public management would bring together the corporations of its industrial set, forming them into a consortium for this limited purpose. The information of the integrated archive would be made available exclusively to the members of this consortium. New entries into the industry could, of course, become a part of this consortium. The information of the integrated archive would be made available to the members of the industrial consortium, but they would be obliged to pay a price for that privilege; a fixed sum as an entry fee, and an annual assessment as a percent of their net income thereafter. The funds received would be used to pay for the annual increments to the integrated archive. Foreign corporations could also be admitted into the consortium provided they would pay the same price for the privilege and would, like the American corporations and under the same terms, make their archives available to the information pool.

Thereafter, the consortium would become self-financing and self-governing in control of the (unpatented) R&D information pool.

Under present circumstances, corporate archives, accumulated over generations at an enormous cost, must be a formidable barrier in certain industries against the entry of new firms; that for new entries are obliged to compete without an information base comensurate with that of their established rivals. What is here proposed would substantially reduce that barrier to entry and hence, to competition.

4. There remains the question as what the archive might contain relevant to science and valuable to technology, beyond the interests of the consortium. The agency of public management should retain the right, in cooperation and consultation with the consortium, to contract for studies of the material in the archive to determine its relevance for science, and for technologies outside the scope of the particular industrial set, and, finding these, to publish in synthetic form that which might have a general value for the development of science or be of particular relevance in other areas of technology.

This has been about the R&D archive accumulated by commercial enterprise, selling their product on the markets of the organizational sector. There is besides an R&D archive produced by the agents of the state, whether by public agencies or corporations working as R&D contractors for the state.

An Archive for Public-Sector R&D

We are referring again neither to published reports nor to patented or disclosed inventions which are but a miniscule elements of the totality of R&D outputs, but rather to the masses of experimental data, calculation, analysis, blueprints, design, and documented speculation possibly retained in the company or agency files. We have just considered the problem of enabling this mass of unpublished proprietary information possessed by corporations operating in the market economy to be organized into a useful, more widely available reference archive. The problem in the public sector is not the same, for these reasons:

1. Inasmuch as profits count, there is for the corporation engaged in the market economy, a motivation aggressively to disseminate the information it possesses when such information can be embodied in products or licensed for a price as patents and know-how. For the corporation working in the public sector as an R&D contractor, there is no built-in motivation to

disseminate the R&D information they possess except, as is generally the case, of that contained in a completed report or prototype delivered to a single governmental client. Furthermore, R&D contractors in the public sector, seeking comparative advantage *vis a vis* rivals for the patronage of the state, will be positively motivated to prevent any general dissemination of any of the R&D information in their possession.

2. On the other hand, while corporate R&D contractors have no inherent motivation to reveal, neither have they any inherent right to withhold any of the information produced through their research and development. Corporations in the organization sector of the market economy must be allowed to acquire comparative advantage through successful R&D, as an inducement for them to continue their investment in R&D. Not so with the R&D agencies of the public sector. The comparative advantages they might gain through withholding information produced through their R&D is neither required for, nor justifiable as an incentive. Their R&D is done at the behest of the state; it is paid for by the state; it will be continued or discontinued depending upon the choice made by the state. The state should decide upon and require that disposition of the information produced through their R&D is considered to be in the public interest.

3. A large part of the R&D in the United States' public sector is done for Department of Defense, where access may be constrained under the rule of military intelligence.

In the light of the above, we propose that an agency of public management, working with the R&D direction or project management of all major R&D contract awards or in-house programs: (1) review the system of internal reporting and data collection for corporate contractors and of governmental R&D operations, and where appropriate, guide or require the development of the system to enable more complete coverage and the standardization of informational formats; (2) select those categories of reports and collectible data adjudged to be of general value; and (3) require that these be simultaneously reproduced and forwarded to a central repository.

Most of the internal reports and data collections of R&D contractors would on examination and evaluation probably be regarded as only of transitory interest and of local relevance, so that no public purpose would be served by making them generally available. Other information might be of great value in developing an understructure for choice and in building an information-basis for technical advance. Negative results of experiments, for example, or tests that have served to narrow the range of choice, while not susceptible to broadside dissemination, might, if properly organized, provide a useful reference base for future research.

Materials received would be organized for and integrated into either the general archive to be available as an information base for all science research and R&D, *or* into special archives open only to those of appropriate security clearance, serving as a reference base for the development of controlled categories of technology.

Military Intelligence and a Science Court

The military establishment sits astride the bulk of science-based activity in the public sector, with the outflow of and access to the information produced through its R&D submitted to the rule of military intelligence; a rule that holds, the fewer who know of any bit of information, the more valuable that information will be; the less that is known, the less that is disseminated, the fewer who have access, the better; a rule epitomized by the military's criterion for access to the R&D information in possession of its contractors. No one, no matter their security classification, no matter the work that they are doing for the military, is to be allowed to know of information unless they can establish a "need to know." And who can establish a need to know what they do not know about?

The enforcement of the rule of military intelligence goes hand in hand with the character of the military censor. Consider the colonel or major or captain or lieutenant who wields the classifactory stamp. His only criterion is whether in some way the revelation of a particular bit of information might do some enemy some good some time somehow somewhere. For whatever great good the revelation of that information might do, he gets not a single brownie point. The benefits of dissemination have no place in his system of accounts. But let there be a hint that the Russkies had an interest, or a suspicion by some professional xenophobe that a secret had slipped, and his head for sure is in the noose. For the censor, the safe and simple answer always is to slap down the stamp, and classify; the fewer who know, the less who know, the better; and in any case what they do not know surely, won't hurt him! All the cards are stacked on the one side only. But there is another side, even strictly from the point of view of military strength and power. For Adam Smith more than 200 years ago, that other side was a key element in his argument against the tenets of mercantilism. And mercantilism, whose whole objective is comparative advantage, was and is an economics of military strength and national power. But Adam Smith saw that military strength and national power depended on accelerating the development of technological capabilities. That, in turn, depends on the rate of technological and scientific advance, which, in our day relies above all, on the incoming stream and availability of the information that research produces. Denying access to that information cuts off the stream that feeds the river that nurtures the strength of the nation. How can this better be demonstrated by a "need-to-know" criterion that cuts even military contractors of the highest security clearance, engaged in developing technologies the military considers critical, off from information that could help them in developing those very technologies? It was as an alternative to this policy that we earlier suggested the formation of an archive open to those with an appropriate security clearance which would be made to contain all relevant R&D data from all R&D sources.

The iron rule of military intelligence is subject at least to rust and erosion, for if the military censor has all of the power, he has none of the reason. He has no workable rationale. He does not know, he cannot know, poor chap, for no one can, what will be the consequences of his choices or in what perspective they will come to appear. Wearing those blinders, he is sure to stumble into pits of ridicule.

The hawks of the American Senate put him in charge of all selling or licensing of technology to those across the bamboo or across the iron curtain. "Yes, trade," they said, "trade is good for business, let there be trade," but nothing must be sold or licensed to the Other that might in any way aid and abet its military capability. Alas, anything the Russians or Chinese might buy or license could conceivably aid their military capability! So what then of trade? Our fatal illusion here is that in trade, we in the United States, have only to give and nothing to get, that we have only to teach and nothing to learn, that we alone possess all the secrets, the techniques, the know-how. Those illusions are rapidly fading now, as our technology is on every side surpassed, and as our allies supply what we, under the imperative of the military censor, deny. There must be a better way to organize our actions in a world where choice, be it commercial, or technological, or scientific, or military, can never be absolute but is, or rationally should be, in the nature of a weighing of pro and con, gain against loss, benefit against cost.

For the sake of military strength and national power, as well as for the other benefits that hang in the balance, we might use for those categories of decision where now we rely on the military censor, the institution of a "science court", secure, juridical, professional, informed, before whom the military and those who represent other and opposing interests and opinions could come as advocates, to present their case and have the ruling of the court handed down.

The Published Outputs of R&D

An R&D project normally culminates in a report or series of reports that answer to a prior set of questions and/or that detail some prototype process, formula, end-product, or instrument as a model for decision or development. The experimental information, including information concerning failed experiments, the techniques, the ideas generated as a consequence of the process that led to the production of the report, are all likely to be sequestered, if they are preserved at all, in the proprietary archive. The report itself also may be relegated to the secrecy of the archive, but not always. Some reports are published or become otherwise available. Especially is this so when the R&D is done by a public agency or under government contract (since the greatest part of R&D is done by public agencies or by corporations under government contract, this is no small matter). The published output of R&D reports is in fact enormous, but aside from the specifics to which the report is addressed, their general value as an element of the archive and for effective discourse in science and engineering, has been minimal.

This for a very good reason. Unlike the outputs of academic science, there is no instrumentality for organizing and integrating those R&D outputs into a disciplined and cumulatively developing, learnable body of knowledge; which is a far cry from the librarian's task of arranging and classifying documents for easy retrieval. There has evolved no apparatus equivalent to that in academic science, which operates very imperfectly to be sure, to obtain a peer evaluation of research outputs hopefully in order to separate the traces of gold from the mass of dross, to find what is general, and to generalize, thence to synthesize significant elements into an archive organized as a continuing reference base, and into an educational instrument that incorporates new information into the "knowledge" of oncoming generations who, in turn, carry that knowledge to the four corners of the economy, applying it in their choices and in their contribution to the advance of science and the development of technology.

If this process of evaluation, selection, generalization, organization of published R&D outputs into a continuing cumulating archive and its synthesis into a teachable body of knowledge to be disseminated through the university nexus is to be done at all, it will be done at the initiative of the state. In that light we would propose the following:

1. Authors of published R&D reports would, in those instances where the research was funded by the government, be required, and in other cases would be requested to respond to certain questions intended to divulge whether (in the opinion of their authors) the information contained in the reports is of a potential significance beyond that to which the R&D was specifically vectored. If so, what elements of their report are in their opinion of a general value for science (and what sciences) or for technology (and what technologies). Inasmuch as the inquiry, with this as a first step, could lead to a fuller appreciation and a wider recognition of the author's work, it would be much in the self interest of the authors to respond carefully and fully to these questions.

2. Using author's evaluation as the indicator, current reports would be divided into categories according to the report's claim of relevance to particular sciences and to the technologies of the industrial sets within the cognizance of the different agencies of public management.

3. Reports, thus categorized, would now be examined by select committees representing the branches of science, and the technological (R&D) interests of the various industrial sets. It would be the tricky and difficult task of these committees to determine whether or not there are significant general values possibly to be derived from the R&D reports within the examined categories; and, if so, whether the cost of an institutional apparatus to exploit that potential would likely more than be compensated for by possible benefits.

4. If the determination is positive, then a system would be organized, through institutional implants in academe on the one hand, and under the aegis and control of the agencies of public management on the other, to work with R&D reports forwarded to them at the discretion and initiative of the authors of the reports, in the first instance to incorporate relevant elements into the active, reference archive; and in the second to encourage and support studies intended to generalize upon and synthesize these elements into convenient working tools and instruments of learning.

Patent Policy in the Market Economy

The sole instrumentality of the liberal state geared to the communication of technologically relevant information and the dissemination of new technologies is the ancient institution of the patent, with the task of grantor delegated by the Constitution to the federal government. The patent conveys for a limited period of time, ownership rights to certain bits of disclosed information. The patent converts an idea, a bit of information into a piece of property with the exclusive right to that property guaranteed by the state, and its illegal use subject to prosecution in the courts.

The liberal dilemma is this. The public good dictates that technologically relevant information be communicated universally and made freely available. But the market requires that information be priced for a profit if it is to be produced and made available at all. In liberal thought, monopoly is the market-destroying malaise, the evil that it must seek to eradicate. But the patent policy, by issuing exclusive control over significant technologies, creates a stream of monopolies to pollute the currents of competition. The patent system is a compromise of sorts between the need for market incentives versus the values of free dissemination, between the detriments of patent monopoly and the constraints and distortions of industrial secrecy.

The patent system operates in all parts of the market economy. Its role is of particular importance in the region of man-sized enterprise, proprietorships operating in segmented markets where small variations in the character of a product or a process can be parleyed into large private fortunes. More than as an incentive to invent, the patent is needed in this part of the economy for the communications and negotiations prerequisite to contractual arrangements. It is hard to see how such arrangements could be made bringing together inventor, engineer, banker, and investor, producers and distributors, (each self-interested and autonomous and able to steal an idea once revealed without opening a safe or depleting any store of material objects) without the safeguards of a patent system.

In the organizational sector, such patent safeguards are not needed to enable the transformation of an idea into a product or process since all parties-at-interest operate within the same corporate frame. There the researcher's design for a product improvement is communicated to the R&D direction; if approved, it is forwarded to the engineers who develop the prototype; which is tested, with results communicated to an echelon of management in command of the financing; who decide whether or not the invention is to be put into production; all within the same operating agency without the need for a patent safeguard. In the corporate organization, the patent may serve not at all as a basis for innovation, but solely as a defense against competitive innovations. It may be, indeed, that without a patent system, competitive innovation would be more intense, investment in R&D would be greater, and the pace of technological advance would be accelerated.

Reams have been written about the pros and cons of the patent system in the market economy. Nor do I intend here to enter into that controversy. It is rather the use of the patent system in the public sector by the great agencies of government with respect to the inventions produced "in-house" or "out-of-house" under R&D contracts that will concern us here. Patent policy in the public sector, however, must be understood in relation to the phenomenon of spillover.

IV. Technology Transfer

Spillover

In the 1950s economists first became aware of the R&D phenomenon.[2] By the end of the decade it had also become clear that economic growth could not be accounted for as a function of capital accumulation as neoclassical theory supposed.[3] And many took the simple step of substituting for "capital," investment in "human capital," that is, educational expenditures, supposing that thereby all would be explained as before. Others would substitute for capital, investment in R&D, supposing that more R&D could be equated directly to more technological advance (more investment in R&D is equated to more "inventions," hence more "innovations," hence higher productivity, hence accelerated growth). By the early 1960s this notion had become widespread so that President Kennedy's announcement of the American intention of beating the Russians to the moon with all the massive R&D expenditure that that entailed, was greeted as bringing good tidings to business and opening fantastic avenues for economic growth. It was supposed that space and military R&D would "spillover" into civilian industry, accelerating technological advance and generating higher productivity and more rapid growth.

It may be helpful to explain my own attempt to influence public policy *vis a vis* spillover, and the periodic nature of my research-based observations in that regard, beginning in 1960 when I undertook a project for the National Planning Association, that was, I think, the first general study of the effects of space and military R&D on the civilian-industrial sector.

In it I did my best to dampen these expectations of great benefits from "spillover," mustering evidence to suggest that the enormous increase in postwar R&D had not accelerated the growth in real GNP. I argued that in draining off the cream of science-trained, technologically oriented talent from work in civilian industry, the continuing increase in R&D, concentrated as it was in the space-military sector, would have a negative effect on the technological advance of civilian industry, hence on economic growth.[4]

The potential values and spontaneous achievability of space-military spillover had to be discounted for a number of reasons. Since World War II, the critical space-military technologies had become very different from those of the civilian-industrial sector; correspondingly the potentials for transfer were reduced. More-

---

[2]Robert A. Solo, "Research and Development in the Synthetic Rubber Industry," *Quarterly Journal of Economics* (February, 1954). So far as I know, this was the first analytic study of R&D ever published in an American economics journal.

[3]After the pathbreaking study by Moses Abramovitz, "Resource and Output Trends in the United States since 1870," *American Economic Review, Proceedings* (May, 1956), rationalized and accommodated into the paradigm so to speak by R. Solow, "Technical Change and the Aggregate Production Function," *The Review of Economic and Statistics* (August, 1957); Luigi Passinetti, "On Concepts and Measures of Changes in Productivity," *The Review of Economics and Statistics* (August, 1957); B. F. Massel, "Capital Formation and Technological Change in United States Manufacturing," *The Review of Economics and Statistics* (May, 1960).

[4]Solo, "Gearing Military R&D to Economic Growth," *op. cit.* The enormous U.S. expenditure in this category of R&D, accounts in my view, in good part, for the precipitous decline in the standing of U.S. technology relative to that of other countries that did not suffer that diversion of skill, interest, and talent.

over, growing differences of skills, outlooks, and institutional organization limited communication between the two communities. As the cross-movement of personnel diminished, correspondingly there must be fewer carriers of technology to perform the task of transference.

Before World War II, essential military technologies were substantially a branch of application of civilian-industrial technology; hence industrial power was quickly and easily transformable into military power. The feeding, clothing, maintaining the health and vigor of millions; the transporting of massive cargoes of manpower and materials and equipage by land, sea, and air; the rapid communication between many points and many persons; earth moving and the construction of airstrips, roads, and bridges; the low cost production of standardized equipment; construction of all sorts; the production and fabrication of steel and metals; and the keeping of records and the development of systems for the control of large and complex organizations were alike critical tasks of military power and of civilian industry. There were specialized military technologies then without significant civilian-industrial counterpart, ordinance, for example; and it is difficult to recall any substantial civilian-industrial benefit (spillover) or any positive impact on industrial productivity deriving from the not inconsiderable advances in these, as with the machine gun, the bazooka, long range artillery, or the bombsight. But generally in those days the two sets of technologies were so closely associated, that a substantial advance in dealing with the problems of the one would be more or less directly of use for the other. World War II and the cold war that followed and the era of space exploration changed all that. For nuclear weaponry and its related science and technology, no civilian counterpart existed, nor for the intercontinental ballistic missiles and the earth orbiting satellites operating not only in an environment beyond the earth's atmosphere but also outside the conceptions, the experience, the practice, the interests of established civilian-industry. So, too, control systems were now created and materials developed with performance characteristics that had no relevance to the needs of business. For these reasons, the potentialities of spillover diminished.

Operating in the context of different orders of risk and incentive, of ethic and standards of conduct, of the means of survival and the requisites of growth, of the preeminence of production costs in the one sector and of performance characteristics in the other, of the fabrication of complex and perpetually changing prototypes in the one, and prerequisite long production runs and standardized outputs in the other, of the buyer-seller relationships, of the nature of organizational controls,[5] there was bound to be particularities of outlook, of language, and of competence as between the two sectors. As these differences deepen, communication becomes more difficult. With the evolution of the demand for and the acquisition of highly specialized expertise in space-military R&D, the cross mobility of technical personnel diminishes. Engineers and scientists who are the most effective carriers between sectors of scientific and technological knowledge and of know how, cease to move back and forth between space-military and civilian-industrial R&D. This does not mean that a policy to promote the "spillover" of technological innovation is not

---

[5]See Merton Peck and Frederic Scherer, *The Weapons Acquisition Process* (Boston: Harvard University, 1962).

important. On the contrary, given our concentration of science trained brainpower in the military sector, what does not spillover spontaneously must be pushed across!

Surely the industrial use of patented invention produced through space-military R&D is but one facet of the spillover phenomenon. It is to be expected nevertheless that a significant transfer into civilian-industrial use of the technologies developed through government R&D, would carry many patented inventions in its wake. Studies of this patent flow demonstrate its rather minimal significance.[6] In what follows I will draw upon a study of my own of the disposition of inventions patented under the aegis of the National Aeronautics and Space Administration (NASA).[7]

NASA was a special case, and both its experience and its potential role *vis a vis* the out-transfer of public sector technologies are of particular relevance here. Unlike, say, the Department of Agriculture but like the Pentagon, it contracted its R&D in order to advance highly esoteric technologies for public sector operation. Therefore, (unlike the Department of Agriculture and like the Department of Defense) because they were extraneous to the purposes for which that R&D was undertaken, any civilian industrial values of NASA R&D must be considered as "spillovers." But unlike both the Pentagon and the Department of Agriculture, NASA had and has no natural clientele, nor any group committed to its survival on either practical or ideological grounds, on whose support it can count on the inevitable day when Congress is tempted to swing its budgetary ax. NASA has been anxious to establish client groups and sought to do so both by offering subsidies and research opportunities to academic science and to business, and also through a *Technology Utilization Program,* and a particular patent policy designed to promote spillover as a service to business. Of all the great public agencies, NASA alone was and remains committed to the development of a system for the promotion of spillover.

NASA took title to the patented inventions of its employees and the (unwaived) patented inventions of its R&D contractors and made these freely available to all who might apply. Also it undertook on request to waive commercial rights, patent by patent, or to grant blanket waivers of the commercial rights on all the patented inventions produced under the R&D of a particular contractor, provided that contractor committed itself to (and submitted periodic reports on)

---

[6]Compare Donald S. Watson, Harold Bright, Arthur E. Burns, "Federal Patent Policies in Contracts for Research and Development," *Patent Trademark and Copyright Journal of Research and Education (IDEA),* Vol. 4, No. 4 (Winter, 1960); *Patent Practices of the Department of Defense,* Preliminary Report of the Subcommittee on Patents, Trademarks, and Copyrights of the Committee on the Judiciary, U.S. Senate, 87th Congress, First Session, pursuant to Senate Resolution 55 (Washington: U.S. Government Printing Office, 1961); Donald S. Watson, "New Information on the Operation of the License Policy in Federal Contracts for Research and Development," *IDEA,* Vol 5, No. 4 (Winter, 1961–62), p. 287; Donald S. Watson and Mary A. Holman, "Patents from Government-Financed Research and Development," IDEA, Vol. 8, No. 2 (Summer, 1964), p. 199; Mary A. Holman, "The Utilization of Government-Owned Inventions," *IDEA,* Vol. 7, No. 2 (Summer, 1963), p. 109; and Mary A. Holman, "Government Research and Development Inventions: A New Resource?," *Land Economics* (August, 1965).

[7]Robert A. Solo, "Patent Policy for Government-Sponsored Research and Development," *IDEA,* Vol 10, No. I (Summer, 1966), pp. 144–207. Part III of this study (pp. 81 to 199) is entirely concerned with recommendations (options) for policy, first for promoting inventiveness or creativity in government sponsored R&D, secondly for assimilating, evaluating, and disseminating hitherto buried bodies of R&D information, and thirdly for transferring invention and facilitating the extension of the use of technology developed through government R&D into the civilian-industrial sector.

the commercial application of the patented inventions on which waivers had been granted.

Following NASA practice, the Presidential Directive of October 10, 1963, proposed a significant innovation designed to promote the commercial application of inventions made under government R&D contracts. The directive required that a grant of exclusive commercial rights to a contractor must be conditional on the proven commercial application of the invention or on the demonstrated effort by the contractor to develop the invention for commercial use and to promote its application. Exclusive rights would be revocable where commercial application or the effort to promote such application was not demonstrated within three years after the grant of a patent. A means for the surveillance of this policy was also established. Where companies were recipients of principal or exclusive rights, it was required that they report at reasonable intervals on the actual or intended commercial use of inventions made under government contracts. A general report concerning the effectiveness of this policy was to be prepared at least once annually by the Federal Council for Science and Technology in consultation with the Department of Justice. Under the Federal Council for Science and Technology a Patent Advisory Panel was formed to carry out these directives.

Thus NASA had in operation two policies for the disposition of commercial rights on inventions produced under government-sponsored R&D and had monitored the consequences of each. The one granting exclusive rights to R&D contractors, and the other offering such rights for the free use of the public. Each had its rationalization; each might claim on a priori grounds that it would optimize the commercial utilization of such invention, and hence, yield the greater social benefits. In 1965–1966, I compared the two policies with reference to NASA's experience. These are the results.

Some $15 billions in R&D contracts producing through 1964 more than 2,600 inventions by contractor employees, involving a complex and costly apparatus for waivers and patents, resulted after six years in the commercial application of six inventions, none of them important: an ionization gauge, a seisometer sold mostly to government agencies, an element of a fuel cell that has been sold for demonstration purposes to universities, a damped accelerator, a subcomponent in a magnetometer, a temperature probe with sales more or less confined to aerospace industries.

Alternatively, NASA offered free to the public 836 inventions for nonexclusive, royalty-free licensing. Some 48 were nominally licensed, but a letter survey in December, 1965, found only one very minor instance of commercial application. For the period studied, there was clearly no significant transference of the patented inventions produced through NASA-sponsored R&D into nongovernmental uses, even though NASA, more than any other government agency, was intelligently experimental and constructive in its efforts to promote, through patent policy and otherwise, the transference into industry-at-large of technologies produced for special public purposes.

The record showed to be fallacious the theory that private companies given a profit incentive in the commercial exploitation of inventions produced under government contract and thenceforth left to themselves, will automatically and spontaneously develop those inventions for commercial application and disseminate the use of those inventions through industry at large. The Presidential Directive of 1963 ruled that when an R&D contractor had an "established commercial position," that, in itself, was to be considered grounds for granting that company exclusive commercial rights to all of the inventions disclosed by that company, automatically, without question or request. Underlying this criterion for blanket waivers, is another theory, namely that when a corporation is both an R&D contractor and has an "established commercial position," it will, therefore, develop and promote the commercial potentialities of inventions made under governmental R&D contracts. The record refutes this theory.

Consider such large NASA contractors with powerfully "established commercial positions" as Chrysler Corporation, General Motors, Bendix, Philco, Honeywell Inc., Transworld Airlines, Union Carbide, Thiokol Chemical, Raytheon, American Machine and Foundary, Motorola, Minnesota Mining and Manufacturing, Pennsalt Chemical, Sylvania Electric Products, Dow Chemical. Not only had they a zero record of commercial application, none of these companies throughout that period of the space effort even troubled to request a waiver.

The strongest impression to be gotten from an examination of the record of waived invention is of general, pervasive sometimes the absolute indifference on the part of the contractor to the commercial potentialities of inventions made under government R&D contracts. Evidently it is very rare that these contracting companies have any internal mechanism to develop and to promote or even to examine and evaluate the commercial potentialities of inventions made under government contracts.

Considered in terms of rational entrepreneurial choice, the indifference of R&D contractors to the commercial potentialities of inventions made under government contracts may be entirely justified. These are huge, complex organizations which, regardless of corporate affiliation, are integral decision-making entities wholly absorbed with competition for government business. Their competence is in the space-military technology. An attempt to reorient themselves into commercial markets in order to exploit the heterogeneous scattering of the inventions in their possession would require a change in the locus of effort and a diversion of executive talent that might debilitate their dynamic force with no clear prospect of any significant payoff in profits.

If the policy of waiving of commercial rights to corporate contractors has failed, and offering the inventions for the free use of the public has been equally futile, what options remain to squeeze the potential for civilian industrial use and economic growth from the fruits of public sector R&D? For an answer to that question, it will be useful to recall, and in the light of the passage of time to reevaluate the policy recommendations published in 1966, and addressed specifically to NASA as the agency uniquely committed to promoting the utilization in the market economy of technology developed for operations in the public sector. *Among* them were the following:[8]

---

[8]Solo, *Op. cit.*

1. Shift emphasis away from attempting to transfer the bits and pieces of special purpose technologies. Instead let NASA identify technologies, understood as integral and replicable capabilities for some purposeful action, and itself develop these technologies "to encompass other activities, to serve new-purposes, to service a different clientele." In explaining and developing this recommendation, I wrote:

New technology is not the same as invention. For what follows it is important that the difference between the two and the relationship of the two be understood.

Technology means here a replicable capability for some purposeful action. A capability (say, for automotive transportation and travel) may include a great many subcapabilities (traffic control, road construction, fueling and servicing capacities) and these in turn could be further divided into subcapabilities down to the competence of the service station attendant in changing a tire. Any capability or subcapability could be conceived of as a technology, and there is perhaps no precise way to draw the line between the small and the large, but here "technology" will mean a capability for purposeful action that is substantial in scope and is significant in the scale of social values. In contrast to technology, which is the sum of all that contributes to a capability for purposeful action, a patentable invention in a novel element of action that can be compacted and expressed in a formula or device. A technology, then, may include a changing multitude of patentable inventions, and a multitude of old and new ideas that are not patentable, and a body of information systematically organized as a basis for choice and the acquired skills and knowledge of those engaged in operations and in the organization of operations, and the accumulation of capital equipment, and the infrastructure of services and utilities.

Through R&D and operations related to it, the government evolves new technologies. These embody an evolving complex of conceptions and theories, of organized information and of learned knowledge and acquired skills, of organizations and control systems, of capital equipment, of techniques and mechanisms and of institutions. Such technologies developed for the special purposes of government also embody numerous inventions.

It is possible that bits and pieces of technologies, in the form of inventions or reports, or mechanisms or devices or methods of organization and management controls, can be detached from the special-purpose technologies in the government sector and shifted into use in other existing technologies in the non-governmental sector. This is what ordinarily is meant by "spillover" or "transference into commercial application." It is this movement of information, technique and device between coexisting technologies that NASA's Technology Utilization Program is primarily designed to promote. Similarly the positive objective of NASA patenting policy is to encourage the movements of isolated inventions, detached from the special-purpose technologies in the government sector, into application in technologies in operation elsewhere. This transference of bits and pieces—of inventions, of information, of devices—developed as part of the special-purpose technologies of government, into other technologies in the nongovernmental sector, is certainly not to be ignored. Transferences of this sort can bring benefits and, no doubt, should be encouraged. Yet such transferences are very difficult; successful and significant instances of such transference are hard to find. They are like looking for uses of a spark plug or a car tire or a piston ring other than in an automobile.

There is another avenue for increasing the benefits from the special-purpose technologies produced through government R&D. What has developed through such R&D are capabilities for purposeful action. Rather than searching these technologies for bits and pieces that can be detached for use elsewhere, the technologies themselves might be reoriented and adapted, their scope extended, to service other social objectives, to serve another clientele, to encompass new activities. It is in this extension of technologies to new areas of activity and not the transfer of inventions between technologies that has historically been of primary significance.

Once a technology developed in the government sector has been successfully extended to activities in the nongovernmental sector, then inventions made in respect to that technology in either sector will flow easily and spontaneously to the other.

The computer is the heart of an electronic data processing technology that was first developed to process military data and was subsequently adapted and extended to process data of many other sorts. With electronic data processing operating in a number of sectors, technical advances achieved in the one can flow easily and quickly into application in the others.

"Aviation" refers to a capability for transporting heavy objects via air routes. That technology was developed first for military purposes where high marginal values justified very high average costs. Subsequently that technology was extended into the transportation of commercial freight and passengers. The extension of the technology of airborne transportation required great efforts and expenditures under public subsidy, the adaptation and development of aircraft and control devices, the building of a vast nationwide then worldwide infrastructure of airfields, feeder roads, servicing facilities, the evolution of viable producing and operating organizations, the training of technicians, the overcoming of consumer fears and inhibitions and, the cultivation of new tastes and habits.

The spillover of information and invention into commercial application from the activities and technologies of the Atomic Energy Commission has been trivial. What has been most significant is the extension of the use of nuclear reactors, at great cost and involving an enormous adaptive, developmental and promotional effort, to fuel power stations and ships. And the AEC created a new radioisotope technology as an offshoot (or extension) of its capability for producing fissionable materials.

Similarly NASA's most significant transference into commercial application has been in the extension of its booster technology, the capability for putting heavy objects into space, first to put Telestar and then other communication satellites into earth orbit.

Rather than by transfers between technologies, the significant social benefit from NASA-sponsored R&D, aside from the intrinsic values of space exploration, will be brought about through the extension of constituent technologies to encompass other activities, to serve new purposes, to service a different clientele. To promote such extensions of technology requires a different strategy of search and promotion than has prevailed hitherto.[9]

Given the development by NASA, of such technologies for civilian-industrial application, two recommendations were made to promote their extension into civilian-industrial use.

---

[9]*Id.* pp. 192–195.

2. All unutilized patented inventions made by NASA employees or obtained through its contractors (with no waivers made to contractors unless there is demonstrated intent to utilize and a proven capability for utilizing such inventions commercially) should be put at the disposition of NASA's agent for technology utilization. The agent of technology utilization should offer exclusive licensing privilege for such invention or for clusters of such inventions (sets that might provide a firm market position *vis a vis* identified and developed space-related technologies) in negotiated agreements with companies willing to undertake a substantial investment in establishing such technologies in the civilian-industrial sector.[10] In explaining and developing this recommendation, I wrote:

Remembering again that the record has shown there to be virtually no social benefits from the solicitude for the privileged position of R&D contractors in claiming exclusive rights on inventions made by their employees, and no benefit either from reserving invention for the free use of the public, it is recommended that a maximum possible flexibility be allowed in the power to grant or withhold exclusive commercial rights in promoting the transfer of inventions and the extension of technology. It is immediately and concretely recommended that exclusive commercial rights on inventions waived to contractors should be promptly voided at the end of the time period stipulated by regulations unless there is by then clear evidence of significant commercial application or of a substantial expenditure on development for commercial application; and that all equivocation and ambiguity on this point be removed. It is likewise recommended that before any waiver of exclusive commercial rights on an invention is made to any large R&D contractor, there must be established in the operations of that contractor a competent group, whether a branch, or a department, or a division, or an office, or a subsidiary, not including the company's patent counsel, assigned the specific task of evaluating such inventions for their commercial potentialities, of developing such inventions and of promoting their commercial applications. It is useless to waive commercial rights to a company that has not organized itself to promote commercial applications. Further it is recommended that blanket waivers of commercial rights on all inventions made by R&D contractors be granted automatically whenever, and for so long a time as that company achieves a 20 percent or better rate of commercial application on the waived inventions in its possession. Otherwise no blanket waivers should be granted. Aside from influencing the policies of R&D contractors, another, and in the long run, a more significant use could be made of the patenting power in promoting the wider utilization of special-purpose technologies. This would be in supporting champions of innovations.

Exclusive commercial rights to sets of related inventions grouped together to afford springboards to innovation might provide strong initial positions in an effort to create a new market, to produce a new product or service, or otherwise to extend a NASA-

---

[10]Federal Property Management Regulations. Amendment A-16, Sector 101-4.101, (b), (c), 1973, specifies that, "it may be necessary to grant an exclusive license for limited period of time as an incentive for the investment of risk capital to achieve practical application of an invention. Whenever the grant of an exclusive license is deemed appropriate, . . . consideration shall be given to the capabilities of the prospective licensee, to the technical and market development of the invention, his plan to undertake the development. . . . (Washington: U.S. Government Printing Office).

produced technology beyond the scope and purpose of space exploration. [For that purpose] *. . . NASA must go out after the business. The universe of disclosures must be scrutinized to select those inventions for patenting which might constitute viable sets, affording a position of market security and strength, to be offered to those who are willing to commit themselves to the effort to launch significant innovations.* [11]

Inventions produced through public R&D where ownership accrues to government should not be patented unless it is intended that the offer of exclusive rights on such patented inventions will be used to encourage a commitment by private companies to invest substantially in establishing new technologies in the civilian-industrial sector. Otherwise, and where the intention is to offer nonexclusive rights to all and sundry, inventions should be simply published. In 1976, for example, there were some 28,000 government-owned patented inventions offered for free, nonexclusive licenses, with no evidence that during the years 1970–1976 more than 175 had found any public sale or use. Consider the costs simply of *patenting* those inventions; at $3,000 per invention, a cost of nearly $100 million! And their dissemination such as it was, into public use could have been better served through publication. Patent lawyers fantasize extreme never-having-occurred imaginary examples to justify a practice very remunerative to themselves. Weighing costs against benefits, the patenting enterprise for government-owned invention has been a gigantic waste.

As an alternative to defensive patenting, that is, where the purpose is not to promote innovation through the offer or exclusive licensing, an intragovernmental board might be established where representatives from agencies having major R&D responsibilities, and including the Commissioner of Patents, would formulate standards of presentation, completeness, supporting data, and breadth of distribution for the disclosure of information on inventions produced through government-sponsored R&D, thus facilitating the dissemination and increasing the utility of such information.

It could be enacted by the law that when the board's standards of disclosure and distribution were met, publication would have the same defensive status as patent applications on those inventions. This would remove any justification for defensive patenting on the part of the government, and would, therefore, eliminate a drain on legal manpower and a burden upon the overloaded Patent Office.

To discern among the great and evolving complexities, those space-military technologies, that might be reoriented, adapted, built into the private sector, there to serve a different set of social purposes requires technical sophistication. To conceive the opportunities for their extension requires imagination. To evaluate those opportunities requires study. To achieve the innovationary thrust that converts an idea into a concrete operation requires motivation and resources. There is hardly likely to be a successful extension into civilian-industrial use of such technology, (1) unless there are resources available to back efforts at innovations, (2) unless the evolving complex of R&D-produced public sector technologies are scrutinized by technically sophisticated observers self-interested in, or charged with, the task of discovering and promoting potentialities for their extension; or (3) unless someone,

---

[11]*Id.,* pp. 196–198.

an individual scientist or engineer or entrepreneur, working within his own firm, within the company where he is employed, or in the public agency, is committed (in Donald Schon's term) as a "champion of innovation" to the concrete achievement of what exists as a potentiality.

To create a field for the development of such "champions of innovation," I recommended that NASA, cum agency for technology utilization, negotiate arrangements with its own in-house R&D operations and its R&D contractors, to bring inventors of or those responsible for significant technological developments, to act for short periods as consultants advising on the relevance, applicability, application of their creative contributions in other areas of the public sector or in civilian-industry, or in proposing a plan for the further development and adaptation of such technology to make possible a more general extension of its applications and values. The agency should be in a position to support or, with the aid of those consultants, to activate such plans.

It should further institute a program of "inventor fellowships" requiring public R&D operations and R&D contractors to offer "leaves of absences" with assured job security for a year or more to a limited number of their research personnel who choose to apply for and are granted fellowships with the objective of developing an invention of theirs, or an aspect of space-related technology, or a theoretical conception considered to have potential general values for science and/or for commercial or new public sector applications. Fellows, who would be free to work in a university or government research center of their choice, would be paid at some fraction (say 80 percent) of their regular salary plus a grant to cover the use or procurement of experimental equipment, travel, and other project-related costs. They would moreover be privileged to receive exclusive commercial rights on any inventions they developed. If the outputs of their research was of another order, the agency would support their publication.

Thus those closest to the emerging technologies would be motivated to scrutinize them continuously for capabilities that might profitably be developed and extended in scope and purpose. In the year or two years covered by the fellowship, fellows would not only have acquired a unique expertise in a special field of endeavor, but also by the very investment of effort and thought, would have become committed to seek the practical fruition of the possibilities they had developed. Back at work in their company or agency, or by entrepreneurial efforts in firms of their own, they would presumably spearhead the extension of a technology developed, created, or adapted through their efforts.

Those recommendations were published in 1966. To recall them permits us to ask what happened then? Explicit, or implicit in those recommendations, are hypotheses, even predictions, of cause and consequence, of the possible, the probable, the feasible. Can those hypotheses be tested now, 15 years later, by reference to course of event?

During the interim years an important Harbridge House study on government patent policy,[12] with a sample of patents issued for all government-sponsored inven-

---

[12]Harbridge House, for the Federal Council for Science and Technology Committee on Patent Policy, Contract No. 7-35807, *Government Patent Policy Study,* 1968.

tions during 1957 and 1962, found that out of the 2,024 contractor inventions covered, 251 (8 percent) were used commercially, all but two resulting from Defense Department contracts. Of these "88 percent of contractor sales, where the invention played a critical role, are attributable to five patents in the fields of transistors, vacuum tubes, numerical control devices, computers, and gas turbines." Significant spillovers were all at that margin where public sector and civilian-industrial technologies overlapped. That overlap would more likely occur with the defense agencies, given the wide spectrum of their interests and tasks, than would be the case for NASA certainly, and also probably for the Atomic Energy Commission.

The clear intent of the Presidential Directive of 1963 was that grants of exclusive or principal rights should be conditional on an effective effort by the contractor to promote commercial application. It was the sense of the Directive that where this did not occur within three years, the contracting agency must "walk-in" on its R&D contractor and nullify the grant of exclusive commercial rights given to that contractor. In 1971, a statement by President Nixon strengthened the Kennedy directive, not merely encouraging but requiring the collection of information on the commercial utilization of such patented inventions where exclusive rights had been granted to contractors, and giving contracting agencies flexibility in demanding that contractors license such inventions whenever this was adjudged in the public interest. I was myself skeptical of these provisions, and in the 1966 publication predicted that there would be no "walk-ins" debouching unutilized patented inventions from contractor control.[13]

The key section of the directive provides that the "Government shall have the *right* [my italics] to require the granting of a license to an applicant on a nonexclusive royalty-free basis," but it is not required that government agencies exercise that right. Nor given the temper and tradition of the Department of Defense, is it likely that the agency (which accounts for about half of all government R&D) will be inclined to do so.

Under the Carter Administration, the Federal Council for Science and Technology, which had monitored the patent control program, was abolished. Prior Presidential Directives were ignored. There ceased to be any monitoring or systematic reporting. Through 1975, there had been not a single "walk-in" by any federal agency to nullify a grant of exclusive rights. The very issue was forgotten, and the question of commercial utilization was swept well under the rug.

The final report of the Federal Council for Science and Technology[14] shows that in 1975 (the last year reported on), there were nearly 28,000 government-owned unexpired U.S. patents available for licensing. The number of unexpired patents held in the commercial portfolios of government R&D contractors was not known simply because the Department of Defense had not required their contractors to report that information![15]

---

[13]*Id.,* p. 151.
[14]*Report on Government Patent Policy,* combined December 31, 1973, and December 31, 1974, and December 31, 1975, and December 30, 1976. Prepared by the Federal Council for Science and Technology in consultation with the Department of Justice.
[15]*Id.,* p. 395.

The data (which is far from satisfactory) provided by this report relevant to the phenomenon of spillover covering nearly two decades of experience, leads to several conclusions and a final policy recommendation.

1. Except for a marginal area of civilian-industrial public-sector overlap, the transfer, extension, utilization of the technologies produced through R&D vectored to public sectoral purposes, has not, does not, will not occur spontaneously. There will not be spillover, but a pushing across, and that must be planned, organized, operated by a public agency responsible for and committed to that task.

2. There now exists a vast store of information and practice forgotten and unutilized which government possesses or on which it has a legitimate (walk-in) claim, which may be of potential value in raising productivity and accelerating growth in the civilian-industrial sector. That potential, if it exists, will not be exploited given the orientation and interests of the agencies now in charge.

3. There is only one agency of government that by historical happenstance and in the effort to create a firm basis for its own long-run survival, is committed to and systematically organized for the transfer into civilian-industrial use of the special technologies of the public sector. That is NASA. And if NASA performance is considerably short of amazing, as the statistics show, it is beyond comparing with that of the agencies of defense and energy. Thus, for example, in the disposition of patented inventions produced under the public aegis, NASA records from 369 to 522 instances of commercial or public sale or use (the data is equivocal) compared to 30 instances for the energy and 9 for the defense agency.

4. NASA has adopted in its technology utilization program (now the Division of Technology Transfer) at least the first two of our recommendations (whether or not the publication of those recommendations was in any way instrumental in this regard, I have no idea). Their emphasis is now (a) on the extension of (the development and promotion of new uses for) their mainline technologies that enable the operation and organization of observation, sensory perception, data gathering, and reporting, from the region of outer space, ("facilitating broader application of remote sensor technology"),[16] and (b) in the deliberated in-house development and adaptation for other public or for market-industrial use, of integral technologies emerging from NASA mainline programs.

It has also albeit in a small way, advertised its willingness to negotiate and has negotiated the grant of exclusive rights to a patented invention or a set of patented inventions, as a means of inducing a substantial industrial commitment to the launching of an innovating technology developed under its aegis. This is in accord with our second recommendation. It can also be deduced from reports in *Tech Briefs,*

---

[16]As explained in the NASA annual report *Spinoff, 1980.*

that NASA now brings in, presumably as consultants or researchers on corporate leave, engineers and scientists involved in initiating the technologies chosen to be developed or adapted for out-transfer into other public or civilian industrial uses. This would be in accord with our third recommendations.

Whatever the explanation, by the record there appears to have been quite remarkable progress in the development of NASA capacities and in the level of its achievement in extending the values and benefits of special-purpose, public-sector technologies.

Which leads to our fourth and final recommendation on this score. Give NASA, and its division of technology transfer, the whole task and the whole responsibility for developing and extending the values and benefits in public and in civilian-industrial use (beyond the agency interest and its initial R&D vector) of all special purpose technologies generated in the public sector. To that end, it should take over all government-owned inventions now in the possession of the Department of Defense and of the Department of Energy, with exceptions (waivers) made where and inasmuch as these agencies intend positive action to utilize those patents for purpose of promotion or control. It would monitor and exercise walk-in rights on all inventions in the possession of R&D contractors and not utilized within the term prescribed by the presidential directives except that beyond requiring free, nonexclusive licensing of such invention, it could negotiate exclusive licenses with those willing to undertake a substantial commitment in launching the innovationary technology. Henceforth all inventions made through R&D sponsored by the defense agencies or by the Department of Energy, unless there are cogent reasons for exceptions, would become the property of the U.S. Government and put under NASA control.

Properly qualified contractors would at their request be given a four year exclusive license for the nongovernmental use of the inventions made by their employees, with the option of having their license extended upon proof of the commercial utilization of the invention and the technology to which it relates. This, too, was the final recommendation published in 1966, when I asked for "A National Role for TUP" [NASA's Technological Utilization Program].

> The Presidential Directive of October 10, 1963, generalized this principal [that exclusive commercial rights were to be granted to R&D contractors only on the condition that contractors applied waived inventions commercially within a stipulated time period or at least demonstrated a significant effort to do so. Otherwise the waivers would be voided.] . . . For groups of inventions the stipulated time period approaches expiration. Will the waivers be voided? Will they join their brethren to languish on the sterile bed of the Patent Registry, offered for nonexclusive royalty-free licensing, and left unused?
>
> In fact, the Atomic Energy Commission and the Department of Defense will certainly do nothing . . . in promoting the wider utilization of special-purpose technologies. But NASA might.
>
> These three agencies, NASA, the AEC and the DOD, together control about 90 percent of all government-sponsored R&D. Each has a distinctly different, mission-based orientation vis a vis the disposition of inventions related to special purpose government technologies. The Department of Defense with the largest R&D program and by far the greatest number of accumulated inventions, is quite indifferent to the disposition of those inventions for nonmilitary use and has no interest itself

in promoting either the transfer of invention or of extensions in the utilization of special-purpose technologies outside of military objectives. The Atomic Energy Commission promotes the general extension of nuclear technologies and tightly controls all inventions related to these, but is not concerned with technologies and related inventions of other sorts that might incidentally be created through the R&D it sponsors. Only NASA is mission-oriented to promote the general extension and commercial application of an unbounded range of technologies and related inventions produced through government-sponsored R&D. NASA uniquely has developed an instrumentality for such generalized promotion and dissemination, the Technology Utilization Program. And, while certainly this has nowhere yet been accomplished, for NASA alone it is conceivable that the licensing and control of patented inventions could be deliberately used in a promotional strategy for encouraging the extension of technology and the transfer of invention.

Supposing the TUP, following the recommendations of this paper, organizes itself to make strategic use of patented inventions as instruments of promotion, for example in influencing the policies of R&D contractors or in granting exclusive rights on selected sets of inventions in support of innovation. Should only NASA-produced inventions fall within the scope of TUP control? In fact the TUP would have a task of nation-wide, not of agency-wide urgency. It would be building a bridge between the governmental and the nongovernmental sectors (the only bridge) and the inventions made and the technologies created through the research sponsored by any government agency should properly be enabled to take passage across that bridge. Why shouldn't the control over DOD patents as well as the control over NASA patents be used to influence the policies of (the same) R&D contractors towards a more vigorous promotion of commercial applications? Why shouldn't the exclusive licensing of DOD as well as of NASA patents be used to fortify market positions as a base for launching those innovations that might extend the application of the special-purpose technologies produced through government-sponsored R&D? And why shouldn't the information packaged in DOD patent applications as well as the information packaged in NASA patent applications be fed into industry through the TUP's channels of dissemination?

It is therefore recommended, not as a NASA but as a national objective, that all of the special-purpose technologies and related inventions produced through Government-sponsored R&D be brought within the scope of a rational and, where feasible, an integral control, in promoting their extension into new spheres of application and use.[17]

V. Organization

Academic Science

Our concern in this section will be with the organization of the traditional, the original science, operating as a closed, self-regulating system detached from, or, at least, unsubordinated to the goals and criteria of practice. That science is located primarily in universities, and remains dominant there though today universities have a substantial enclave of R&D as well.

---

[17]Solo, "Patent Policy for Government-Sponsored Research and Development," *op. cit.,* pp. 198–199.

Before weak, parasitical upon that of Europe, after World War II, academic science in the United States has prospered vastly and expanded enormously, dominating the science of its genre throughout the world.

Since it does not sell a product nor otherwise generate income, academic science must rely on external supports; and its support in the American mode, has come in the form of grants from the state and from private foundations, with self-subsidization at the margin. The prototype system of support in the United States, characteristic also of the private foundations, is that of the National Science Foundation. Though nominally an agency of the federal government, the NSF is in fact and by design the agent, instrument, and servant of established authority in the various sciences. It represents their interests in the conclaves of government. It specifies their demands, pleads for the funding of their activities; and, receiving funds from the state, divides these, always in accommodation to the established scientific authorities, first as between the sciences, then as between the subbranches of each of the sciences, then as between applicants for grants within each of the disciplines. The latter is done through the submission of "proposals" for peer group evaluation and award.

Certainly the activity of academic science in the United States during postwar decades has been vast and vigorous. Operating at the university nexus, it deserves high marks as an educational instrument. Indubitably it has produced a great number of competent workers and even some prize-winning virtuosi, including many who labor in the vinyards of R&D.

And yet in another sense academic science in the United States has been extraordinarily sterile. For a time span of more than two generations, even approaching half a century, encompassing the work of more scientists, more richly endowed with scientific instrumentation, publishing more than all prior generations through the centuries taken together, academic science in the American mode has produced no scientific revolutions (none of what laymen like to call "the big breakthroughs"), not a fundamental change of outlook and mind set, no paradigmatic shifts or transformations, opening new horizons of inquiry. None!

This is an immensely significant and terrible fact, for by the measure of public betterment, scientific revolution is the justification of academic science. Academic science exists, it might be said, to produce scientific revolutions. This is not so only because of the values that inhere in extending the frame within which the mind operates and the universe is comprehended, but also because it is thus that academic science yields, or could yield its greatest (and perhaps its only) practical payoff. Fundamental change of cognitive structures produced through academic inquiry, (as, for example, in the case of Einstein), transforms the cognitive understructure of R&D as well. It therefore opens new passages for the pursuit of social goals and creates a new potential for the solution of problems of long- or short-term social interest.

For, if academic science does no more than proliferate outputs within an established framework of thought, serving simply to perpetuate and to elaborate upon these, then why shouldn't all those energies operating within that approach and with that apparatus, be subordinated to problems of practice, focused upon and evaluated by reference to the goals, and the long or short term interests of society at large?

Why, under those circumstances, allow it to continue as a closed, self-directed system, rather than deliberately geared to the problems of praxis? Why, in a word, shouldn't all science take the form of R&D, with that of the university different from the rest only in its overlap with higher education and its integration into a universal discourse?

Two scientific revolutions might be identified in our time. One, the birth and development of solid state physics related to the transistor technology, was the product of R&D. The other was in the birth and development of microbiology. There the culminating or initiating step is attributed to the Englishman, Crick, and the American, Watson, working together at Cambridge, in Great Britain, in an institutional context very different from the American system of academic support. Watson records in his book *The Double Helix* that when he decided to move in the direction and to undertake the inquiry that would lead to his extraordinary achievement, *because of that decision* he was cut off entirely from what had been before a steady stream of American foundation funding. So also, Linus Pauling, that giant in American science whose work had prepared the way for Crick and Watson, and of whom alone, they perpetually feared (as recorded in *The Double Helix*) might steal their thunder, is a lonely battler in perpetual defiance of established authority, denied foundation funding even at the apogee of his glory. Nor are these mere anomalies; rather they point to the heart of the matter in explaining the terrible sterility of academic science in the United States.

What is required to produce scientific revolutions? Whatever else, and there is, no doubt, much else besides, there is this: scientists of ingenuity and high competence must be free to pursue a hunch, a sensed potential, a lurking doubt, to undertake and to persist in lines of inquiry outside the paradigmatic boundaries, running counter to the assumptions, challenging the presuppositions, putting in peril the foundations of the discipline. That is a first prerequisite. Without that freedom, how can the enormous inertial force of an established science, staunchened by the work of generations, supporting an enormous superstructure of logical elaboration and experimental achievement, ever be upset or displaced?

The *potential* value of academic science is that, more than would be possible for R&D, it can, or it could permit the free maverick inquiry by scientists of proven competence in a pursuit, perhaps illusory, perhaps real, beyond and outside the laws, the rules, the presuppositions and the established practices of their disciplines. Academic science in the prewar European mode did institutionalize a space (small, exclusive, sometimes very narrow; Einstein self-subsidized his own critical inquiries from the income he earned as a clerk in the Swiss Patent Office) for such free inquiry, from which a series of scientific revolutions was forthcoming.

But if that freedom for maverick inquiry is the progenitor of scientific revolution, the enemy of such inquiry is the established scientific authority. Scientific authority throughout the centuries, always, everywhere, inherently, necessarily, is the enemy of that freedom and hence, scientific authority throughout the centuries, always, everywhere, inherently, necessarily is the first and greatest barrier to scientific revolution; for it is the function of scientific authority to preserve, to perpetuate, to elaborate upon and to develop an established apparatus of thought (which is its stock in trade). Hence it is the business and the role and the self-interest of scientific authority to delineate the boundaries of the paradigm and to allow nothing alien to enter its gates, and in every way to fortify and to defend the assumptions, presuppositions, foundations of the discipline.

As maverick inquiry is its necessary progenitor, scientific authority is the natural enemy of scientific revolution, and scientific revolution is the *raison d' etre* of academic science. We in the United States have so designed our system of support so as to enthrone the power of scientific authority and, thereby, to frustrate the possibility of scientific revolution. Our academic science is not free; it is directed, directed not by the moguls of enterprise or by those who speak for public goals and social need. Rather it is thoroughly subordinated to the whim and will of academic authority, friend of technical virtuosity and enemy of scientific revolution.

Consider the process of academic support. The individual scientist or, more likely, a team working under one or more "principle investigators" submits a complex statement specifying what they intend to do, how they intend to do it, what will be the results of their activity, what will be their reference base, that is, what similar or related work has been done before, and why their project is interesting and significant. The stream of incoming proposals are reviewed by sets of scientists selected through the NSF secretariat and considered as *authorities* who serve voluntarily with no other reward than a bit of prestige and a taste of power, acting at a distance as referees or coming together as a committee, and bearing no responsibility, nor exercising any follow-up on the consequences of their decisions. In the light of their large numbers, those who perform the reviewer's task must on the whole be yeoman workers representing norms of judgment, outlook, expectations as these prevail in their disciplines. Since grants are made not to individuals but to the institutions with which they are affiliated, there is likely to be yet another level of evaluation and selection, with proposals obliged to pass the muster of department chairmen, departmental, college, university committees, institute directors, institute committees, and such like agents of authority, before they are forwarded for consideration to the source of funding.

This process we have chosen of allocating resources for the purposes of academic science is very costly and very wasteful. Aside from the costs of the foundations' hierarchies and their secretariats, and the costs of the administration (the universities take 60 percent of every grant to cover "overhead" allegedly related to administering and accounting for the grant), there are the days spent in reviewing and refereeing, and there are the uncounted weeks, months of scientist's labors required for the preparation of proposals (sometime volumes thick) for this is a game where the skill in proposing counts more than the record in achieving. With the hundred proposals prepared and evaluated, one succeeds; and immediately the grantee must orient himself to the task of preparing for the next round of proposing. It is a process moreover that even aside from the force it gives to the resisting power of academic authority, will of itself select out and extinguish the inquiry of any creative maverick who is groping for a truth in the shadows of the unexplored, for the burden of choice is exercised by those for whom the task is a chore and who in their hurry will look for, and will find a common denominator of the acceptable in the safely authenticated, the well-precedented, the familiar and comprehensible, eliminating out of hand that which is still inchoate, unarticulated, uncertain, un-familiar, half-baked—which is to say dismissing all and whatever is truly at its beginning.

As if by design, the American system of academic support extinguishes the flame of scientific revolution. To rekindle and nurture that flame—what option?

At issue, it must be remembered, is an academic science which has not, does not, and should not be expected to focus on the solution of problems of practice. If society has an interest in supporting this genra of science, in contrast to R&D, it is this: among scientists of proven skill and competence, who labor for a lifetime, each free to seek and search for what he deems to be of interest and significance, there may be a few who can turn the trick of revolutionizing science and thereby making possible the solution of a range of practical problems and opening avenues of technological achievement to which there is no access now. That is a reasonable hope, a worthwhile gamble except that now the rules of the game are such that the chance of winning is almost nil.

Our objective must be to change those rules to increase society's chances of winning the prize of scientific revolution. And this requires that we institutionalize a protected space for a free choice of paths of inquiry, unconstrained by the con-servative, antirevolutionary hand of scientific authority. To that end, scrap the whole complex, costly, wasteful apparatus of project proposal and peer group re-view. Simplify, get to the essential transaction. Society is taking a gamble, making a bet on the lifetime labor and free inquiry of a selected, science-trained group. Recruit them. Select them. Support them. There is nothing more, nothing else.

The trick is in their recruitment, their selection, and in preparing the institu-tional context of their labor. Society has the right to demand, to recruit, and to test for the highest level of scientific competence. If it is possible also to test for creativity, or, by the record to bring in some who have already demonstrated that quality, so much the better. Those so selected, who are ready for a lifetime commitment should be guaranteed a modest but sufficient level of support, provided only that they actively participate in the discourse of science, in pursuit of whatever level of inquiry they might choose to. For the rest we should endeavor simply to facilitate their interaction, their capacity to communicate, to associate, and their full, free access to experimental facilities.

Public Sector R&D

Before attempting a discussion of R&D in the public sector, organized by or under the aegis of the Department of Defense (DOD), of the National Aeronautics and Space Administration (NASA), of the ex-Atomic Energy Commission, (AEC) now incorporated into the Department of Energy (DOE), of the Department of Agriculture (DOA), of the Department of Transportation (DOT), of the Bureau of Standards (BOS), of the Department of Health and Welfare (DOHW) particularly in its Institutes of Health, and in a great many other agencies, qualifications are in order and apologies are due. This is a vast and complex area of activity. Some of it is entirely closed from public view, and all of it is outside the reach of common observation. I have myself been able to study in depth only facets of its operations and performance and then only for the brief periods of 1960–1962, 1965–1966. No doubt some of the changes in the years since then have escaped my notice. All that would be more serious if this were intended as a comprehensive analysis. It is not so intended. We hope merely to bring out of the shadows of public unawareness, certain important, policy-related problems, taking a few agencies to exemplify those problems, and policy options for dealing with them.

At the outbreak of World War II and for the decades before then, public sector R&D, large in comparison to that of private enterprise, miniscule in relation to what it would become, was concentrated in two fields—agriculture and aviation.

During World War II the United States developed the atomic bomb, and in so doing crossed a number of thresholds. For one it entered an era of weaponry entirely outside of current trends in science or in technology, and beyond the reach of any established industrial competence, so that the development of an entire system from the science at base to the production and utilization of the complex end products of new technologies, became a national imperative. In all of this, it is sobering to recall that Leo Szilard, who initiated the development of atomic weaponry, was repeatedly rebuffed by the military authorities and their "science advisor" and only succeeded in setting the critical development in motion through the intervention of President Franklin Roosevelt spurred by a letter from Albert Einstein (they then made Szilard the munificent grant of $5,000). The development of the bomb itself was never at the behest, or under the control, or planned, or organized by the military. The military simply kept on the security wraps. That Faustian achievement was entirely due to an autonomous group of scientists who relied above all on the contribution of refugees from Hungary, Germany, and Italy. After the bomb and after the war, that creative and autonomous group who had developed the science and created the technology dispersed into academe (hurried along by the politicians, quasipoliticians and ideological inquisitors now in possession), to establish atomic science there. The Nuclear Establishment, routinized, bureaucratized, served now as a contractor to the Pentagon.

Postwar events must be understood in the light of a new phase of American nationalism. For more than a century and a half, the United States had, more or less assiduously attended exclusively to its own knitting. Its occasional foreign interventions in Mexico, in Central America, "From the Halls of Montezuma to the shores of Tripoli," the Spanish-American misadventure in the Carribbean and the Philippines were ugly and unfortunate, but entirely marginal to the energy driven center of American interest and concern. World War I was America's first participation in a war of the major powers. There the dependence of its allies on its industrial and agricultural outputs, and the brief but bloody use of a hastily assembled expeditionary force which probably tipped the scales against the armies of the Kaiser, might have given it a decisive voice in postwar arrangements. The United States preferred to withdraw from commitment and involvement. During the 1920s and 1930s, its military shrank again into a peripheral enclave, very small, in no way distinguished, technologically static. And yet with the advent of World War II, with all its initial setbacks, its total unpreparedness, its planning failures, the United States rapidly emerged as the greatest military power on earth, entirely as the consequences of its civilian-industrial power. It was able at once to transform itself into the world's greatest military power not merely in spite of *but because of* the long decades of no military preparation, because of the years when no massive military establishment drained off society's industrial potential and its technocreative capacities. Just so France, that had for those long decades been prepared, maintaining the largest, most powerful military establishment in Europe (and drained to the bone by that) collapsed in an afternoon.

After World War II, American nationalism assumed a new and entirely novel posture. Possessing the bomb, underwriting the industrial reconstruction of Western Europe and Japan, it took on the imperial trappings of the greatest of the great powers, "leader of the free world," proclaiming "the American Century." Churchill's rousing imagery of all the dangers and evil alieness of the Other behind his "iron curtain" produced a deep American response, that mingled the ethnic prejudice and xenophobia of the common man and the ideological outrage of the elites (Truman with Acheson, McCarthy, and Dulles). We became the cold warriors who, guarding the ramparts, hunted down pinkos, leftists, and commies at home and carried on anticommunist crusades abroad. We created the CIA, something entirely new in the American system, and a total anomaly in a democratic society; the massive, secret enclave for activities unobserved and unaccounted, where scoundrels, fanatics, madmen could act out their fantasies and shape our policies without constraint.

What a glorious time for the military! The little men in Congress blinked their eyes and bowed their heads before the blazing brass. Neither Congress nor those in Executive authority had the competence to gainsay military demands, nor were they equipped to comprehend, monitor or evaluate the vast, complex technological activity under military aegis. It was a time of virtually unlimited military expansion.

A word about military establishments, all of them, here and elsewhere. They are alike of the nature of what I have called "institutional systems,"[18] which, belonging to the selfsame category of the churches, academic science, or communist parties, are rooted in and derive their coherence, orientation, and force directly from an ideological commitment; with the ideological basis of commitment to be understood as a construct of shared imageries, values, and valued things. The ideological root of military commitment, by any philosophical, ethical, intellectual criterion, is hardly an exalted one, but it is clearly capable of invoking a powerful and tunnel-visioned dedication "to the Navy" or "to the Air Force" (or once upon a time) "to the Cavalry" wherein a valued way of life is inextricably related to a given technology, the battleship, the manned bomber, the horse. With the outset of atomic weaponry, the nature of warfare was on the edge of revolutionary transformation and, of more concern to the nabobs, it was clear that military superiority would depend on a complex, rapidly developing technology produced through R&D; and that the fate of each of the services would depend on its capacity to advance its own core technology. Consequently there developed an intense interservice rivalry at the

---

[18]Solo, *Economic Organizations and Social Systems, op. cit.,* pp. 302–307.

level of technological development in the drive to command the R&D resource. In that light, one can identify a number of policy problems.

Appropriation and Allocation

Congress budgets, which is to say allocates resources between the public and the private sector and as between the diverse agencies, programs, projects of the public sector, using the dollar as the denominator of value: with so many dollars worth of resources taken from use in the private sector through taxation, and then with so many dollars worth of resources to be used for public purposes, for example, for education, or for health care, or for space exploration, or for armament.[19] Given the imageries of ideological liberalism (and of microeconomic analysis) this is all quite unexceptional for in that vision of things the dollar (price) constitutes an adequate measure of the value of resources taken, and comparative dollar expenditure constitutes an adequate measure of the relative real value of the resources used. But for the allocation of certain resources that measure does not suffice; for example, with respect to the current use of petroleum. Inasmuch as the significant consequences that follow from the accelerated depletion of that resource are not conveyed by its selling price, rational choice requires a budgeting, not in dollar terms, but directly in terms of the resource itself.

Especially a *resource budget* is required in the instance of the use of science-trained manpower in public sector R&D. An appropriation for "defense" amounting to to 3 or 4 percent of the gross national product does not seem to Congress or to the public to be of much significance. But if that 3 or 4 percent of GNP represents the employment for military purposes of 60–70 percent of the nation's active scientists and research engineers, then the consequences of that appropriation are of enormous significance, with costs to be reckoned in the slowdown of economic growth, in an incalculable loss of productivity, in the radical reorientation (as Herbert Holliman has shown) of an engineering curriculum that ceases to prepare young talent for work in the civilian-industrial sector, in a change in the character of the archive. And indeed that is what has happened as the consequence of Congressional appropriations thoughtlessly draining the motor force for technological advance from the civilian-industrial economy, with *no budgetary signal* of the consequences of such Congressional choice.

Nor can it be thought that the value of science-trained manpower is a function of the civilian-industrial demand for that manpower and hence that its value is adequately measured by its price, which is, in turn, indicated in the system of dollar-budgeting. For the unique quality of that manpower is that, in the potentials it could develop, in the technologies it might produce, in the enterprises it would initiate, in its inventions and innovations, it creates its own demand. Without that resource there is no demand for it, just as a stalled engine calls for no fuel. Its task is to provoke the spark, so sadly lacking now, that spurs advance and creates and widens the avenues of opportunity.

---

[19]Leaving aside such programs like social security that do not allocate resources between the private and the public sector, but that transfer income between groups in the private sector.

Science Subordinated

The military allocates resources, its manpower categories, its civilian and military personnel, its materiel, its equipment, its stores of clothing and its rations of food, its arms, its real estate, always in relation to the *mission* of some service arm, branch, bureau, division, task force, army, carrier, and so forth. Each component has its mission, every mission has its requisites, and resources are assigned to satisfy these. And during postwar decades R&D has been so assigned as logistical support, mission by mission. This has been the essential organization of defense-oriented science.

The inherent defects and weakness of such an organization of defense-oriented science should be at once apparent. Scientific activity is totally fragmented, eliminating any coordination towards common goals as well as the possibility of effective discourse. Experimental replication must be endless. And, most debilitating of all, the character of scientific inquiry becomes inherently defensive. Science is subordinated to missions. The mission is the responsibility and is under the control of a service, of a branch, of a task force, of an operation, but always built around the mastery of some core technology or existing set of established technologies. Hence science geared to the mission is necessarily a science subordinated to the servicing, adaptation, and development of given technologies: attached to the tank corp, such a science must devote itself to the operation of tanks; attached to the artillery, such a science must devote itself to the fabrication and fire power the big guns, and so forth. Such a science cannot in toto but become an instrument for the defense and perpetuation of those existing core technologies. It cannot, by the nature of the case, introduce basic innovation (which would eliminate and replace the core technologies), nor can it provide for the reconceptualization, redesign, and transformation of the military system or its subsystems, in accord with potentialities generated through science. Nor, so far as I can discover, has the immense investment in the mission related R&D of the military establishment produced any basic military innovations. Certainly atomic weaponry was imposed from the outside, so was the intercontinental ballistic missile, with a jolt by the Soviet sputnik.

A more rational organization of defense-oriented science would subordinate the military system and the design of its missions to the offerings of science. For that, autonomous science groups at the center of the establishment would have the task of ingesting and exploring the emerging potentials of all the sciences and technologies, and of developing these potentials in the light of existing circumstances and current needs, for the design of missions and the transformation of systems. Science components attached to military operations would act as a receptor to inputs from, and as a linkage with the science center.

Contractor Dominated

The military is, I suppose, the largest and most complex enterprise of our time, needing for its tasks, a high level of organizational and technological competence. Operating as a command center that must transmit orders over vast networks rapidly and precisely to produce rapid and precise response, to the end of deploying a great array of element in any of an infinite number of combinations anywhere around the world, the military must go by the book, with no room for equivocation or uncertainty. Hence the requisities for and the context of the military enterprise, is the very antithesis of that required for creative R&D. Therefore, the military has preferred to procure its R&D from the outside, just as it procures GI underwear from the outside, and by the same method, tried and true, of bid and buy. This advertising for bids with specifications given and accepting the low cost offer by a reputable producer may work well enough in the instance of undergarments for the troops. It cannot work with R&D, the more so must it fail to the degree that research is real and creative development is required. This for at least two reasons. Where the technology has no customer but the state, those who supply that technology are entirely dependent on the state and are necessarily its agents. Hence, there are no reputable bidders whose competence has been tested and whose productivity has been demonstrated through market competition. If there is to be testing and evaluation of competence and productivity at all, it must be the state that tests and evaluates.

Nor is there a specifiable product, nor any ascertainable costs. What the military bargains for in the case of R&D is not a product but for a proposal, a statement of intention, of aspiration, or expectation, of pie-in-the-sky. Because the what, how, and when of real research and creative development cannot be known beforehand, neither can costs. Hence, the contract that is, with one variant or another, required, guarantees to cover costs plus a profit.

Seen in its bare bones beneath the bid and buy flummery, the transaction consists of three quite inescapable functional elements. First the state does not bargain for and buy a product; it must select a producer. Second, since only the state is responsible or can be accountable for consequences, the state, evaluating alternatives must select the direction of research inquiry and technological development, and should stand responsible and be held accountable for that choice. Otherwise there is no locus of responsibility or instrument of accountability. Third since there is no competitive incentive for low cost and high productivity performance (the necessary cost-plus contract builds in only the converse incentive), the state must monitor and control performance and act to minimize costs.

To an extent, procurement authorities have been driven to the realization that it is for them to evaluate the creativity and competence of the contractor, and on that basis to award the contracts; institutionalizing "source evaluation," and gathering data on past performance. Certainly they admit at least to a responsibility for setting the direction of R&D, if not to that of monitoring performance and controlling costs. Yet, in the nature of the case, all are essential as the fundaments of public R&D procurement. *But* to analyze and to evaluate the creative capabilities and developmental effectiveness of gigantic corporate enterprise and their relative suitabilities in satisfying the particularities of public need; and to possess the skill and have the vision to set the course of R&D; and to exercise the authority and possess the capacity to monitor the performance and control the costs of vast and vastly complex operations of corporate contractors—to do these things and to do them well requires a particular competence of the highest order. Without it, the state will not direct and control but will be dominated and controlled by its contractors.

There's the rub. For that requisite mastery of science and of technology and of industrial process coupled with a commitment to public purpose and sensitized to the table of social values, is not possessed by the borrowed businessman. Nor will it be acquired by the time-serving, quick-in, quick-out military officer whose heart and aspiration points him in a different direction, nor by desk-bound civil service hirelings peripheral to the military establishment, the toughest and most capable of whom will be hired away by the high paying, high flying corporations with whom they must deal. Again the need for the autonomous agency of public management (coupled here to the proposed science center) recruiting, training, and offering a lifetime of career opportunities to climb the ladder of authority and responsibility: and the need as well for a public control of the salaries and payments to contractor personnel, not only because such control is intrinsically appropriate but also in order to balance the recruitment of talent as between the public agency and its corporate agents.

NASA and the Value of Organization

The two other agencies that have been massively involved in public sector R&D are the ex-Atomic Energy Commission (AEC) now integrated who the Department of Energy, and the National Aeronautics and Space Administration (NASA). During the Eisenhower Administration the Nuclear Establishment, beyond its contracting for the military, was charged with the (peaceful) development of atomic energy for civilian-industrial use. More about this when we deal with the energy infrastructure.

NASA was established under President John F. Kennedy's directive to beat the Russians to the moon. With a team of ex-nazi scientists and engineers as its technological core and under the administration of James Webb, a savvy and foresightful politician with great organizing abilities, NASA developed into an enormous and highly effective agency for the exploration of outer space.

Webb was aware that, unlike the Department of Defense and the Atomic Energy Commission, NASA had no natural constituency, no clientele bound to its support by an ideological commitment or by a demand for the services it rendered. Under his administration, NASA worked hard to create such a clientele. Beyond its space mission, Webb sought to make of NASA a center for science and technology, able to adapt and revector its capabilities to a range of public uses, and engaged in identifying and developing the potentialities of high science and of advanced technology for civilian-industrial needs. We earlier reviewed its achievement, unique among the great agencies engaged in public R&D, in promoting "spillover." In that light we proposed that it be given the role of general agent for "technology utilization" in the dissemination of accumulating technological values outside the special focus of public sector R&D.

What Webb feared did come to pass. After the television spectaculars, after we had pronounced ourselves winners of the "space race," after the moon walk had satisfied the pride of cold warriors, the budgetary axe came down upon NASA, disemploying thousands of highly skilled and specially trained personnel and shattering the agency. How and to what degree it managed to salvage its parts and to preserve its integrity is a tale beyond my telling. It contains a lesson nevertheless that must be learned.

Under Presidential directive, to Congressional applause and with public approval, the agency was savaged and shattered, under the logic of dollar budgeting and the criterion of taxpayer relief, with no consideration whatsoever given to the values of established organization.

More than spacecrafts, more than moonshots, the essential product of NASA expenditures, and the only one of potentially lasting value, is of an organization that was able to design and produce the spacecraft and to make the moonshot. Billions were spent and well spent in creating that organization, capitalizing on enthusiasms and aspirations not likely to be replicated, in recruitment, in training, in building the reference archive, in acquiring consensus, community, discipline, in developing the processes of decision and of coordination, and the instrumentalities of control, communication and information feedback, and of linkages to the other constituent elements of public choice and power, and all the running stream of efforts and experimentation with its failures, partial failures, partial successes supplying the grist for organizational learning. And yet in the hard-nosed naivete of dollar budgeting, all that counted for nothing!

We inhabit the universe of systems, where organization, the particular, the unique, and nonreplicable organization, the rare development-generating entity that itself is capable of development and can integrate the work and striving of thousands with the potentials of high science and technology, constitutes a critical social resource. The casual willingness to destroy such an organization with no question raised as to opportunities lost and of potentials diminished, marks our ideological bankruptcy and the inadequacy of our processes of public choice. Great opportunities have been lost. NASA might have provided the broad, multifaceted spectrum of energy-related R&D, in place of the total disarray and directionless fumbling of the present Department of Energy; and it could have spearheaded a realization of the still hidden potentialities of a national, communication/electronic-processing infrastructure.

Systems of Technological Advance in the Market Economy

For each sector of the market economy the role of the state and the character of policy will differ. But always it will be necessary to act in relation to elements of a *system* of technological advance, taking account of the sources of technologically relevant information; the means, channels, costs of acquiring, and the motivation to acquire a mastery of information, and of technology; and the means, channels, costs, and motivation to disseminate techniques or product-embodied technologies, and data concerning the experience of innovation and, conversely the means, motivation and costs of preventing such dissemination; and the means and motivation to seek out, the receptivity to, the social capacity for a response to a knowledge of technique; and the nature and locus of power to transform or to resist the transformation of technology; and the character of and constraints upon the transformation process, whether by piecemeal adjustment or requiring a multiplicity of simultaneous or coordinated changes; and the source and availability of investable resources to cover the costs of transformation. Something of this and of the role of the state in facilitating and supplementing the operation of such systems can be shown in the instance of American agriculture.

Of all the sectors of the market economy, the agricultural most closely approximates the classical model of pure competition. The man-sized farm brings a complex and integral set of technologies within the scope of individual observation, so that they can be learned by the observant individual on the job as part of the job. And the farm offers to its owner the opportunity to experiment and to innovate as he chooses within its confines. It is possible in that context for invention, innovation, transformation to occur in the classical manner, with the farmer-entrepreneur drawing upon his experience and ingenuity and building upon his self-acquired mastery of the technology, to conceive of an improvement, to try it and develop it through experiment, and then to install it in his own operations. Observed by his neighbors and learned about by others who follow suit, the innovation might spread into a general transformation of agricultural practice.

Spontaneous advances, generated out of the experience and ingenuities of a farm community do occur, for example in the important post-World War II development of factory-like operations for the environmentally controlled mass production of poultry, initiated by refugee German Jews who had taken up chicken farming on meager, barren New Jersey land sites, serving the metropolitan market. In this instance those refugees brought to their work on the farm a knowledge of chemistry and pharmaceuticals learned at school. And while nothing would prevent the dissemination of the new technology, it did not spread spontaneously through observation and imitation, but rather was disseminated to the grain producing regions of the south and the midwest through the intermediary of corporate feed producers for whom farm-owners worked as contractors.

There are particular lacks, problems specific to the operation of a system of technological advance for a decentralized, price-directed industry, as agriculture. Thus:

1. When the mastery of complex technology is acquired through observation and imitation, then practice is learned without understanding that which is practiced. Hence the consequences of variation, of changes in practice (the mental experiment, as the first step towards invention) cannot be conjectured. Of another mind set, such masters of technology are closed to the data of science. They are profoundly resistant to deviation from their learned and established practice.

2. To the degree that there are greater numbers of individual decision-makers, more widely dispersed in space, the difficulty and costs of reaching, communicating with, demonstrating, persuading on the side of the disseminators, and of testing, evaluating and deciding on the part of the receptors is correspondingly magnified.

3. Under conditions of decentralized price-direction, spontaneous investment in R&D (in long-range, professional science-based studies to produce tech-

nologically-relevant information) is virtually precluded (a) by the extreme dispersion (hence fragmentation) in the control over investable resources, hence in the capacity to finance R&D; and (b) by the greater likelihood, as a consequence of dispersion, that the benefit of such R&D will accrue to others than those who invested in the production of such information, that is, that benefits of such investment will be externalized.

In response to these inherent deterrents to any spontaneous operation of technological advances in agriculture, the state established the system of land grant colleges, (and I write from the campus of the first of these), the initial effort at higher education for the common man, here undertaken for the purpose of cultivating agricultural receptivity to the inputs of science; and it established a publicly-supported R&D network and regional experiment stations to produce useful information and better technologies for agriculture; and it organized publicly supported extension services responding to farmers need and queries to carry that information and the knowledge of new technology directly to farmers, demonstrating its use and values. All this was established and in practice from the last half of the Nineteenth Century. An yet, when we examine the record of productivity from the earliest data available, it would appear that in spite of the land grant colleges, experiment station, R&D network, extension services, and in spite also of the mechanized and motorized equipment made available to agriculture by industry during this period, technological advance in agriculture was, by the measure of productivity, almost nil. Thus

TABLE 1-Farm Productivity in the United States

Period	Output Per Man-Hour (annual rate of increase)
Pre–1899	1.1
1899–1909	0.0
1909–1919	0.0
1919–1929	1.2
1929–1937	0.8

Data are from John Kendrick *Productivity Trends in the United States* (Princeton, N.J.: Princeton University Press, 1961) p. 152.

Then in the mid-1930s something happened. Two elements were added by the state to the land grant education, the R&D, the extension service, that made the system of technological advance suddenly viable. First, by making resources available to finance a key innovation in the electrification of rural America, initiated through low interest loans to farmer cooperatives. Second, by the guarantee of minimum (parity) prices for major farm crops, which gave to farmers the security they needed to undertake long term investments in new technologies. Thence forward, for the next four decades, the system of technological advance operated in high gear, and agriculture became the star performer of the American economy.

TABLE 2-Farm Productivity in the United States

Period	Output Per Man-Hour (annual rate of increase)
1937–1948	3.8
1948–1953	6.2
1953–1958	6.2

Data are from John Kendrick *Op. Cit,* and *Trends in Output Per Man-Hour in the Private Economy 1909–1958*. (Washington: Bureau of Labor Statistics, for 1950–1958).

Now again it is slowing to a halt for reasons yet to be explained.

So much for an overview. Something also is to be learned in examining a microincident as well. For example, pickles! I live in Michigan, the center of the country's pickle industry and, since pickles are made from cucumbers, this is the state where most cucumbers are raised and harvested. During and in the aftermath of World War II, cucumbers were picked by a high quality farm laborer brought, under special dispensation, from Mexico. Anticipating the end of that program (it was ended in 1964), farmers and especially processers looked for the development of a mechanical cucumber harvester to replace the departing braceros. Agricultural machinery manufactures tried, and failed to develop a commercially viable machine. Michigan State University was approached, and it succeeded (and this is the critical point) because it was able to set in motion three parallel developments. First, it developed the harvester which, following the prevailing prototype, does not pick the cucumbers from the vine sequentially as they ripen as the departing farm laborers did. Rather it uproots the vine and carries it in its entirety back to rollers that separate large fruit from all the rest. For this to work effectively, a new species of plant had to be and was developed, producing preponderantly large (hence harvestable) cucumbers that all ripened more or less at once so that the entire crop could be harvested, with all the vines uprooted in a single swoop. Finally it was necessary to design an appropriate mode of cultivation, and to disseminate and teach it to the farmers.

We have used the agricultural example to illustrate the macro and the micro operation of a *system* of technological advance, in part because only in agriculture has the state significantly intervened to create and to develop such a system in the private sector. Nor did this represent any comprehensive and purposeful plan. It emerged bit by bit in response to the farmer's demands. No one, for example, had any notion of the critical relation of parity pricing to the successful functioning of that system. When in John F. Kennedy's administration, an effort was made to provide a similar set of services (experiment station, regional R&D, extension service) to support technological advance in the laggard construction industry, the project was killed by the builders themselves, or at least by the objections of an articulate few who feared to lose comparative advantage. Comparative advantage is of no concern to the farmer. He does not compete with or seek the custom of his neighbor, but sells all he has to sell at the market price and sees his benefit in lowering his costs and in higher market prices.

And now in the face of productivity slowdown and a frightening loss of the technological preeminence that was our heritage, what collective action to supplement, to support, to accelerate, to create and develop viable systems of technological advances in the market economy?

The Category of Nonscience Based Corporate Technology

It must be accepted from the start that any program for positive action in developing the systems of technological progress in the market economy, no matter its intrinsic merit, must withstand opposing, negating cultural, political, ideological forces; this aside from those of public and political ignorance and indifference. There will be the opposition and resistance of those who fear that technological change will cause them to lose some comparative advantage. And there will be those who resist and oppose collective action in support of technological advance because it is collective, because it is intervention by the state, for them casting shadows of socialism, communism, totalitarianism, and other demons from the pandora's box of their fantasy. Those of the first category have been with us always. If their attitudes had prevailed, we would still be scratching the earth with pointed sticks. There is nothing for their opposition but to bulldoze it down. The taboos of the ideological purists, of the fanatics of free enterprise, signals a deeper malaise. Against their idea must be posed another, of a universe wherein the activities of individuals, of antonomous groups (like trade unions and corporations) and of the agencies of the state coexist, and need to coexist symbiotically with form fitted to function, where the alternative systems of choice and action, whether individualized, corporative, or public, should be judged and chosen only to the doing of that which they can do best.

To chart a course of action, the terrain of technological advance must be surveyed thus to identify the missing elements, sector by sector, industry by industry, great firm by great firm. And to discover by the record where the system of technological advance is working badly or not working at all. And to mark out those areas of technology where there is no system, no means, no vectoring of the forces for advance. Such is a task, and a continuing one, for the agency of public management.

The operations of the man-sized firm enables the individual to master an integral technology (as a basis for experimenting, inventing, innovating) through observation on the job as part of the job. But in the massive modern corporation all those engaged, whether their status is high or low, occupy but tiny niches in a very complex system, where technology is extended vastly beyond the reach of individual observation, its elements fragmented and where the role of each is fixed by an encompassing directive. In that context, the individual cannot comprehend the integral technology by observing it, nor learn it by doing it on the job as part of the job. To master that technology requires a stepping back, an act of abstraction, a mental reconstruction of the whole viewed from the outside. Normally the mastery of such technologies must be acquired through formal education. For this reason the university has a necessary and natural role in recruitment and training for the operations of the modern corporation; and the acquired knowledge of scientists and engineers is of direct relevance to those operations which was never the case for man-sized enterprise in decentralized markets. Nor under the encompassing directive, within the corporate plan, can there be any spontaneous experimentation or individually motivated, self-directed innovation.

In sum, given the context of massive corporate enterprise, neither learning by the individual of an integral technology, nor organizational learning in the sense of systematic development of technological potentials, nor technological invention or innovation can occur spontaneously. In this context individual training, organizational learning, processes leading to technological advances and innovation must be planned, institutionally developed as separate functional components installed in a complex operation. Unless such functional components are planned and installed, there will be no individual training leading to the acquisition of technological mastery, no organizational learning cumulatively increasing the operating potential, no processes leading to, and no invention or innovation.

R&D, itself a variety of things, is normally intended to function as an instrument of organizational learning, and of technological receptivity, scanning the horizons of science for, or itself producing technologically relevant information, and developing applications of that information for the operations and activities of the company of which it is a part. R&D need not succeed. It may be a failure and a waste. But without R&D or an equivalent, the vast body of activities encompassed by the corporation will generate no technologically relevant information, will contribute nothing to the general stream of technological advance, and will be unable to search the archives or respond effectively to emerging technological potentials.

In fact there are great areas of corporate enterprise, massive technological aggregations, whole industries, the American railways for example, that are not functionally equipped to search out and themselves to generate the informational stuff of technological advance, barren of invention, contributing not at all to the stream of technological progress, without the capacity to seek out, effectively to evaluate or adopt emerging potentials or technologies offered to them. Among the industries that have failed effectively to gear the R&D function into the systemic advance of their *core* technologies, one would number even steel and automobiles.

There is a reason for this. There are certain (science-based) industries whose core technology is a product of science, or even whose core technology is a science paradigm that has been given a particular product or problem vector. It is thus for chemicals, pharmaceutics, synthetics, electronics. There some genra of R&D is itself the core technology or at least it is that which links the development of operations to the enlarging, evolving archive of the mother science out of which operations came.

There is another, older, very important category of corporate industry whose core technologies were developed entirely outside of science, (nonscience based) without a link to any mother science or any science archive. Such technologies were initially developed spontaneously through the self-learned technological mastery and inventiveness of individuals in the domain of a man-sized firm. Those technologies evolved and were extended into mammoth enterprises, in part because of real economies of large scale operations. Those who came later to control those vastly extended operations had learned the technology not as scientists but as engineers committed to the exactitudes of established practice. With the growth of such industries beyond the individual's observational compass, self-learning and spontaneous invention as the spur to technological advance, ceased to be possible. Something was needed to take its place.

How to design, develop and build a learning function that systematically searches for and generates the information relevant to technological advance, producing innovation and the transformation of industrial practice, in industries where the core technology is not science-based, and where R&D cannot, therefore, be a projection or refocussing of an established paradigm of science? The Japanese must have created something of the sort, for they consciously and systematically and over generations undertook to learn and learn about, scanning, studying, testing, evaluating, adapting, and building upon information from every corner of the Western World, in order to develop their own science-based and also nonscience based industries.

In any case the design and development of a learning function appropriate to the nonscience based industry and the creation of the archival center into which such instrumentalities of corporate learning might gear and from which they might draw informational sustenance, is a critical and unresolved problem. Nor is it one that can be dealt with by the individual enterprise. It requires collective effort, and it should be approached by the agency of public management.

Lacuna

There are areas where technology has no vector of advance, where systems to generate advance must be created in toto, and others where missing elements must be supplied, and there are general conditions which can negate the operation of all such systems.

Thus the policy of high *nominal* interest rates pursued with particular rigor in the late 1970s intended as an antidote to inflation ("nominally" high because the ascending interest rate forced an even more rapid rise in the rate of inflation, so that the higher cost of money was offset by its declining value), starved the systems of technological advance of the resources they required. Demonstrably investment agencies were unwilling to enter into long term commitments. Instead their focus shifted to the rapid payoff in the short term, especially to the barren fields of commodity, of land and of gold speculation. Thereby they further deprived R&D and all that relates to the transformation of technology of the investment it requires. Independent R&D-based companies were squeezed to death or died stillborn.

So, too, the institutional context can affect the operation of the systems of technological advance throughout. Thus the engineering curricula in American universities, reshaped to satisfy the esoteric demands of public sector R&D, fails now to produce the skills and creative competencies required on the civilian industrial side; in this regard, it is claimed, the development of the curricula and of the engineering sciences in the United States lags far behind that of other countries spared the overwhelming pressure of military R&D.[19]

A comparative study of technological education (both engineering and voca-

---

[19]The National Research Council, *Technology, Trade, and the U.S. Economy* (Washington: National Academy of Sciences, 1978), pp. 60, 61.

tional) here and abroad, at the level of a presidential commission is surely in order to know if, when, and how we have lagged so that we might better get on with the business of catching up.

In particular important regions of technology, for example, that of urban transit, or related to urban transit, that of tunneling and underground construction or in the development of more efficient hospital care technologies, the need is to create a whole system of technological advance, including education, R&D, the development of an archive, the establishment of loci of responsibility, of interest and of power, and sources for the financing of innovation and transformation.

Transnationalizing Science and Technology

Our "advanced" science and technology presages the end of the nationalist state, presages the end of a world of national states, each a sovereign, admitting no right, no law, no interest save its own; for the destructive power that this science and technology has given to the individual national state is now so enormous that when it is unleashed, and the question seems not whether but when it will be unleashed, the world of nation states must destroy itself. Is there any way out of that trap? At least we can, bit by bit, create ties, and relationships of function that transcend the domain of the national state creating the sinews of an encompassing society within which perhaps the force of the nationalist can be submerged. And in no other set of functional activities is the logic of supranational or transnational organization so clear, or the opportunity of establishing those ties so great, as with the systems of science and of technological advance.

Aside from compassion, aside from all our human concerns, what simple, clear, self-interest have you and I in the science and technology, and the prerequisite level of economic development of the vast impoverished and backward masses of the third world? There is this self-interest and perhaps this one alone, that when the yoke is lifted that holds them in an ancient darkness bound like oxen to a wheel that turns on the edge of survival, then their normal proportion of talent, intelligence, creativity, genius will be released adding to the force of science and technology as a world system that raises the potentials of being for all. In the propelling forward of science and technology, we are all passengers on the same ship.

There are good reasons to regionalize, localize, disperse particular activities in science and in the development of technology inasmuch as those activities integrate with and serve to upgrade higher education, industrial *cum* agricultural organization, and the processes of economic development. But the locale or personna of discovery and development is irrelevant to what can be the benefits or who can be the beneficiaries thereof. It matters not at all for the recovery from a disease that the cure was developed in Paris or Moscow or Rome or Delhi or Houston or Boston. To recruit the ablest, to make the best and fullest use of available resources, to optimize the human values of the outputs of science and technology, in sum to optimize the public good, the nation by nation organization of the system of science and of technological advance, makes no sense at all.

On the face of it, national boundaries should have no relevance in the organization of these systems, nor should their output bear a national label. Except that one begins not with a clean slate but with a world already possessed. The command and control of resources, the agencies and instruments of collective choice and of re-source allocation, the agencies and instruments of institutional control and of techni-cal transformation in fact operate within and are sometimes a part of the national state. Differences in language and culture whether generated by or only correlary with the division of society into nation states, nevertheless exist as barriers to association and communication. Particularizing interests, drives for comparative advantage, and the hovering xenophobic suspicions, aggressions, and fears all coun-tervail against a science that seeks for the universal as water seeks its level. And in technology too, the extension of the international company and, indeed of trade itself, serve to rationalize in transnationalizing the system of technological advance. There are some programs linking the R&D of these multinationals with that of R&D agencies in the socialist states. We have no real knowledge of the actual breadth, constraints upon effectiveness, or significance of any of these.

How further to promote the transnationalization of science and of the systems of technological advance, to realize upon intrinsic values and also as a step in the development of a global state? Certainly there is place for the transnationalization of elements of the science infrastructure, that is to say, of the science-based services that constitute a context for a host of individual and corporate choices and activities, for example, in meterology (R&D and related services geared to problems, processes, and services of testing and measurement, such as we would associate with our National Bureau of Standards and including the testing of toxic substances), or in the forecasting of climatic conditions and of geophysical phenomena, or in oceano-graphic, or hydrological, or soil and other surveys and surveillance. Why, for exam-ple, should there be X number of national patent offices replicating a particular patent search, X number of times? There ought to be but a single world agency searching for prior publication and earlier invention out of a universal file. (In these days of the microfiche, that file should be made widely available as a library tool for education and for the dissemination of technology.) It might be appropriate for such an agency to have a number of search centers correspondingly as scientific literature appears in different languages. The principle search centers should be located when possible in countries where there is an oversupply of qualified, science-trained per-sonnel, as in India, where the cost of operations could be covered through the use of counterpart funds. The search agency would not issue patents. It would supply the information to national authorities who would or would not do so in accord with their laws.

There is room as well for transnational programs of public R&D vectored to problems of agriculture, of fisheries, of forestry, of mining, of pest and pollution control, of medical development, and of space exploration. Yet I know of no signifi-cant and successful programs of transnational, public R&D, at least not in which the United States has participated. The immediate cause of this failure has been in leaving the organizational task to diplomats and politicians (including "scientists" co-opted into agencies of diplomacy). Arrangements made thusly will amount to no more than ritual liaison and publicity gestures. Behind this approach to the public organization of transnational R&D has been a diplomacy empty of substance and jealous of prerogative, and perhaps a certain arrogance on the part of American science and technology (vanishing now) conceiving of itself as having only to teach with nothing to learn.

To make public programs for transnational R&D work, avoid the channels of diplomacy, the political intermediaries, the high level administrators. Let their role be simply to bring together defacto directors and the shakers and movers of organized R&D operations, laboratories, institutes; give to these the responsibility for devising a common program, and let them bring that program to the diplomats and politicians who can then argue over the sharing of costs.

Prior to the organization of R&D, there is the question of allocating resources as between the broad avenues, the roads, paths, and byways open to choice. How to decide the direction of inquiry, on what project, on what set of experiments, should the public put its money? We refer here not to academic science, but to the research and development where product and practice is the objective and the payoff. That allocations choice must always be very hard to make and, in fact, a real and rational choice on this score is rarely made. Nor is there any way to eliminate uncertainty. There are, nevertheless, good bets and bad ones. Our objective should be to make this set of bets, whose consequences are critical for society, as rational and as informed as possible. What can it mean, to be informed?

Suppose the objective was to increase the quality or to lower the cost of the meat available to consumers, or to lower energy costs, or to raise the quality or lower the costs of home construction, or to develop more secure and lower costs methods of toxic waste disposal, and so forth. What information would be useful for a rational allocation-of-resources choice as between alternate R&D paths to such an objective? At least the following:

1. To learn what the alternatives are, from a survey and specification on a world basis, of the avenues of search, and within these avenues, of alternative methodological and experimental approaches: ongoing, proposed or considered potential.

2. With respect to each of these to have an estimate of costs and of the time required for a positive or a negative determination.

3. To have an informed range of judgment as to the degree of uncertainty, and the probability of a successful solution of the problem posed.

4. To analyze positive values in the information sought for or in the solution of the problem posed, suggesting where such information or solution fits in a larger scheme of things. Too often R&D is supported where costs are considerable, risks are low, but where the fullest and most complete success will produce information that is almost worthless.

To prepare such an assessment of R&D alternatives, for any area of choice would be costly and difficult nor could it be made once and for all, The data of choice and the alternatives for consideration are continuously changing. Hence, assessment too must be continuing, and with all the fields that might reasonably be surveyed! Very difficult, inherently uncertain, it is nevertheless the only possible basis for an informed and rational choice as between alternative paths of inquiry and experiment.

This immense task of preparing the information base for the R&D allocations choice need not be done by the single national state alone. It could, as will be shown, be shared among the nations. Let the public authority of each select a set of experts, a commission assigned the task of preparing in depth an assessment of R&D alternatives for a particular field of inquiry, with commissions from each of the associated nations undertaking the survey and assessment of a different R&D field. The individual commission would, in due course, report before and enter into a discourse with those of the associated nations engaged in the allocations choice. Given their differences in priorities, in their research resources, in their evaluation of risk and payoff values, it is unlikely that the allocations made by the various national authorities would ever be the same, but the survey and assessment information could serve (a) to upgrade the quality of decision of all, and (b) could provide the basis for transnational planning to assure a wider range of R&D pursuits and the full and effective dissemination of its results.

Chapter

11

A POLICY FOR ENERGY

I. To Regulate Monopoly or to Shape the Infrastructure?

Infrastructure as a term in common usage, referring to the social or economic context of particular choice and behavior, must be new in the language. Nor is its meaning unequivocal. Equivocal or not, the idea it conveys of the structure that underlies and determines the character and direction of a broad spectrum of activities and choices, is an important one. What then are the systems of the infrastructure? The law and its enforcement? Health care and disease prevention? Money and credit? Education? Here we will be concerned with two of the critical infrastructural systems of the economy (1) communications, and (2) energy, which overlaps that of transportation.

The State and the Infrastructure

The American state has had its long period impact upon the critical systems of the economic infrastructure, (communications, energy, and transportation) at two distinctive levels. The one has been in pragmatic, residual, collective responses to pressure and need largely by local government and quite outside the zone of conceptualization and rationalization. The other expressing an ideological blueprint, rationalized, formalized, taught in the classroom elaborated in the courts, is institutionalized as the regulation of natural monopoly. Both the character of policy *vis a vis* these systems of the economic infrastructure and the cause and consequence of the current collapse of that policy, needs to be understood in those terms.

The Regulation of Natural Monopoly

In the imageries of ideological liberalism, the envisioned universe is of boundless competition by individual self-seekers with their interactions orchestrated through the free, autonomous movement of price. Such is understood to be the natural condition, and the one that must inevitably prevail so long as things are left to themselves. Except that here and there, in odd corners of the economy, because of some special circumstance of resource availability or of technological peculiarity, efficient production requires a degree of concentration not compatible with competition, and where not competition but monopoly is natural. If there is to be competition, then costs will be unacceptably high; but without competition the consumer is at the mercy of monopoly's predatory power. What was to be done?

In Europe, under the most libertarian regimes, where the state nevertheless retained a measure of authority and a degree of competence denied to it here, the answer was to nationalize the important loci of natural monopoly.

But in the United States during the period of industrialization and of libertarian orthodoxy, with an impotent state in ideological thrall, American liberalism devised its own peculiar solution based on these axioms.

1. Since capitalist enterprise is the natural source of all efficiency, all ingenuity, all productivity, all initiative, production must remain in the hands of capitalist enterprise.

2. Since the salutary force of market competition is absent, something must be substituted to protect the consumer.

3. Since politicians are inherently corrupt and the state is inherently ineffective, neither the operation nor the control of natural monopolies should be allowed to politicians or left to the state.

4. Experts are expert, however. Experts are knowledgeable, wise, detached, objective and scientific. Hence the natural monopolies in the hands of capitalist enterprise should be regulated by commissions of experts; nonpartisan, autonomous, detached from the political system of electoral answerability and control.

5. The regulated enterprise was the property of its owners. The courts must regulate the regulators to protect the sacrosanct prerogatives and powers of property.

By 1927 every state save Delaware had such a commission engaging particularly in setting rates for electric power and gas. The federal government created the Interstate Commerce Commission (ICC) in 1887 and the Federal Power Commission (FPC) in 1920, though not until 1936 was it given the right to regulate the interstate transmission of electric power, and in 1938 the right to regulate the interstate movement of natural gas. In 1933, the Federal Communications Commission took over the functions of two earlier commissions, to regulate interstate telephone communications and radio, later television. The Civil Aeronautics Board

(CAB) and the Federal Aviation Agency (FAA) were both established in 1938, to regulate the commercial airlines.

The regulation of natural monopoly was to be in the nature of a contract. The monopoly enterprise was recognized as necessary, was legitimatized, franchised, shielded from competitive incursion. In return, the enterprise would accept the commission's right to protect consumers from its monopoly power over price by setting rates that would cover operating costs plus a "fair" return on investment, presumably equivalent to "normal" prices under competitive conditions. The courts, alas, imposed criteria especially with regard to the value of investment (the rate base), under which a clear, unequivocal administrative determination of fair return was not possible. The ICC is a case in point.

The Act passed in 1887 required the Interstate Commerce Commission to set railroad rates that were "just" and "reasonable." Almost at once the Supreme Court emasculated its effective powers. Not until the Hepburn Act of 1906 and the Mann-Elkins Act of 1910 did the Commission receive the legislative basis it needed to regulate rates according to the classical conception, so that for each railroad costs would be covered plus no more, no less than a fair return on the value of investment. For that the complex of properties in the possession of each railroad must be valued; and the Valuation Act of 1913 authorized the Commission following the criteria laid down by the courts, to undertake such an evaluation which, after opportunity for public hearings and appropriate revisions, would be pronounced as final, kept up to date, and used thenceforth as the rate base in determining fair return.

It was supposed to take three years to make that valuation. It took twenty. And in 1933, when a tentative valuation as of 1913 was ready, the issue was moot. The problem, no longer one of constraining rapacious monopoly, was to get the bankrupted railroads out of hock. In any case, the intent of regulating rates for each railroad by reference to its costs and the value of its rate base was inherently incongruous since railroads in the same region have myriad operating costs and different capital structures but their rates must be competitive when shipments are parallel and serve the same market. Nor was such a determination compatible with the requirement that there be some general cost-mileage relationship for the system as a whole so that the development of one region would not be favored at the expense of another.

Indeed, under ideal conditions, if regulation worked exactly as it was supposed to with rates continuously adjusted so that return on investment was never more and never less than "fair," there would no longer be any profit motive to produce efficiently or hold down costs.

Monopoly was legitimatized, competitive entry was excluded, and yet there was never effective regulation of rates according to the famous recipe. As for the politically neutralized commissions, only the regulated companies had a powerful and continuing interest in their transactions. Not surprisingly the regulated industries became in due course, the clients, and the supporters of the regulating commissions; and the commissions came to represent the interests of the regulated. In the horrified eyeview of ideological liberalism, those whose task it was to control monopoly, had become instead the quasiofficial appendages of industrial cartels. It was becoming increasingly evident moreover that those areas marked out as natural monopoly were no more or less monopolies, no more or less in need of regulation than other great industries of the corporate sector. Hence the movement to *deregulate,* cheered by Academe, warming the cockles of every libertarian heart, launched by the Carter Administration, to be accelerated no doubt under President Reagan.

Requisites of the Infrastructure

The imageries of liberalism were wrong. Natural monopoly is not the issue, and never was. What has been and what remains critical is the character of an infrastructure on which the direction and development of all the rest depends. The requisites of its systems, instrumental in the formation and development not only of the economy but also of the community, of the society itself, cannot or cannot always be met through the interplay of market forces alone. The founding fathers knew this when they laid down the establishment of a postal service as a constitutional imperative, and as a task of the infant federal government; for to make that service universally available under uniform conditions, was a basis and means of making a nation.

It is in these terms that we would understand a continuum of interventions and actions by the state, all outside the conceptual reach of prevailing ideologies (collectively subliminal, if you like) the ad hoc and unrationalized response to pressures and to sensed needs and opportunities, in the massive subsidies that underwrote the transcontinental railways, in the R&D that created the technology of modern aviation, in the subsidies and support that prepared the context and made possible the development of the commercial airlines, in the clearing of harbors and the dredging of rivers and the building of canals, in the organization and building of multipurpose flood control, irrigation and hydroelectric projects wherever the water flows, in spearheading the electrification of rural America, in the TVA that demonstrated and developed the use of low cost energy as an instrument for overall regional development, and in defiance of market practice, established not only the social advantages but also the corporate profitability of a bold reduction in electricity rates, and in the development and dissemination of a nuclear technology.

The instrumental requisites of the systems of the infrastructure are still sensed rather than specified. They need to be brought to the level of general awareness, explained, explored, rationalized, debated, made the subject of inquiry and of discourse. It is by reference to those requisites that we should now judge the record and take account of the consequence of the demise of utility regulation.

True the commissions represented the interests of the industries they regulated rather than of the consumer; but these were important industries, important interests, and to represent them had its values as well as its dangers. Surely the same can be said for the role of the Department of Agriculture, the Department of Defense, the Department of Labor, the Department of Commerce. There are *industry* interests, in contrast to the interests of the individual firm, interests in the general rate of industry growth and development (certainly the CAB and the FAA were committed and contributed to the growth of commercial aviation), in the resolution of internecine disputes (which was a continuing preoccupation of the ICC), in a general conformity to some code or standard of "fairness" as a precondition to a long-run public acceptance of industrial practices (an ongoing concern of the FCC). And the commissions did sense the need for, and did promote conditions required for the developmental values of these systems: standards of safety and service, of universal availability, of uniform and stable pricing that did not discriminate against any region's or group's *potential* for development, and that provided a secure base for the future planning by recipients of the service. Those conditions precisely have been thrust into disarray by the current policies of deregulation.

The first triumphant deregulation has been of the airlines. From the eyeview of this middletowner, midwesterner, its consequences have been far from beneficient. Fares have skyrocketed. There has been a sharp decline in scheduled flights; for some places, service has been eliminated entirely. On-flight service deteriorates, accidents increase, everywhere the margin of safety is less. Price discrimination proliferates to an unheard of degree so that there ceases to be any general relationship between mileage and costs. Prices veer wildly and drop precipitously in airline competition between a few established metropolitan centers and rise as precipitously elsewhere; thereby subsidizing and supporting the concentration of population and business in those urban centers, correspondingly, suppressing and penalizing potentialities for the dispersion of population and of industry. In very short order this system of the infrastructure has ceased to provide a secure and rational basis for locational arrangement, for future planning, and for regional development. The very notion of a common carrier has gone.

What follows will focus on the infrastructural systems of energy and communications. This must to an extent be a synthesis of arguments made earlier concerning policy for the corporate sector (we will be concerned with the arbitrary power of autonomous corporations), concerning policy for science and technology (to upgrade and sustain these infrastructural systems above all requires the development and installation of new science-based technologies), concerning the organization and reform of the instruments and agencies of public choice, and control (a competent public management is here an absolute prerequisite).

II Energy

Failures of the Market/Failures of the State

The failures of the state are manifold, and we have tried to trace them to their organizational and ideological roots. Those failures, however, for the most part are failures to anticipate, failures to ameliorate, failures to find a way out of disasters produced through free enterprise in the market economy. The destruction, the degradation of the environment, the stinking effluents of affluence, the poisons upseeping the earth, the pollution of the air and the waters, the wholesale annihilation of species, the threat to the biosphere has, save for the sins of the military, not been the work of the state. All that is the product of free enterprise on the market economy.

So the energy crisis is a crisis of the market, a failure of enterprise. Oil embargo brought an abrupt awareness of the closure that operations of the free market economy had created, a realization of the fragility of an economic base where, with a single prop removed, we no longer could sustain ourselves. Through free enterprise

operating under the sacrosanct laws of the market, we had squandered our sustenance. The well we were told was bottomless, is running dry, leaving us with no other
technological recourse. Surely the state failed to foresee, to prevent, to find a solid
path around the morass where free enterprise and the market economy had led us.
The crisis, the morass, the lack of any viable technological fallback are the gifts and
consequence of free enterprise in a market economy.

The question is not whether the state would have done better than free enterprise
did. The state, our state, in doing nothing did badly. But, in matters of this proportion, in protecting or, in a positive sense, in enhancing the environment, or in taking
into account the grave depredations that threaten the very system that enables the
existence of life on this small spot in the great dead universe, or in giving weight
to the values of social continuity and to the survival of the whole, or in acting in
awareness that the thread of energy by which our destiny hangs is thin, trembling
and beginning to tear—only the state can do it at all.

One of Jimmy Carter's rallying cries in his initial presidential campaign was the
need for an energy policy. There was no energy policy, he complained, but if elected,
he would have one. The only significant change in this regard brought about by his
election, reflecting that yearning to return to the golden age of laisser faire, was to
accelerate the decontrol of the price of oil—a process brought to its triumphant
culmination by his successor. All was to be left to the market. Then (academics
applauding) everything would be solved through the miraculous manipulation of the
invisible hand.

What then can, and what cannot be expected of the market?

Leaving It All to the Market

In trying to explain and express that argument and policy position deriving from
the set of cognitive structures we call economics, we will refer to the arguments of
two very capable, intelligent, sophisticated economists, Lester Thurow[1] and Richard
Schmalensee.[2]

The price of natural gas has been controlled from the start of the industry by
the former Federal Power Commission (now integrated into the Department of
Energy as the Federal Energy Regulatory Commission) and by the public utility (or
public service) commissions of particular states, as a part of the regulation of natural
monopoly. Petroleum prices were not controlled (though natural gas and petroleum
are normally joint products of the same process) until the formation of OPEC and
the shock of the oil embargo. A complex system of controls was then imposed, with
a lower price for oil from wells in operation before the OPEC crisis, higher but still
controlled prices for oil from new wells in established oil fields to take into account
increased costs of deeper drilling, and uncontrolled prices pegged by the oil companies to the price of imported petroleum, from oil from new wells in new fields.

---

[1]Lester Thurow, *The Zero Sum Society* (New York: Basic Books, Inc. Publishers, 1980), Chapter
2.

[2]Richard Schmalensee "Appropriate Government Policy Toward Commercialization of New Energy Supply Technologies," *The Energy Journal,* Vol. 1, No. 2 (April, 1980).

Through a series of taxes and subsidies, the prices of petroleum from these three sources were combined, with consumers charged the average of the three. Natural gas prices which can be linked to imported oil on a basis of Btu equivalence, followed approximately the same design.

All this meant that the controlled prices consumers paid for their gasoline and natural gas were below the price paid for imported oil, which constituted about 20 percent of the energy total. Hence consumer prices in the United States were below the marginal cost of the petroleum product—a cardinal sin, according to accepted doctrine, against *efficiency.* On that account, price control was condemned by virtually every type and species of economist.

Was there anything detrimental in lifting price control? It would, in raising prices and profits, constitute a massive transfer of income from consumers to producers (from a vast number of gasoline and fuel oil consumers to a few petroleum companies). Thurow calculated that to have removed price controls:

> In 1978 an additional $120 billions or 6% of GNP would have been transferred from American consumers to American producers if all energy prices had been allowed to follow the price of imported oil . . . given an expected increase in the price of imported oil of about 100% during 1979, the 1979 transfers would have been correspondingly larger. . . .
>
> . . . While a 100% increase in the price of energy would reduce the real income of the average American by 9.9%, it would have reduced the real income of the poorest decile of families by 34% and the richest decile by 5%. The real income effects among the poor are almost seven times as large as they are among the rich . . . most of the income transfers among Americans will go to the top 10% of the population . . . , the income of the remaining 90% will go down.[3]

Thurow views the redistributive impacts of decontrol with misgiving, but rather as a barrier to rational political action in decontrolling the price of petroleum than as a reason for avoiding decontrol and searching for an alternative policy.

Schmalensee, judging social preference by political behavior, sees the problem not as one of distributional inequity, but rather of avoiding too sudden and severe a "shock" to group expectations and the organizational arrangements long established in the economy. It is on that ground that he rationalizes an (indeterminate) gradualism in the movement towards decontrol.

Schmalensee takes:

> [W]hat seems to be a common approach among policy-oriented microeconomists, but one that is rarely made explicit. I look for the sorts of imperfections in market operations that the formal analysis identifies as relevant, but I prescribe government intervention only when those imperfections are of demonstrably unusual importance. Energy markets are imperfect in many ways, but so are markets for textiles and most other goods and services. The many imperfections that society chooses to ignore in the case of textiles should also be ignored in the case of energy, unless the two cases can be qualitatively or quantitatively distinguished.

---

[3]Thurow, *op. cit.,* p. 29.

> . . . The market system's generally good performance justifies imposing a nontrivial burden of proof on those who would modify its operation.[4]

Thus while market imperfections are not denied, the imperfections in one industry are presumed to balance out against the imperfections in another with the consequence that market is regarded as "on the whole" performing well, so that any specific intervention in that market must a priori be judged as a source of distortion except only when extraordinary imperfections of "demonstrably unusual importance" can be *proven.*

Aside from the issue of equity mentioned earlier, Schmalensee conceives of two energy-related policy objectives; first, that energy be used efficiently, and second, that imports should be reduced as a proportion of total consumption for reasons of national security. The first would require that the domestic price of petroleum and of its natural gas equivalent be equal to the price of imported oil, hence satisfying the law of marginal costing. The second, according to Schmalensee, would require the imposition of a tariff on imported oil, raising domestic prices above the imported (efficient, marginal cost) level, to some socially optimal price that reflected the greater real value of domestically produced energy. The higher the tariff, the greater the security, with "careful quantitative analysis of cost/security tradeoffs yielding an optimal tariff,T^*,"[5] thereby reducing consumption and thence constraining imports, and increasing the possible profitability, hence encouraging the installation of new, or unconventional sources of energy supply.[6]

The security twist and the notion of a socially optimal price level produced through the imposition of tariff T^* may be considered as Schmalensee's own. The proposition and policy inescapably to be derived from the economics paradigm is (1) that efficient prices, serving as an index of real scarcity and hence providing a rational basis for the entrepreneur's, the investor's, and the consumer's choice, is equated to marginal costs, hence in this instance to the cost of imported oil[7]; and (2) that efficient pricing is a sufficient and the best available mechanism for the allocation of resources, for the organization of production, and for consumer's conservation choices.

Assuming efficient prices, that is, decontrolled prices of petroleum and natural gas pegged to the price of imported oil (and with the price of imported oil possibly adjusted upward through a tariff for reasons of national security), and assuming a

---

[4]Schmalensee, *op. cit.*, pp. 4,5.

[5]*Id.*, p.9.

[6]Schmalensee's logic is obscure. Given that domestic prices are pegged to the imported price of oil and that a tariff would simply raise the price to which domestic production is pegged, consumers would be indifferent as between consuming domestically produced and imported petroleum. Hence no clear inference can be drawn as to the effect on domestic production or on the domestic/import ratio in petroleum consumption. The result may be simply a proportional decline in domestic production of petroleum and substitutes. Nor is it made clear why a general reduction in the consumption of energy should increase national security. Quite the converse could be argued.

[7]The embarrassing paradox of the "second best," that other market prices do *not* reflect marginal costs, hence that a price reflective of marginal costs is *not* an index of relative scarcity, and it is relative scarcity that counts as a criterion for rational resource allocation, is invariably assumed away. At least it can be safely assumed that other market prices are not below marginal costs, which may suffice in the argument for decontrol.

basic reliance on market forces, Schmalensee asks whether any public intervention
or support for the commercialization of "particular new or unconventional energy
supply technologies,"[8] that is, synfuels, can conceivably be justified. Again only by
reference to extraordinary imperfections proven to be of "demonstrably unusual
importance." Otherwise intervention must be presumed a distortion of rational
choice and a reduction of efficiency. Is there in these terms any general justification
for the public support of such energy technologies? Schmalensee examines and
rejects arguments that such intervention and support is justifiable on account of the
very heavy capital costs and long lead time sometimes required (as in the case of
synfuels), or because of the obstacles posed by the environmental legislation to the
establishment of such technologies, or by the riskiness attributable to the establishment of energy-related technologies. This on the grounds that none of these attributes are peculiar to energy-related technologies, and to provide a special dispensation
for them on such grounds would bias choice against alternative options for investment and organizational design.

> While some unconventional energy supply technologies are apparently notable
> for their capital costs and for the lead times likely to be involved in plant construc-
> tion, they are hardly unique in these respects. There apparently does not exist any
> solid evidence or theory indicating that private capital markets are *biased* against
> large projects with long lead times. (In a world of uncertainty, some aversion to such
> projects is rational and reflects real costs of protracted risk bearing.) More impor-
> tantly, even if such a bias could be demonstrated, . . . the rational policy response
> would not be to use that bias as an excuse to single out the energy supply sector
> for special treatment, but rather to attempt to offset biases against large investments
> with long lead times throughout the economy.
>
> Finally, it has sometimes been contended that strict environmental standards
> represent an excessive obstacle to potentially important new energy supply sources,
> an obstacle that should therefore be removed. There are two possible supporting
> arguments. First, the main costs of complying with environmental regulation might
> reflect a breakdown of the regulatory/legislative process, rather than perceived high
> social costs of environmental degradation. (One thinks of delays in getting nuclear
> plants approved, for instance.) This argument, however, provides a rationale for
> reform of that process across the board, *not* for singling out individual sectors or
> technologies for special regulatory treatment. Second, the OPEC-produced fall in
> U.S. real income may have made us sufficiently poorer as a society that we feel we
> cannot afford the very clean environment aimed at by current regulation. This
> argument rationalizes lowering environmental standards across the board, however,
> for textiles as well as energy, and for conventional as well as unconventional energy
> supply technologies.[9]
>
> [P]rivate capital markets generally do a good job of handling risk. There is
> empirical and theoretical support for that assumption; and, in any case, if it were
> false, the "Why not textiles too?" test would suggest that we should be debating a
> general policy concerned with *all* risky private sector investment, not just commer-
> cialization initiatives in the area of energy supply.[10]
>
> These and other complications related to technical uncertainty do not by them-

---

[8]*Id*., p.11.
[9]*Id*, p. 13.
[10]*Id*, p. 25.

selves argue for government intervention, however, either in energy supply or in textiles. Technical risk may introduce complex and difficult problems, but the private sector has been dealing with such problems under market pressures for years. There is simply no general reason to suppose that government administrators will be able to manage technical risk better than private firms can.[11]

In sum, where the most efficient use of resources is the criterion, and given a free market, an "approximately competitive economy," and efficient pricing for the domestic consumption of oil, there is no a priori justification for any public intervention or support for establishing any category of energy-related technologies.

> If the economy is approximately competitive, government actions can neither improve overall efficiency nor lower the real cost of energy without raising other costs more. If the economy does not operate well, policy attention should focus on the source of that problem, not on new energy supply technologies.[12]

However when the interplay of interests or public sentiment does not permit the imposition of the tariff T* to raise the price received by domestic suppliers to the level considered necessary to meet national security needs, then, as a second best measure, subsidies in support of the establishment of domestic energy sources including new and unconventional energy technologies may be justified. Such subsidies should not exceed the difference between actual and socially optimal price per unit of output. With P* as import costs plus T*, and P_b as the price paid by domestic consumers:

> The efficient policy is thus resonably obvious: a subsidy of $(P* - P_b)$ per unit of output should be paid to suppliers using unconventional technologies. As prices adjust to P* over time, this subsidy vanishes. Equity considerations might mandate announcement of a list of (conventional) technologies not eligible for subsidy, but there is no general reason otherwise to discriminate against particular energy supply technologies. This policy would clearly *subsidize* commercialization but would not *manage* that process.
>
> It should be clear that this is not a fully efficient policy. . . . Subsidizing one set of supply technologies, while in effect taxing another, means that the real costs of domestic energy production are inflated and that investment in the energy sector will not flow to the socially most productive uses.[13]
>
> The usual reason given for holding down suppliers' prices in energy markets is to avoid windfalls manufactured by past OPEC price hikes. The same windfalls issue can hardly be raised by energy supply technologies not yet in widespread use, so there is unlikely to be any persuasive equity argument against paying P* for energy from new or unconventional sources. There is a strong efficiency argument for doing so. It follows that a natural and sensible commercialization policy, when domestic prices are being held inefficiently low, would be to employ output subsidies to raise net receipts per unit to P* for *all* domestic energy supply sources except those politically affected by the windfalls issue. Only such a subsidy program, which is

---

[11]*Id*, p. 27.
[12]*Id.*, p. 12.
[13]*Id.*, p. 13.

as broadly focused as possible and avoids prejudging the market's choices of technique, can be called *balanced* in any meaningful sense.[14]

Any system of subsidization or support will mean that market forces are to be in some way and to some degree shaped and influenced. Schmalensee poses as a general rule that the system of subsidization that least constrains the breadth of entrepreneurial choice and of consumer and investor options, will *ipso facto* be the most efficient (or least distorting) system. On this ground, it is always better to support output prices that particular input costs, and always better to support the larger, more encompassing rather than the more specific, narrowly vectored output range.

If some commodity, like domestically produced energy, is more valuable to society than its market price indicates, the natural remedy is to use an output subsidy to increase its market value. Other devices can never be superior to such a direct approach; if they build in extraneous incentives, they are strictly inferior in cost and efficiency terms.[15]

At the commercialization stage, the most efficient form of government support for the resolution of technical uncertainty would seem to involve competitively determined specific output subsidies or price guarantees. As before, these do not distort design or operating choices. Competitive bidding should serve to select the firm that can most cheaply resolve the uncertainties connected with commercial-scale operation of some particular technology. The government would, of course, have to compensate that firm for bearing risk, but it would learn in the process how important the risk was.[16]

Some guidelines for such subsidies follow more or less directly from the analysis above. First, the amount of the subsidy should be directly tied to and justified by comparison (in per-unit-of-output terms) with subsidies elsewhere in the energy supply sector. There is no obvious defense for differentials between technologies that make equivalent contributions to reduced imports; subsidy dollars should yield equal returns in these terms (on the margin) wherever they are applied. Second, the subsidy should be phased out as domestic prices adjust to P*. Third, the form of the subsidy should be as neutral as possible; it should have the least possible effect on project design or on more fundamental strategic choices among alternative techniques. . . . Finally, the subsidy should be visible. Visibility makes it easier to phase out a subsidy and more likely as a practical matter that the other guidelines will be met.[17]

These and related effects make minimizing the real cost of domestic energy consumption over time more complex, but such increased complexity by itself cannot strengthen arguments for government management of the commercialization process. The general case for broadly focused output subsidies to offset socially inappropriate market prices carries over to a dynamic world. The greater complexity of such a world does nothing to make it more likely that government administrators can improve on private firms' response to such subsidies, however.[18]

---

[14]*Id.,* p. 36
[15]*Id.,* pp. 14, 15.
[16]*Id.,* p. 29.
[17]*Id.,* pp. 18, 19.
[18]*Id.,* p. 20.

Aside from subsidies offsetting a socially inappropriate market price, what conceivable market imperfections of "demonstrably unusual importance" might justify public intervention and support for the commercialization of new or unconventional energy technologies? Schmalensee conceives of two possibilities, both instances of significant *externalities,* both related to the production and dissemination of information for the benefit of others than the corporate recipient of the subsidy or of other forms of public assistance and support, and both only equivocally related to any special support for the commercialization of energy-related technologies. There is first, that learning produced through the experience of operating new or untried technologies where such learning would be available to others than those engaged in the supported operation.

> The widely discussed 1975 Synfuels Interagency Task Force Report, for instance, identified subsequent cost reductions as the largest single benefit from rapid construction of synthetic fuels capacity, though absolutely no quantitative support was presented for the magnitudes of the predicted learning effects. . . .
>
> For policy purposes it is at least as important to know what fraction of the benefits of experience will be captured exclusively by the firms that generate them and what fraction can be freely enjoyed by others. If all benefits are captured or internalized by the producing firm, future cost advantages over competitors can provide a powerful incentive for accelerating exploitation of new technology. On the other hand, if the lessons of experience cannot be kept from others, there is a strong incentive to wait and allow someone else to pay for those lessons. In this case there are spillovers or externalities, which imply that the unaided market mechanism provides an inadequate incentive for expanding output, because existing producers neglect part of the cost reduction benefits of such expansions in their calculations.[19]
>
> There is a deep problem with all this, however: not only does it seem to be quite impossible to predict accurately the overall effect of experience on future costs; there currently seems to be no way to predict the fraction of such effects that will fail to be internalized. If there is no way to predict learning-related spillovers, there is no reliable way to set any such subsidy. More importantly, at the present state of knowledge, there is no way advocates of commercialization support can supply any reliable proof that learning-related spillovers are of unusual importance in any particular case. If no such proof is required of them, however, these spillovers can be invoked to justify subsidizing almost any evolving industry or new technology. In light of all this, it would seem sensible to consider as inadequate arguments based on learning or experience effects that favor special treatment of particular energy supply technologies, at least until a good deal more is known in general about those effects.[20]

There is, secondly, on the part of consumers, producers, and government a learning to accommodate to, to circumvent, or to eliminate barriers and resistances to innovation. Consumers learn how to use and to appreciate a new product. A cadre of experienced workers learn a critical set of skills and acquire the capacity to impart

[19]*Id.,* pp. 20–22.
[20]*Id.,* pp. 22, 23.

those skills to others. Public agencies learn of the inadequacies and responsively adapt their regulations and systems of control to the requisites of a new and different technology. Thus a demonstration project could produce and disseminate the information needed to obtain consumer acceptance and thus clear the way for other firms to enter the industry, and so on.

> [W]hile it is very difficult in specific cases to predict the importance of learning-related spillovers, the kind of technology-specific (but *not* firm-specific) obstacles to commercialization we are now considering can apparently be more or less readily identified. Private sector market research routinely seeks to identify this type of obstacle, which need be overcome only once during startup. It does not seem difficult to assess the importance of problems identified in this fashion, nor to decide whether they have nontrivial associated spillovers. There is thus the option in energy supply, textiles, and other sectors, of asking whether the cost of overcoming important startup obstacles to commercialization should be borne by the government or left to a pioneer firm. This may be a particularly good question to ask when the startup costs are related to the legal or regulatory environment, since direct government action may be more cost-effective than protracted private litigation in dealing with such institutional obstacles. But it is important to reiterate that the logical justification for government action of this sort is the existence of an *unusually important* spillover associated with overcoming obstacles to the commercialization of a new technology, *not* that technology's role in energy supply.
>
> Demonstration projects set up as examples (rather than as experiments) can, under certain conditions, deal well with informational obstacles. A smoothly operating demonstration project may be more persuasive, especially to an unsophisticated audience, than a thousand technical articles. As a Rand study concluded, demonstrations "are most successful when diffusion would otherwise be hampered by potential adopters' lack of knowledge about the use of the technology under commercial operating conditions." There have been some spectacular failures among federally funded demonstrations, of course, often associated with premature large-scale use of processes with serious unresolved technical problems. But demonstrations may nonetheless deserve careful consideration when the main obstacles to commercialization are informational, when there are obvious associated spillovers, and when the technology is very well in hand.[21]
>
> Direct federal legislative or administrative action would thus seem more appropriate when the main barriers are institutional and there are obvious and unusually important spillover effects associated with letting pioneer firms overcome those barriers unaided.[22]

Again a possible justification of the grounds that information might spillover to the benefit of others.

> One can make an economic efficiency case for government intervention in some situations involving technological risk, but only because of major spillovers or externalities associated with the resolution of uncertainty. If, for instance, one can

[21]*Id.,* p. 24.
[22]*Id.,* p. 25.

learn the costs of high-Btu coal gasification only by building a commercial-scale plant, and if knowledge thus gained cannot be patented or kept secret, there may be a case for government support of such a plant's construction. (Patents or trade secrets generally remove the spillover and thus the rationale for subsidy.) . . .

We allow the private sector to bear such risks in other industries, however. To be at all persuasive, then, it would seem that an argument for specific support of a particular energy supply technology's commercialization, based on technical risk, should at least offer some empirical support for the implicit assertion that the case at hand involves exceptionally important spillovers related to the resolution of those risks. To remove this burden of proof is apparently to admit that *all* private plants embodying any new or unconventional technologies are entitled to subsidies.[23]

While conceding the *possibility* of justifying support for the commercialization of energy related technologies on the aforementioned ground, Schmalensee finds no compelling reason for so justifying support for any "major energy supply commercialization proposal."

In all these descriptions, the key word is "unusually." Most innovations that become widely used commercially do so in spite of some difficulties with buyer ignorance, institutional barriers, residual technical risks, and unpredictable government policies. In order to justify government support for any particular innovation, in energy or in textiles, proponents of this support should be required to show that it is affected by these types of problems to an extraordinary extent. I do not think this has yet been done for any major energy supply commercialization proposals. Since all markets are imperfect, if this burden of proof is not imposed, a competent policy analyst will be able to find some imperfection in any politically selected market and so support detailed intervention in the corresponding innovation processes with impressive jargon-laden incantations.[24]

It is always more sensible to focus on undoing a price distortion directly than on trying to beat the market system at its own game unless major, relevant market imperfections are present. I have yet to see much evidence that such imperfections are a major problem for any new or unconventional energy supply technologies.[25]

We have tried in this section to delve the rationale of the conventional economic analysis, and to replicate the logic of its argument in dealing with the problems of energy supply; an argument which comes down in the end, to "leaving it all to the market." We will critique this approach, but in order to assess its practical relevance we must understand the present context of choice and the options that are perforce before us. For that, and in order to specify where we are and, for the short run at least, what are our policy constraints, we turn to the chronology of events under successive administrations that shaped the existing context of choice, the forum for evaluation and the springboard for change.

---

[23]*Id.*, pp. 27, 28.
[24]*Id.*, pp. 35, 36.
[25]*Id.*, p. 37.

An Energy Chronology

Under the impact of the oil embargo and the OPEC price squeeze and mounting trade deficits and the inescapable shrinkage of the domestic oil reserve, the locus of so-called energy policy and control like a kaleidoscope turning, has rapidly changed itself into new and fantastic shapes of many colors, affecting nothing. In rapid succession under successive administrations, a political hack and lame duck politician, a loud mouth bond salesman, a third order economist, an ex-chief of the CIA, a big political contributor from Atlanta, then (under Reagan) back again to the political hack and lame duck politician, rapidly succeeded one another on the throne of the "energy czar." Under President Carter, all the bits and pieces, large as the ex-Atomic Energy Commission, small as the fossilized fossil energy R&D of the Department of the Interior, were gathered together into a Department of Energy. Under Reagan this ramshackle structure seems slated for dismemberment. Then as now the upper echelons of control have been purged and purified of any who might even pretend to political experience and a dedication to public and social purpose combined with technological *cum* scientific savvy. Characteristically policymakers are and have been second rate corporation in-and-outers, upholders of free enterprise, antagonists of the state, seeing their task as that of servicing a business clientele. Never has a thought been given, or the slightest intention shown of systematically, deliberately working towards the establishment of a high level, professional competence for public evaluation and control, and for the public planning and organization of complex and vital programs in the transformation of the energy infrastructure. Again to recall the declared purpose of the high official charged in the Carter Administration with the development of new energy technologies, of "moving it all out to industry and getting the hell of of the business."[26]

There is and has been only one locus of autonomous action and of technological competence established by extraordinary happenstance in the framework of the American State, and oriented towards the development of an energy infrastructure: the (ex) Atomic Energy Commission, bureaucratic and technical successor to the soon-departed scientists of the Manhattan Project that built the atomic bomb. For security reasons the Commission was obliged to create and develop nuclear science and its technologies within the secret enclaves of an agency of government, not "moving it all out of industry and getting the hell out of the business." Only after its activities had been institutionalized and its capabilities developed, was it oriented towards the "peaceful use" of nuclear energy in the private sector.

During the decades following the end of World War II, the Atomic Energy Commission was *the* energy agency of the American state, the only one with a responsibility for developing better, lower-cost energy sources and technologies. Year after year for more than three decades, all of our energy eggs, billions upon billions of dollars worth of them, went into that single, fragile, contaminated basket,[27] with no effort whatsoever to evaluate the costs and benefits of investing

---

[26]*The New York Times,* December, 1977, Sec. 2, p. 61.

[27]See "U.S. Subsidized Growth in Nuclear Power by $37 Billion Over 30 Years, Study Says," *The Wall Street Journal,* December 15, 1980, p. 8.

resources into alternative avenues of energy development. This demonstrates what we earlier called the force of a "technological imperative," wherein all great organizations that have vectored out from a technological root and are built around an integral set of technological competencies, whether that of General Motors, or the Atomic Energy Commission, or the U.S. Air Force, will be driven by that built-in technological imperative that defines their path, delineates their purpose, and determines their role as an interest group acting upon public choice and policy. Here the danger is not of monopoly or bureaucracy. It is of great organizations hurtling down a predetermined track, dragging society into an unwonted future; precisely the threat of the nuclear establishment in the framework of the energy program today.

What is astonishing has been the fixity of that technological imperative, not simply between nuclear and other avenues of development, but even within nuclear. The retrospective record suggests that nearly all nuclear R&D resources were concentrated on engineering, upgrading, and installing light water reactors, an unsafe technology based on a depletable resource, which, even if all R&D objectives were obtained, could not be more than marginally competitive with conventional energy sources. Meanwhile, during those decades, critical problems like the disposition of nuclear wastes were never solved, and the development of an energy source that is radiation-free and inexhaustible, as nuclear fusion is supposed to be, remains still in the domain of rosy promise.

Second, the lack of any systematic evaluation of energy-oriented R&D alternatives demonstrates again the incapacity, and the indifference of those who govern, including the academics who sat as "science advisors" to the president, for evaluation and choice on crucial matters of technology or even of a sense of any need for choice, or of the need to develop a competence for choosing. The nuclear establishment, its tunnel vision fixed upon and finding the ultimate solution in the breeder reactor dominated energy policy even after the petroleum crisis. Left to themselves, those in charge would not have given much attention to any other R&D objective. This pattern was broken for two reasons. Nuclear energy is a substitute for coal in the production of electric power. The critical need is not for a coal substitute, but for something to replace gasoline as a fuel for autos and trucks. Finally, politicians could not ignore the rising grass roots opposition to a dependence on nuclear energy. The response of the Department of Energy (DOE) and its predecessor agency was to organize programs for the development of nonnuclear (primarily solar) energy technologies, and technologies for the conservation of energy following the paths of (1) *scattergrants,* and (2) demonstrations.

What is distinctive and particular about these two approaches, the scattergrant and the demonstration project, is that they are above all designed as an escape from public planning, public answerability, public accountability, public responsibility. They avoid the exercise of public responsibility. They rely on the enterprise of "free enterprise," on individual choice, on business response. They preclude the development of a planning and managerial autonomy and competence in the political system.

In the instance of solar energy, numerous private contractors, even public agencies like NASA or the national laboratories that had operated as agents of the Atomic Energy Commission were engaged to set up and develop familiar, if unpracticed, prototype technologies ostensibly for the purposes of public demonstration.

These initial demonstrations ranged from grandiose ocean thermal units that use the hot/cold relationships of surface/deep waters of the ocean, to generate electric power to the simple solar heated homes, including solar collectors and concentrators for power production, windmills, photovoltaic cells, and the harvesting of agricultural residues or water-grown plants, algae, for use as fuel or as a chemical feedstock. Hopefully somehow, someone might do something with that which has been demonstrated.

In the strategy of scattergrantsmanship, proposals for projects are invited, and the money is passed out among chosen proposers, to corporations, institutes, architects, professors, builders as the case may be. The scattergrant like the demonstration project is an easy way out, imposing no responsibility and requiring no clear objectives on the part of those nominally in charge, needing neither hard decisions nor hard to acquire skills on part of the state. The inherent character and the inevitable consequence of scattergrantsmanship can be illustrated in a concrete case. We have already examined albeit briefly the World War II establishment of a synthetic rubber industry in the United States,[28] an achievement so often proposed as the model for the establishment of a synthetic fuel industry today. Consider then the postwar disposition of that industry.

After the war, a petroleum-based synthetic rubber industry existed intact. It was operated by the tire and oil companies for a fee, but owned by the government and controlled by a government financial agency, Rubber Reserve. The private corporations involved did not consider the industry to have a commercially sound future and would not buy the plants. But for stategic reasons, the government was not ready to junk or abandon them. Instead, a massive research and development program was launched, with two principal goals: to reduce operating costs and improve quality so that the product might become competitive with natural rubber; and, for reasons of national security, to develop a true substitute for natural rubber. Such was the first effort by the American government to advance a civilian, industrial technology through the support of R&D.

To these ends, Rubber Reserve initiated the scattergrant approach in the promotion of technological advance. Operated by minor technicians and bureaucrats, it was directed by advisory boards of company representatives who divided up the government cash among alternative proposals, with results to be pooled and made available to the industry. Each company took its share. Court favorites, formerly employed by Rubber Reserves, set up shop as consulting firms, and got their hands in the till. Academics in Akron flourished. New institutes grew like mushrooms. In sum, a grant-eating industry quickly developed.

But the results—$40 million later—were zilch, zero, nothing. By the measure of technological achievement, the research and development program was useless. The developments that came eventually to make the industry commercially viable all came from outside the scattergrant zone of the Rubber Reserve program. One of the two most important of these innovations, the so-called cold rubber process, had been fully developed in Germany during World War II. Under the terms of the

---

[28]Appendix to Chapter 7.

occupation, the record of German technical achievement was open to Allied inspection, and enthusiastic reports of the German method were sent to the United States. But evidently no one in the Rubber Reserve operation or in the program that it sponsored thought to consider them.

In later years this type of R&D operation—administered by minor and subservient bureaucrats without responsibility for the program's outcome, dominated by advisory committees with representatives drawn from industry, and scattering grants among flocks of incoming proposals—would be used repeatedly. So far as I can tell, it has never produced significant technological advance and innovation. When George Romney became the first secretary of the Department of Housing and Urban Development, it was used with the important objective of introducing modern systems-building and other technological advances that would, it was hoped, revolutionize the laggard construction industry. But the revolution never came, nor did the program have any visible impact on technology or productivity.

It is hard to believe, but true, that for years there has been an R&D program on fossil energy—hence on synfuel—operated through the Department of Energy and its predecessor agency. Organized in exactly the manner of the Rubber Reserve model, managed by minor technocrats or bureaucrats, subordinated to an advisory board of industry representatives, it has been scattering the grants and also setting up demonstration projects with private contractors. If any technological contributions have resulted, they have been exceedingly well-hidden. It is significant that, in the face of this program, designed to promote the development of low cost, nontoxic, fossil energy technologies, the cost of producing oil from shale (as reported in *Science,* July 17, 1979) has increased from $4.50 a barrel in 1973 to $25 a barrel in 1979. Cost up 556 percent in six years—there's technological achievement for you!

The consequences of such demonstration projects has been "demonstrated" in the two instances of the evaluation of such projects under Congressional oversight. There was the Coalcon Project, termed "the first federal attempt to demonstrate a synthetic fossil energy technology by converting coal to a clean burning liquid fuel."[29] This was part of the Clean Boiler Fuel Demonstration Program of the Energy Research and Development Administration (ERDA), predecessor agency to the Department of Energy; a program which was initiated in 1974 by the Office of Coal Research of the Department of the Interior. The objective of the program was to demonstrate by 1983, that coal can be converted to a clean boiler liquid fuel in an economical and environmentally acceptable manner. On January 17, 1975, the Department of the Interior, as a first step in this program, awarded the Coalcon Company (formed out of a partnership between Union Carbide Corporation and the Chemical Construction Corporation) a $237 million contract to design, construct, and operate a synfuel plant. The contract provided that the work was to be done in four phases, with the federal government retaining the right to terminate the project at the end of any of these successive phases. The first two phases were to be funded by the government on a cost-plus-fee basis. The first phase would provide a conceptual design for a commercial operation, and the preliminary design of the

---

[29] *Report of the Comptroller General of the United States,* August 17, 1977. All that follows regarding Coalcon is taken from this report.

scheduled demonstration plant, including pilot plant tests to provide the basic process data needed for the start of phase two. It was to cost $4.75 million and to be completed by March 31, 1976. After a $10 million in cost overrun and a 14½ month schedule slippage, the project was deemed a failure and terminated on June 15, 1977. Scheduled pilot tests needed to provide basic process information were never completed. The Government Accounting Office found, that because of this failure the objective of establishing by 1983, the economic and environmental viability of coal-based synfuel must be abandoned because "it takes 8 to 12 years from project conception through successful demonstration."[30] In his critique of the program, the Comptroller General emphasized the lack of any "effective system to monitor and control the contractor's progress and project costs," and the major substantive recommendation of the Comptroller General to the ERDA Administrator was to "require the establishment and implementation of formal project monitoring systems" which would enable public management to track and control progress and costs.[31]

Failure or not the project was a sweet deal, riskless and profitable, for the contractors.

The Consolidated Coal Company of West Virginia presented a proposal in 1961, and in 1963 received a contract through the Office of Coal Research of the Department of the Interior, to design, construct, and operate a pilot plant with a capacity of slightly less than 60 barrels a day of synthetic crude oil. This allegedly would "develop a process for converting coal into gasoline at an economically attractive price."[32] The pilot plant would be used to determine the commercial feasibility of Consolidated's synthetic fuel (CSF) process, providing the data for the design of a full scale commercial plant. Constructed in 1966 near Moundsville, West Virginia, on the Ohio River, it was known as the Cresap Plant Facility.[33] With less than 500 hours of actual operation during the years between 1966 and 1970, the plant was shut down in 1970 because of mechanical failures and, allegedly, labor problems. Between 1970 and 1974, it lay dormant. During this time a great part of its piping and equipment was destroyed through failure to purge the system of corrosive elements or adequately to protect it from the environment. In 1974, a contract was made with Fluor Engineers and Contractors, to reactivate the plant, at first on a limited scale, and then in 1976, to refurbish and reactivate it entirely. Total estimated costs escalated from $13.5 million in 1974 to $69.4 million in 1978, yet through May, 1978, the longest run was only for six days, and then for only a portion of the plant.[34] Written off as a failure, it was recommended to the Committee that "The CRESAP Coal Liquification Test Facility . . . should not receive any additional funding beyond fiscal year 1978, except as might be required to terminate operations and 'mothball' facilities."[35]

---

[30]*Id.,* Appendix I, p. 14.

[31]*Id.,* Letter to Congressman John D. Dingell, p. 3.

[32]*Oversight: Staff Study on Management and Cost Issues Associated With Construction of the Cresap Coal Liquification Facility,* prepared for the Committee on Science and Technology of the U.S. House of Representatives, Ninety Fifth Congress, Second Session, Serial NN, Vol. IV, October, 1978, p.3.

[33]Not an acronym. The name stems from a town in West Virginia, named after the Cresap family.

[34]*Id.,* p. 4.

[35]*Id.,* p. 16.

In its "findings," the report emphasizes that "no single individual was assigned to the Project as overall project manager and held accountable for overall success or failure," and that "no government representative was assigned to the construction site to verify contractor performance."[36] In its major conclusion, the report of the Comptroller General asserts:

> The management of CRESAP facility construction and rehabilitation were unacceptable in terms of current management practice in the construction industry. The project was entrusted to a private firm and the government completely failed to exercise any real supervision over the project. Cost, schedules, and technical control were almost totally absent in that the government did not assign a project manager with authority to make decisions across the technical, administrative, and contractual spectrums. In other words, no one was in "charge." To make matters worse, a government inspector was not even assigned to the site as millions of dollars of equipment were installed. The project was permitted to wander along at the whim of private forces.[37]

and, we may add, to the profit of private companies.

Failure of effective surveillance! Failure to monitor! Failure to supervise and control! Failure to be "in charge"! Failure to verify contractor performance! Failure to create a locus of public accountability and responsibility for overall success or failure! But let it be understood that as an absolute prerequisite to overcome all or any of this, there must be created a level of public management with a dedication, a competence, a degree of authority and autonomy that does not now exist and has not been allowed to come into existence.

Demonstrations and scattergrants fail, as any enterprise fails and must fail that operates without answerability, with no criterion of purpose, nor any measurement of achievement, nor any locus of power and responsibility that evaluates, eliminates, coordinates, vectors energies and efforts, and bears the onus and pays the price of failure.

Synfuels

Before the Ayatollah proclaimed the seizure of the American hostages and in so doing roused patriotic passions in brief and transitory support of a beleagured chief-of-state, Jimmy Carter and those around him, then at the nadir of their fortunes, with the political groundwork collapsing from under them, were spurred to undertake some "bold new initiative," something that would "mobilize our national energies," something to "realize the American genius," something that might capture popular imagination and in so doing save the President and his entourage from certain defeat in the forthcoming days of electoral reckoning. But what?

Their choice was a massive program to produce synthetic fuel—gasoline from coal. Nothing small this time (not peanuts)—something huge. They raised the ante from the millions to the billions, to more than a hundred billions. In broad outline,

---

[36]*Id.,* p. 13.
[37]*Id.,* p. 15.

this was their plan. The positive action to establish a new synfuel industry would be coupled with the complete decontrol of petroleum and natural gas prices. With the rise in oil and gas prices, the profits of the oil and gas companies would rise correspondingly. So would public revenues through a tax on excess profits. These new revenues would be used to finance the establishment of the synfuel industry. Hence the industry could be created without threatening the will-o'-the-wisp of balanced budgets. Allegedly taking as their model the establishment of a synthetic rubber industry during World War II, an agency would be established (sic) like the War Production Board to clear away unwonted obstructions (read environmental and safety considerations and regulations). Another agency would serve, as the old Reconstruction Finance Corporation once had, to finance, on safe commercial terms, the establishment of the industry.

What of the gross failures of the Coalcon and Cresap projects, demonstrating the incompetence of those enfolded within the Department of Energy and the ineffectiveness of its habitual approach and the absence of the knowledge required for synfuel decision and design? The Administration would not allow itself to be distracted by such small concerns. The scheme was too important as a last moment, last chance bid for public approval to allow for that. It was a scheme calculated to please the many and diverse interests who provide the props of political power.

It would presumably please the economists crying out for decontrol of oil and natural gas prices, and to all who rallied around their banner, LEAVE IT ALL TO THE MARKET. Most certainly it would please the oil companies and those feeding at their table; for with it the company coffers would continue to swell to overflowing. It would give no offense to to those who consider balanced budgets as the "open seseme" to inflationless prosperity. It would offer the carrot, indeed a harvest of prime carrots, rich and crunchy in grant money and government-backed, price-guaranteed industrial opportunities to a vast potential business clientele. It should yield besides a bumper crop of press and public approval for what was after all a "bold initiative" made in strict imitation of World War II heroics to the drumbeat of a "moral equivalent of war." It appealed to common sense. The North American continent was the greatest known repository of coal reserves. The South Africans, using a system developed by the Germans in World War II and installed by an American engineering firm, were producing gasoline from coal and allegedly at a cost well below that at which gasoline could be purchased on the open market. Why not ourselves as well?

Out of the interplay of Congressional and Presidential politics, the following policy design emerged. Several billion dollars would be spent (scattering grants) to subsidize the establishment of a number of feasibility studies and demonstration projects.[38] These would widen the spectrum of technological choice, and provide an information base and operational familiarity as a springboard for the commercializa-

---

[38]For details of the program see PEDCo Environmental, Inc., *Verification of Data on Synthetic Fuels Initiatives: Summary of Findings,* Cincinnati, Ohio, EPA Contract No. 68-02-3173 PN 3450-21, Project Officer: Michael Bergman, September, 1980; and National Coal Association, *Coal Synfuel Facility Survey,* August, 1980. The latter includes a survey of a synfuel program in West Germany.

tion of synfuel technologies and the establishment of a viable synfuel industry. For commercialization and the establishment of the industry, policy would rely on market forces with the synfuel corporation as the underwriter of private investment.

Schmalensee, it will be recalled, sees this as a conceivable justification for the subsidizing of projects providing it can be proven that there is or will be a substantial body of new and relevant information accruing to others than those, beneficiary of such subsidies, who, for example, operate the demonstration plants so "that learning-related spillovers are of unusual importance." We would, for reasons that will be developed later below, reject Schmalensee's demand for hard proof; and, because we do not consider corporations in the private sector the only relevant body of decision-takers in this game, we would add as a potential value and possible justification for such demonstration projects, relevant information that might accrue to public policymakers and planners, for example, of the Environmental Protection Agency, or the Department of Energy, or Synfuel Corporation.

Suppose that such feasibility studies and demonstration *qua* experimental projects operated by private contractors could produce information that is highly relevant and useful to government policy makers and decision takers, and also information that is highly relevant and useful for choice and waste avoidance by private corporations who are in or who might enter the industry. Would they produce and disseminate such information spontaneously? It is nonsensical to suppose that operations and study would be geared to answer complex, policy-related questions without those questions being asked, and without operations being specifically designed and monitored to seek the answers. Nor can one accept the popular notion of some easy and spontaneous spillover and intercorporate flow of the critical or significant information produced in experimental projects; available studies indicate the opposite, that in the normal course of events only the doers learn by doing.[39] The cow must be milked; the questions must be asked; the feasibility studies and the demonstration projects must be organized deliberately, monitored, squeezed, their inquiries directed to produce the information required (Why else, for example, would any feasibility study or demonstration project produce and make available that range of information relevant to the policies of, say, the Environmental Protection Agency?). So, too, the dissemination of that information must be organized for dissemination

---

[39]Schmalensee, *op. cit.*, suggests that "the U.S. nuclear power industry provides an instructive and particularly relevant example of learning effects. Beginning in 1963, General Electric and Westinghouse began to offer reactors to electric utilities on attractive, fixed-price terms. Both firms apparently expected losses on these early "turnkey" plants, losses that they expected to more than recoup as learning reduced their construction costs and thus provided competitive advantages. In a recent statistical study, Mooz shows that learning did occur; power reactor construction costs fell with experience. More interestingly, Mooz tests for spillovers but does not find them; apparently only the firm constructing a particular reactor learned from that project how to reduce costs on later plants. Similarly, a recent study of learning by nuclear plant operators, by Joskow and Rozanski, points to the importance of plant-specific, not industry-wide, experience. If there are no spillovers, there is no case for subsidies even if overall learning is very important." p. 22.

Cited studies are Paul L. Joskow and George A. Rozanski, "The Effects of Learning by Doing on Nuclear Plant Operating Reliability," *Review of Economics and Statistics* (May, 1969); Edward Merrow, "Constraints on the Commercialization of Shale Oil," R-2293, Department of Energy (Santa Monica, California: Rand Corporation, 1978); William E. Mooz, "Cost Analysis of Light Water Reactor Plants," R2304, Department of Energy (Santa Monica, California: Rand Corporation, 1978).

with systematic information sharing between participants of the program and a systematic feedback from nonparticipants.

Certainly a demonstration program might have been rationally designed for the sharing and universal dissemination of "learned experience," for advancing the general knowledge of technique and of costs of operating requirements as a basis for risk evaluation, and organizational planning by corporate enterprise. It could conceivably have been designed to provide the Environmental Protection Agency with the information required for its cautionary planning. It could have been designed conceivably to provide the Department of Energy with information useful in anticipating and planning ahead to avoid bottlenecks in equipment and manpower, or to prepare for the problems that must arise when the clustering of plants pushes the totality of effects beyond some danger threshold, as in sudden concentrations of industry and population where the infrastructure and the political competencies needed to deal with the problems that inhere in such concentrations are lacking. The program might have been designed to provide the Synthetic Fuel Corporation with information it would require to evaluate the commercial prospects of proposals in the light of alternative technologies in late stages of development, and especially with that which might give guidance to public action should the assumption critical to the Corporation's present plans and strategies prove false; if it turns out, that is, that there aren't those firms "out there" with technologies in hand, ready to undertake the big risks, chafing at the bit to get into the synfuel business. What if all who come knocking at the Corporation's door are interested instead only in sweet deals, and good meals eating at the public trough?

Alas, there was no provision for sharing experience between participants. None for the systematic dissemination of technical learning. None to direct inquiry into relevant channels; none that specified questions for the asking; none that would require and pipe information useful or necessary for planning and choice by the Department of Energy or the Environmental Protection Agency, or the Synthetic Fuels Corporation or the oversight agencies and committees of Congress. Nor did there appear even to be a consciousness that the systematic provision of information was an issue. Even the matter of who owned the data and the inventions produced under public grant was left in limbo. No system was established nor, so far as I could tell, had anyone in authority thought to seek for the development of any such system to monitor, to organize, to dessiminate, and rationally to utilize information producible through a massive demonstration-feasibility study program.

But, after all, in order to choose between experimental options in the development of an information-producing network, in order to direct and monitor inquiry, and in order to evaluate operations and results and to gear information into planning and choice, requires a formidable competence on the part of the agency of public management. Where was that competence? The Department of Energy gave no evidence of possessing it, nor of ever having tried to develop it. So the demonstration program turned out to be another case of the scattergrant, without any locus of responsibility or control. When Mr. Reagan's budget cutter axed the program into virtual extinction, one could hardly mourn for what it was; only, perhaps, for what it might have been.

The Carter plan, as now the Reagan Administration, relied on a Synthetic Fuels Corporation as the key agency, now perhaps the sole activator of a synfuels program. Its character reflected the hard boiled "get on with job" "leave it to business" outlook of Scoop Jackson and his colleagues on the Energy and Natural Resource Committee of the United States Senate. It assumed that "out there" in the corporate world there were firms aplenty with the technology in hand, with good old American know-how, chafing at the bit to get on with the job, ready for the big risks, willing to put their own money on the line, needing only partial financial support for these enormously costly ventures where an optimal size plant might require an investment of $4 billion or more.[40] The Synfuel Corporation[41] was a small independent agency operating like a private investment house with a Wall Street pay scale and a banker's outlook. Its total employment of full-time professionals was limited to 300. Initially allotted $20 billions, it was scheduled to receive $88 billions by 1984. It was to consider only projects based on proven technologies, that must pass technical as well as financial muster, with the anticipated (though not the only possible) support to be made in the form of loan guarantees. The corporation receiving such support must shoulder a considerable share of the risk on its own. At least 25 percent of the total investment must be in the equity of the corporation undertaking the project. A charge would be made for these loan guarantees. Sound, commercially viable technology, reputable companies with their own money on the line—a surefire formula for repayment. Costs of the Synfuel Corporation would be covered. The government might even come out with a profit. Such were to be the rules and such were the expectations. What rock ribbed conservative could cavil at that?

But by Schmalensee's criteria, the Synfuels Corporation combines the worst of all possible worlds. It is narrowly (rather than broadly) vectored, introducing a formidable bias against other than coal-based synfuel energy alternatives. Within synfuels, it introduces a powerful bias against investment in novel, "unproven" technologies, excluded from consideration under the rules of the Synfuel Corporation. Its loan guarantees would bias investment in the direction of capital intensity, mitigate considerations of riskiness in the choice between alternative avenues of investment, and take no account of the value of information spillovers as the benefit possibly justifying public support.

> If the government is to aid commercialization because of extraordinary spillovers associated with resolving technical and cost risk, it follows that its object must logically be the purchase of valuable information (for use by other suppliers) on the most favorable terms. This has some immediate implications for the form of government support. First, loan guarantees and other related devices that shift risk to

---

[40]Ben C. Ball Jr., "New Challenges to Management in the Synfuels Revolution," *Technology Review* (August/September, 1979); and for a fuller analysis "Synfuel Supply Issues from the Commercial Perspective: New Kinds of Decisions," *Workshops on Energy Supply and Demand* (Paris: International Energy Agency OECD, 1978).

[41]Richard D. Grundy, "Synthetic Fuels: A View of the Energy Security Act from the Inside." Paper presented at the Seventh International Conference on Coal Gasification, Liquification, and Conversion to Energy, University of Pittsburgh, August 5, 1980.

taxpayers have very severe drawbacks in this context. Information about the real cost of risk-bearing is hidden; design decisions are biased toward capital intensity; both design and operating decisions are biased toward risky alternatives; and a disincentive for follow-on investments is created.[42]

For Senators McClure and Jackson and the practical men who devised the Synfuels Corporation such consideration surely must carry little weight. For them the question is whether it will "do the job." But will it? So far the only firm to surface with a positive interest in establishing a commercial synthetic fuel operation has been the American Natural Resources Corporation, through its subsidiary the Great Plains Gasification Corporation. This company, primarily in the pipeline business supplying natural gas to consumers in the east and midwest, had invested heavily in the purchase of low grade coal deposits in North Dakota. In order to open a market for this coal, it wanted to establish a gasification plant there, and ship the gasified coal via its pipelines to the utilities in the east and midwest. It applied to the Department of Energy for a massive subsidy to support the establishment of this plant as a demonstration project. But the demonstration program was limited to experimental (second generation) technologies; and an experimental, second generation technology this was not. Yet the Carter Administration and the Department of Energy were understandably anxious to see the project started. After all, there was nothing else. Without this, the page on which so much brave rhetoric was written would be quite empty of concrete achievement. So the Department of Energy and the Federal Energy Regulatory Commission (no longer independent and autonomous as it once had been, but now a part of the Department Energy) arranged a very peculiar deal. The customers of the American Natural Resources Company were ordered by the Commission through an increase in price at which they purchased natural gas to pay the billions of dollars required for the company to build its gasification facility. These payments must include a substantial profit to the company. And these consumers would be obliged to buy the synthetic gas that it produced no matter that the price would vastly exceed the current price, and probably prices that in the future could be negotiated with natural gas producers.[43]

The arrangement had been imposed at a time of natural gas glut, so great that consuming states were refusing quantities of natural gas for which they were nevertheless obliged to pay under existing contracts. The glut was brought about by a shrinkage of demand, the consequence of industrial recession and a fast climb in natural gas prices in the process of public decontrol, and by an increase in natural gas availability as a consequence of a sharp upturn in the rate of new discoveries, the consequence of an exploration that was no longer tied as a by product to search for oil and by radical developments in the technology of search.[44] This change in the

---

[42]Schmalensee, *op. cit.,* p. 28.

[43]The *Detroit News,* February 11, 1981, p. 10-D, reporting on "the consortium's latest and possibly final project financing plan" stated that "service costs of the private pipeline would have to be added to the $6.75 per cubic feet base price the consortium wants to charge participating pipelines for its gas . . . the base price would escalate . . . giving equal weight to increases in the price of home heating oil and the consumer price index."

[44]*See The New York Times,* December 1, 1980, p. A-1.

prospect of natural gas supplies stimulated consumer groups to resist the imposed arrangement. It is notable, nevertheless, and it says something about the character of the natural gas "market" that gluts did not slow the climb of natural gas prices which rose as fast as decontrol permitted, and where the "free market" price appeared to be pegged to the energy (Btu) content of imported petroleum. Nor did glut induce the development of means of supplying regions of natural gas shortage in the northeast.

Major consumers of natural gas serviced by the affected pipelines including public representatives of Michigan, Ohio, and New York and the General Motors Corporation brought the matter to the courts. On December 8, 1980, the Federal Court of Appeals of the District of Columbia invalidated the arrangement as based on an order that was beyond the juridictional powers of the Federal Energy Regulatory Commission. New risk-free devices are currently being sought by the company to ram the project down the consumer's throat.

Enter the new Reagan Administration that, in a stroke, brings the jerry-built scheme for the development of a synfuel industry tumbling down like a house of cards. The demonstration plant program based on government grants was totally dismantled. The status of the Department of Energy was put in limbo. The Synthetic Fuel Corporation (under new management) remained, with the ante raised on the private investment required before loan guarantees could be made. All price controls on domestically produced petroleum were abruptly terminated. We are thus obliged to end our chronicle long before the tale is fully told, and to return to our own thoughts on the ineluctable problems of energy and the policy options that may, in due course, enter into the spectrum of choice of a positive state.

Extraneous Distortions

Schmalensee's central contention follows ineluctably, logically, from the economist's paradigm, that if and inasmuch as the disposition of the synfuels industry and any other sort of investment is to be left to the market, extraneous subvention or intervention will distort the rationality of entrepreneurial choice and should therefore be avoided. This is a sensible rule. The argument behind it is persuasive. But alas sources of such distortions, consequences of extraneous subvention, intervention, influence are already built into the system. The 10 percent investment tax credit is there; so are depletion allowances; and as provided by the Windfall Profits Tax Act of 1979, the 10–15 percent business energy (investment) tax credit is in place; plus the tax credit allowed by the 1980 Windfall Profits Tax Act, on synfuel produced from coal, oil shale, and biomass, of $3 for every Btu equivalent of a barrel of petroleum sold. Couldn't these coupled with riskless (government guaranteed) borrowing, make for an investment package that would be a business plum in itself, regardless of commercial prospects?

But surely the most invidious, destructive, profoundly distorting extraneous intervention of all is in the interest rate, controlled in doctrinaire madness by the "Fed," axing the economy in a blind and futile fantasy of "fighting inflation." Consider for example the impact of the skyrocketing rates of interest in effect a tax levied by the Fed with bankers' connivance and with bankers as the recipients and beneficiaries of the tax on the cost of synfuels. With "capital requirements . . . estimated to range from $30 to $45 thousand per daily barrel of equivalent oil from coal" and assuming a six-year construction period and a 20 percent interest rate, then *interest costs alone* would be in the range of $26.30 to $39.45 per barrel of synfuel produced—itself greater than the OPEC price for petroleum.[45]

Given the existing thicket of extraneous interventions, we return to the paradox of the second best; there is no way to know a priori whether the net effects of additional intervention or subvention would, by reference to the market criterion of efficiency, be beneficial or detrimental.

Unacceptable Assumptions

Our economist considers himself moderate, reasonable, pragmatic. He insists that in "discussions on energy policy . . . one must go beyond explicit textbook assumptions to obtain tools useful for policy analysis."[46] While he quite rejects the textbook theory that

> . . . assumes a perfect government and an almost perfect economy, describes and classifies harmful imperfections in the market mechanism, and prescribes government action whenever such imperfections occur. In the present context (and in others), this framework can hardly be taken literally. Market imperfections relating to risk and information are common, if not ubiquitous, in the process of technical change, so that naive application of textbook theory simply serves to rationalize any and all proposed government initiatives in research development, or commercialization. On the other hand, if one replaces formal theory with uncritical faith in the competence of markets and the incompetence of administrators, one arrives at the polar opposite prescription: the government should touch nothing. It is hard to doubt that the truth lies somewhere in between.[47]

He seems willing to consider, even to support positive public action in establishing a synfuels industry provided it can be *proven* that such action is warranted by market imperfections of "demonstrably unusual importance." Otherwise one must rely on the "generally good performance of the market system" with all its admitted imperfections. He holds that

> The alternative to this approach would involve either blind fai'h in the market system's approximate perfection or in the ability of government to improve upon that system. In both these quasi-religions, economics is effectively decreed unfit to provide analysis relevant to important decisions; it merely serves as a source of jargon.[48]

---

[45]The estimate is from TRW, Inc., *Environmental Issues Associated with Synfuel Utilization* (draft) 1980, p.20. The price calculation was made as follows: $30,000 (or $40,000) $\times$ 20% $\times$ 3(years of accumulated interest payments for the period of construction) + ($30,000 (or $40,000) $\times$ 20% divided by 365 (days).

[46]Schmalensee, *op. cit.,* p. 3.

[47]*Id.,* p.4.

[48]*Id.,* p.5.

Granted all this, a way of thought is a way of thought. Whether expressed in shrill, fanatic hysteria or in quiet and reasonable tones, its logic leads to the same destination precisely; in this instance to no action, to no policy save of leaving it all to the market. What we would question is not the logic of the argument, but the assumptions, hidden or explicit, from which the economist's thought proceeds.

There is the assumption that the operation of the market must be accepted (without *proof* but on faith) as perfect, or as good, or as "reasonably good," or sufficiently good as not to be interfered with, modified or replaced except on a *demonstration* of imperfections of *unusual importance,* and on *proof* of the greater benefit or better performance or higher values that will be forthcoming from any proposed intervention, subvention, control, or replacement of the market mechanism.

This offer to balance that which need not be proven against that which must be proven, provides no entry for public intervention in the market system. For such "proof" is never possible, no more proof that public intervention will yield higher values than proof of the "market system's generally good performance." In this instance, Schmalensee's phrasing itself excludes the possibility of "proof." In fact the credibility of all large propositions concerning society or the economy must in the end rely, if not on sheer faith or the acceptance of authority, on an assessment, a judgment that is inherently intuitive, of a shifting mass of the evidence, pro and con.

> When Paul Samuelson wrote *Foundations of Economic Analysis,* his declared intention was to recast economic theory into a set of mathematical propositions *in order that those propositions could be tentatively verified or definitively refuted through experimental test,* thus giving to economics the same empirical base that physics had. In one sense, Samuelson was enormously successful. He set the tone and direction for his generation. He became a man of great influence and affluence, a Nobel Prize winner and a millionaire. In another sense he failed completely. He and those who followed him succeeded certainly in recasting the whole of economics in complex and esoteric mathematical symbolism, *but not a single one of the propositions of theory has, as a consequence, been exposed to refutation through experimental test.* The basis for the acceptance or rejection of the propositions of economics remains as much a matter for intuitive judgment as ever before.
>
> The problem in trying to establish and disestablish statements concerning social phenomena is that there are no precisely quantifiable relationships that are universal and continuing. Individual behavior, group action, social policy—all are functions of ideas, images, imageries, and ideologies that may be created out of nothing and vanish into nothing. In the social realm, every entity, every relationship is unique. Any general statement can do no more than refer to phenomena or relationships that are merely analogous to one another. Very untidy all that; inconvenient no doubt, not *comme il faut* at all. Still statements are and must be made concerning social phenomena, and those statements will be accepted or rejected. The real question under those circumstances is how best to establish or disestablish the credibility of such statements[49]

---

[49]Robert A. Solo, "New Maths and Old Sterilities," *Saturday Review* (January 22, 1972), p. 52.

Certainly the evidence to be culled from current observation permits the judgment that the market system in the United States has been performing not reasonably well but very badly; and that rather than the imperative—no second guessing the market, the market system needs to be second guessed, and third guessed, and fourth guessed.

Besides the assumption of a "perfect-to-reasonably good and certainly best available" performance of the market system, long an article of faith in Western capitalism, there is another assumption, not a part of the economics paradigm, not articulated as theory but fixed into practice by commonplace observation, acted upon in pragmatic response to need, crisis, and the experience of Western societies for centuries. It is the assumption that that which I have called here systems of the infrastructure—communication, energy, transportation—are basic to the evolution and development of all the rest, constituting the base upon which that whole edifice depends, and hence that the social stake in the viability, continuity, and development of these systems far transcends the interests of the income earners or entrepreneurs or investors engaged in their operation. In the jargon, they are surfeit with externalities. For centuries no "proof" has been needed to establish that they require another order of policy concern than does "textiles."

Nor is there any recognition of the deficiencies, functions of decentralization and inherent in market-based choice, the more pervasive and devastating the closer reality approximates the ideal model of pure and perfect competition where the externalization true costs and true benefits from the calculus of choice is bound to be the most pervasive and most distorting, and where those uncertainties activated by the operation of the economy itself will be the greatest and most destructive of foresightful and rational choice, and where the tables of group and social values are most completely excluded from expression and consideration, and where the highest pain and the greatest costs are implicit in the process of response and adjustment to fundamental change in the context of economic and social activity.[50]

Our economist as a sound middle grounder rejects the "textbook theory . . . of perfect government." I know of no such textbooks available to an American clientele. Be that as it may, so far as "government" is concerned, the important and characteristic implication of his way of thought, beyond its faith in the intrinsic superiority of the market's judgment, is the absence of assumptions concerning its nature, character, potentiality, imperfection, or perfectability. The state remains X, invariant and unprobed. "If the market economy does not operate well, policy attention" we are admonished "should focus on the source of that problem,"[51] which is to say that if the market system does not operate well, then rather than bringing extraneous subvention or intervention to bear to redirect market choice, the market itself should be restructured, reorganized, reformed so that it will operate well and without intervention. Who or what is to "focus on the source of the problem?" Who or what is to evaluate the options for action? Who or what is to perfect the "demonstratably important imperfections?" Who or what is to restructure, reform, reorganize (as an alternative to substituting its own initiatives and

[50]Robert A. Solo, *Economic Organizations and Social Systems* (Indianapolis, Indiana: The Bobbs-Merrill Co., Inc., 1967), Chapter 3.
[51]Schmalensee, *op. cit.,* p. 12.

judgments for that of) the market economy? The state, of course. No other locus of evaluation and action is possible. Must we not be concerned then with the competencies of that state? Are not these competencies to be understood and evaluated before we can prejudge their capacity to intervene in, or to restructure or to reorganize the market system? Since what can be done with, to, and for the market economy will depend on these competencies, isn't the development of those competencies a proper subject for economic policy? What the state can or cannot do is not given. It will depend on what is given to the development of the character and competencies of the state.

Before we pose counter assumptions as a basis for a positive policy *vis a vis* the energy infrastructure, there are two lacunae in the economic discourse that remain to be remarked upon. One is a genuine absence from the paradigm itself; economics as a mode of thought has nothing to say and is indeed incapable of grasping the constituents of a system of technological advance, and here the advance of technology is the core of the problem. The other is not foreign to the paradigm but seems forgotten by its epigone. This is the character and consequence of resource depletion.

The Depleting Resource

Half a century ago Harold Hotelling said what can be said about depletable resources within the frame of the economist's paradigm.[52] Just as it was supposed to arrange for the optimal distribution of any resource as between alternative uses at a point in time, so also it was supposed, the free and competitive market would arrange for the optimal distribution of the fixed quantum of a depleting resource over time. As the resource was used it would become scarcer, and as greater scarcity loomed in the future that would be anticipated as higher future prices. Correspondingly, owners of a depletable resource would be inclined to withhold it from sale (and hence slow down its depletion) in order to sell the resource in their possession at the higher price anticipated for future sales. This withholding of resources would cause current prices to rise until current prices became equal to all anticipated future prices discounted by the rate of interest. Since, according to the doctrine, the rate of interest exactly expresses society's preference for present as compared to future benefits, and since prices so discounted are the actual values to society of consuming the resource at every point in the future and the present, the free market would thus have equalized the value of future and present benefits to be derived from its consumption so that there can be no increase in utility by a further shifting of consumption as between present and future. Hence the distribution of consumption will be optimized over time.

So also the distribution of income payments would be optimized (discounted profits would be maximized) over time. This meant, assuming rational and informed choice, that the rate of resource depletion and prices over the period of depletion would be exactly the same whether the ownership of the resource was widely dispersed and the market competitive or whether ownership was concentrated and

---

[52]Harold Hotelling, "The Economics of Exhaustible Resources," *Journal of Political Economy* (April, 1931), pp. 137–175.

the market monopolistic. Either way price would have nothing to do with the "costs of production."[53]

A century of experience with price and depletion rates for petroleum on the free market in no way confirms or is explicable in terms of this theory.[54] No one would deny at the level of academic discourse that petroleum is a depletable resource. But the assumption basic to practical action and policy was quite the contrary. In practice the resource was considered as depletionless. Market choice, business practice, and public policy turned on the assumption that the well was bottomless. For the depletion decision, the critical data were the costs of exploration, drilling, refining, distribution, in other words, the cost of production. It was considered an industry like any other, like steel, or machine tools, or shipbuilding, or automobile manufacture, where the cost of production was at issue and the proper objective of public policy was to encourage production and the expansion of production capacity.[55] Only in understanding that, are business attitudes, public policy and the advice of economists explicable.

Conceiving the formation of OPEC as the critical threshold of change, wherein the monopoly power of the new cartel was used to raise oil prices above the "competitive level" betrays a shallow sense of events and is hardly consistent with the efforts of the Saudis, major partner in the cartel, to stifle free wheeling, free marketeers from raising their selling price on spot markets. Rather the critical change is in the transformation of the great territory of the original 48 states, for

---

[53]Conservationists unhappy with the disposition of depletable resources by the market economy and imagining that actual events could be rationalized by reference to theory argued that while the free market properly reflected the interests of living individuals, it failed to reflect the wants and needs of future generations. Hence the state should in some way act as guardian of the welfare of future generations, and for their sake constrain the rate at which resources are depleted. (See Alfred Pigou, *Economics of Welfare* (London: Macmillan, Inc., 1946). To this the hard nosed economist, idealizing the market, replied that there was no society than that of living individuals, and that the state, as its instrument, had no function other than to serve their views and interests. Stephan Marglin, "The Social Rate of Discount and the Optimal Rate of Investment," *Quarterly Journal of Economics* (February, 1963), pp. 95–111, reconciled the two views; arguing that while the market permits the individual to decide on the values of present as against future benefits on the condition that there is no general constraints imposed on the use of the resource, it does not allow the individual to opt for the imposition of such constraints for the benefit of future generations. That individual preference can be expressed through voice and vote in the political system, and thus a social preference for postponed consumption can be articulated and reflected in a social discount rate different from that which would occur through the market interaction.

[54]Over this long period there is no evidential support to the notion that depletion rates have been paced out in the calculus of anticipated scarcities, with a rising schedule of anticipated prices discounted by the rate of interest as the guiding rule. On the contrary, observation suggests that such a calculus has never controlled nor can it in any way explain the rates of depletion. Thus, for example, when in recent years, outpaced by inflation, the real rate of interest sometimes hovered at around zero indicating presumably a nil preference for present *vis-a-vis* future consumption. With the prospect looming of critical shortages and higher future prices coupled with a zero time preference, the theory would predict a decline toward a zero level of current consumption and resource depletion. In fact, consumption and depletion increased continuously and at a dizzy rate.

[55]Thus oil depletion allowances subsidized and continue to subsidize at taxpayer's expense, the output of oil, presumably reducing the price paid by consumers, increasing consumption and accelerating depletion. The same is true of the practice of allowing the royalties paid by oil companies to Middle Eastern shiekdoms as a full tax deduction rather than considering those royalties as a sharing of profits with indigenous owners. Again at taxpayer's expense, costs are subsidized and prices reduced and depletion accelerated. Inasmuch as rate regulation in natural gas succeeds in its professed aim of holding down rates, "production" and consumption are increased and depletion is accelerated.

long the largest producer of petroleum in the world and a major exporter of oil, into an economy that requires massive imports of petroleum from abroad, and where in spite of an extraordinary increase in price and profit and in drilling, the level of output continues, year in, year out, steadily to decline; and where research scientists, taking account of the higher costs of deeper drilling and specialized extraction, writing in *Science* estimate as a high order of probability, that by the mid-1980s the day will come when the "energy cost of obtaining a barrel of oil is the same as the energy in that barrel."[56] Since there are other costs than that of energy involved in this process, the well to all intents and purposes will be dry before that point is reached.

This transformation, this sudden encounter with global limits, was the tremendous event that forced the world across the threshold of realization that not production but depletion was at issue, and that scarcity must increase and increase, and market price must go higher and higher. The rationale of choice that Hotelling described becomes silently operative. And in this regard, more important than the formation of the cartel was the decisive shift in the decision-making power from the processing interest to the interests of resource ownership. In the days when their voice was decisive, the interests of oil companies *vis a vis* the rate of depletion, was equivocal. Whatever return they must seek as owners, inasmuch as their profits derived from refining and distribution, their interest was in large volume throughput. And inasmuch as the oil fields in their possession were under threat of expropriation, they had a positive interest in rapid depletion. But with ownership in the saddle, the

---

[56] *Wall Street Journal,* February 3, 1981, p. 8, reporting on the article published in "this weeks" *Science* by Charles A. S. Hall and Cutler J. Cleveland, stating that "This break-even day of reckoning won't come for about 20 years if industry holds drilling to its 1978 rate. . . . But if that rate continues to increase, 'the break-even point for oil could occur in the mid-1980s'." Thus " 'The Cornell scientists' study statistically correlated the industry's yearly volume of drilling for exploration and development and the amount of oil found. That correlation doesn't show what is commonly assumed, however.

"The team found that the amount of oil and gas (measured in equivalents of barrels of oil) discovered per foot of well drilled is dropping precipitously. They cited studies more than a decade ago by M. King Hubbert, an oil exploration consultant to both the industry and the government, that showed the industry in the 1930s extracted about 250 barrels of oil for every foot drilled. This dropped to about 40 barrels per foot drilled in the 1950s.

"The trend was reversed briefly in the 1960s, causing many to cast aside Mr. Hubbert's analysis, the researchers noted. The new analysis, they said, shows that the downward trend resumed in the mid-1960s. By the late 1970s, the industry was finding only 10 to 15 barrels of oil for every foot drilled.

"At the same time, they said, the energy cost of exploring for, extracting and delivering oil has been increasing steadily. It currently equals about 1½ barrels of oil energy for every foot of well drilled.

" 'The time at which domestic petroleum will no longer, on the average, be a net fuel for the nation isn't when all the wells run dry but rather at some point before that time when the energy cost of obtaining a barrel of oil is the same as the energy in that barrel,' they said.

"If the yield of oil per foot of well drilled continues to drop—and the energy cost of drilling continues to rise—this break-even point will be reached fairly soon. How soon, they said, depends on how intensively the industry explores for oil.

Break-Even Year

"If the industry slows its drilling rate to about 130 million feet of well a year, the break-even point could be staved off until the year 2004, their analysis found.

" 'Were we to continue to drill at the 1978 levels of about 200 million feet a year, the linear extrapolations would intersect in 2000,' they added. This is for both oil and its equivalent in natural gas. 'For oil alone, we could reach the break-even point in about a decade.'

"If the industry continues to increase its drilling rate at the pace it has in recent years, the break-even point for oil and gas could be reached in the mid-1980s, they concluded."

logic of depletion turned on the axis of future scarcity and current prices. The needs or demand for imported producer or consumer goods by those in possession of petroleum, might make a difference in the rate at which they would be willing to deplete. In the case of the Saudis, with claims on imported products far beyond their current power to consume them, it is simply a question of the form in which they prefer to hold their assets, underground as oil or as securities or cash in foreign banks. Under the circumstances, it is a wonder, on the grounds of economic self-interest, that they allow any oil to be produced at all.

But if the sense of an ineluctable limit has at last been driven home, we in the United States, our politicians, our businessmen, our savants, are the last to realize it. They still cannot comprehend that we cannot increase the production of petroleum. All we can do is to accelerate its depletion.

What public purposes should enter into the formation of energy policy? In this regard great noise is made about "national security" understood in the military sense,[57] Consider first the issue of national security and an energy policy for our depleting resource.

National Defense and the Depleting Resource

Aside from the general interest in a stable, low cost supply, there might be these energy concerns which, if not particular to military security would, in relation to the oil resource, be concerns upon which a rational policy of national defense would place special emphasis.

1. That *in case of an emergency* at least a critical minimum (and as large a proportion of total requirements as possible) should be available from domestic sources and hence invulnerable to external interuptions.

2. That there be a reserve supply of petroleum over and above that which would be normally available for use *in periods of emergency,* or in order to ease the pains of civilian-industrial and military-industrial transition.

Both objectives would indicate a slowing down in the rate at which domestic petroleum reserves are normally depleted; and conversely, as would be required in order to protect domestic reserves, a relatively *greater* nonemergency reliance on oil imports from abroad. No genius is needed to realize that strategically, militarily, it is safer for us that the black treasure of the earth be exhausted in Arabia or Nigeria or Iraq or Iran than in Texas or in Louisiana. Every increase in home production means the accelerated depletion of the domestic oil resource and therefore must reduce that which could be made available to ourselves from domestic sources in times of need and crisis. Nevertheless, the Eisenhower Administration imposed quotas on the importation of crude oil from abroad, thereby necessarily accelerating the depletion of domestic reserves; and did it deliberately, purposefully in the name

---

[57]The Synfuels Corporation was established under The Energy Security Act, and was charged with promoting the creation of an industrial capacity able to produce 450,000 barrels of petroleum equivalent synfuel a day by 1985. Why 450,000 barrels? Because allegedly that is the daily requirement of the armed forces. Pure charade.

of national security. That quota policy was kept in place and supported by subsequent administrations and not a single voice in Congress or the Senate was raised against it. In 1959 I wrote

> The synthetic rubber experience shows that a government is ill advised to rely on a competence shaped to the criteria of commerce in formulating its policy for national security. Yet, today as yesterday measures purporting to insure the national security continue to be based upon the demands of those who have commercial stakes in public action. And today as yesterday, the government continues to rely on a technological competence for the formulation of national security policy that is shaped to the purposes of private profit. Thus, air transport and the merchant marine are given aid and subsidy for the supposed purpose of insuring national security. It is folly to assume that, inasmuch as such aids and subsidies are freely used by the recipients according to the criteria of good business, a maximum return in national security will ever be derived per dollar of public expenditure. The oil companies demanded and received protection for their oil ownership overseas—this on the ground that our limited and depleted domestic reserves must be preserved in the interests of national security. Yet at the same time, domestic oil producers were demanding and getting protection against the import of foreign oil into the United States—again, on the ground that it is necessary for national security to accelerate the rate at which we use up our known reserves as a stimulus to the exploration and the development of new domestic reserves. We must expand our foreign commitments and spend billions for overseas bases to protect Arabian oil so that our domestic oil will be less rapidly depleted, at the same time that we impose quotas against foreign imports and permit higher prices to consumers in order to stimulate the use of our domestic supply.[58]

If the quotas upon the importation of crude oil had not been imposed, the Saudis would not now be so well endowed and the United States would be able fully to supply all its needs from domestic sources in any period of emergency.

The imposition of quotas against the import of Arabian crude in the name of national security seemed to me inexplicable on rational grounds. How much more incomprehensible that the same outlook, the same reasoning, the same policy design, accelerating the depletion of domestic supplies in the name of national security, should still prevail. Yet it does. It underlay Jimmy Carter's Project Independence. It is at the heart of Reaganite policies. It is implicit in the economist's rending of garments and beating upon breasts to bewail and cry out against the price control of oil, lest such control subsidize the importation of petroleum from abroad. It is made explicit in Schmalensee's proposal that a tariff be levied on the importation of petroleum in order to increase the proportion, hence the production, hence accelerate the depletion of the domestic oil resource, and that for the sake of national security! Caught as in a mind-trap, prevailing thought cannot break free from the calculus of production, to realize that the issue here is of depletion.

In response to the second objective, we are following the curious practice of paying vast sums to have oil pumped out of one hole in the ground in order to pump

---

[58]Robert A. Solo, *Across the High Technology Threshold: The Case of Synthetic Rubber* (Norwood, Penn.: Norwood Editions, 1980), pp. 125–126.

it back into another hole in the ground where, as a strategic reserve, it could be pumped out again in case of special need; a practice that is surely more than a little mad. A rational policy would take selected oil fields out of production, cap their wells, and stand ready to start the outflow up again in case of special need. Or we might undertake to explore the public lands to discover and to bring new oil fields there to the point of exploitation, with the requisite infrastructure in place, poised to produce should a crisis warrant, but not for purposes of private profit. For this, and for other reasons as well, the state should develop a geophysical capacity at least equal in competence to that of the great oil companies.

A Geophysical Capability for the State

What is needed to deal effectively with the arbitrary power of the great international oil companies whose policies and activities may or may not be in the public interest? Certainly a highly competent and autonomous agency of public management, but in order to countervail against their monopoly of critical skills and capacities, something more is called for. The state itself should develop as in France or in Germany or in Italy its own geophysical establishment able to explore, discover, mine, drill for, refine, and distribute the mineral resources in lieu of or in competition with the great companies. That experience would support the development of competent public management as well.

For generations the Soviets have tried to sell or barter their petroleum at bargain prices. The great companies denied them access. In the initial grain deal, the Soviets offered natural gas for American wheat, an exchange which might have been very much in our interest. There was no way to activate such an arrangement except through these companies, and for them it was anathema. Only the existence of a governmental geophysical establishment able to undertake the task, would have made the exchange possible. But given the existence of such a public agency, the private corporations would have been in hot competition for a contract with the Russians. Only through a governmental geophysical agency can we explore and evaluate the reserves in our coastal waters and of our public lands without surrendering public rights to their control and exploitation.

Demystification

There is an underbrush, thick and dark, of mystification concerning oil that needs to be cleared away if we are to take a clear look at the terrain of choice.

1. We are importing more foreign oil that we did before and we are paying a higher price for it than we used to. That is what has happened and that is all that has happened—the sole objective change in those economic circumstances to which we must adapt.

2. We are therefore more vulnerable to external events and pressures than once we were. There is nothing unusual, nothing extraordinary about that. Great Britain and Japan have been and are totally dependent on resource imports. All the countries of Western Europe are and have been far more

dependent on foreign sources for their energy supplies than we now are or are likely to become.

3. It is no more "patriotic" to conserve or to use imported (or domestically produced) oil efficiently than it is to conserve and to use efficiently imported (or domestically produced) automobiles, television sets, cameras, coffee, tea, or what have you.

4. We import goods from abroad and we are obliged presumably, eventually, to pay for what we import with the goods that we export. If we import more, we presumably must export more; and whether it is importing more cars from Japan or coffee from Brazil or oil from Arabia, the choice, the problem, and the means of its resolution are essentially the same.

5. If because we must buy more oil at much higher prices than before, we are obliged to produce and export more than before to pay for it; we would on that account be poorer than we were. We would have less real output to divide amongst ourselves. In that case the problem to be faced is that of poverty, and, given the character of the depleting resource, of increasing poverty as time goes on: how to cope with it, distribute the burden of it, and overcome it.

6. Such would be the case if those from whom we import oil used their earnings to purchase corresponding quantities of goods and services from us. Already surfeit, they have not done so. In good part, they have allowed unused claims to accumulate as funds or securities, thereby no doubt introducing considerable uncertainties into the system of international trade. Meantime the oil we import has *de facto* been a kind of gift. And if as a consequence of all this we have become actually poorer (and I think we have as a consequence become actually poorer), it is not because the product of our labors has been siphoned off to be consumed by others in distant lands, but because of our own actions in the way that we have responded to the new circumstances.

Who Collects the Rent?

We are dealing here with a depleting resource that must in real magnitudes continuously diminish in the face of and as a consequence of increasing demand. Classical economics knew very well what must happen on the market when a resource cannot be increased (land) in the face of growing need for its use (because of larger populations). The absolute and relative share in production accruing to the few in possession (landlords) must increase, concentrating more and more wealth in their hands, while that which remains to be shared among all the rest (who work the land and consume its fruits) would decline until all save the few in possession, would exist on the perpetual edge of starvation. Such according to the theory was the certain consequences of leaving it all to the market when increasing needs of the economy and society depended on the use of a fixed resource. Here we are dealing with a resource that not only cannot be increased but that in its real magnitudes must continuously diminish in the face of the soaring demands of an industrializing world.

The classical economists called that share accruing to those in possession of the fixed supply of a scarce resource, rent; and they knew that a rent has no incentive value, and that to expropriate, siphon off, and redistribute rents would have no effect on the supply of the resource and hence on production. The enormous income, the vast new wealth accruing to the domestic producers of petroleum and natural gas as a consequence of decontrol, is a rent superimposed upon prior rents, all without incentive value, that could be expropriated, siphoned off, redistributed without changing existing outputs. The price of domestic oil and natural gas could be allowed to rise to the OPEC level or beyond or below that level, with the public in whole or in part collecting the rent. The excess profits tax is a way for the public to collect a part of the rent. Or the price of domestic petroleum and natural gas could be recontrolled, and rolled back company by company, or field by field, or well by well, with ownership allowed to recover normal operating costs plus a fair return calculated as a fixed percentage of the selling price. Selling price would be allowed to rise to OPEC (or any other chosen) level, with the difference between the allowed return on wellhead output and the selling price accruing as government revenue, replacing other revenue sources, hopefully eliminating the sales tax. Why not?

It could in the name of legitimate expectations be argued that so to deprive the oil companies of their rents while other rents were left untouched, would be unfair. Against that alleged unfairness, must be balanced the inequities implicit in an enormous, functionless transfer of income as the consequences of a windfall unrelated to the investment calculus and no part of the business game.

Or it might be said that aside from the oil produced from established fields and existing wells, oil companies need (a) the cash flow to finance and (b) the incentive to explore, or to deep drill, or to ocean-search for new petroleum and natural gas supply sources.

Beyond the specifics of petroleum and natural gas, there is something wrong with this argument. For it proposes a system that would divert vast wealth and thereby would concentrate the power to effectuate changes which could conceivably overcome the condition of (energy) scarcity into the hands of those who are uniquely beneficiaries of this condition of scarcity, whose wealth and income will continue to increase correspondingly as the condition of scarcity worsens. The market concentrates the power to effectuate change in the hands of those least motivated to change the condition of scarcity.

Under the former system of price control, oil from new fields could be sold at world prices, and oil from new wells in old fields could be sold at a price above that allowed on oil from old wells. Such "incentives" to explore could always be allowed; though clearly the extensive exploration of the mid 60's was activated at far lower levels of anticipated prices and profits. And the profits to be made on new discoveries, when (as here suggested) return is reckoned as a fixed percentage of the selling price, might quite suffice. In any case, the question remains: how much ongoing exploration and new drilling is desirable; or rather, how to pace out the rate of resource depletion? If through subsidy, high profits or otherwise the level of exploration and drilling is increased this year, supplies available in the future will be less;

conversely a lower level of exploration and drilling today will preserve that which is discoverable and available tomorrow.

The rationale of ownership choosing how much of a scarce resource to deplete will not be a function of absolute return (rent) but will depend on the costs of depletion (drilling, exploration) and on the relative returns over time, or in other words on the price anticipated for tomorrow as compared to the price that can be gotten today regardless of the absolute level of today's and tomorrow's prices. In any case, if it is considered desirable to increase exploration and drilling for natural gas, without affecting the wellhead price of oil, then the exploration function and the drilling function might be set apart in different business organizations and differently supported.

Bounties could be paid to exploration companies for their discoveries, tied to the extent of the proven reserves, without the necessity of exploiting those reserves. Especially important would be the public support of R&D to develop the technologies of exploration.

If more drilling is wanted, the costs of incremental drilling or of a specified type of drilling could be tax-subsidized, or subsidized through low interest loans for the procurement of drilling equipment, or especially through public R&D investment in the development of lower cost and more effective drilling technologies.

What we have proposed would avoid or reduce the massive income transfer from the public at large to the oil and natural gas companies in particular. The questions of why decontrol at all, of why create the rents subject to redistribution at all, or why raise the price of domestic supplies to OPEC levels (as economists have demanded and as two successive administrations have decreed) remains to be answered. And before that the question of how rapidly or how slowly should we allow this energy source to deplete?

The Price of Energy and the Zero Sum Game

Lester Thurow writes

> From the perspective of Americans, higher oil prices represent a mixture of gains and losses, For the country as a whole, Americans lose since they had to pay an extra $30 billion (in 1978) for imported oil over and above what they would have had to pay if prices had stayed at 1972 levels. Since $30 billion represents about 1.5 percent of our GNP, average real incomes have to fall by about that amount. But domestic energy producers also gain if domestic energy prices are allowed to rise. Since about 80 percent of our energy is domestically produced, this transfer between Americans from energy consumers to energy producers is much larger than the transfer to foreigners. In 1978 an additional $120 billions or 6 percent of the GNP would have been transfered from American consumers to American producers if all energy prices had been allowed to follow the price of imported oil. On the average, Americans are not poorer on account of this transfer—it is from one American to another—but particular Americans will experience large income gains and other Americans will experience large income losses.[59]

---

[59]Thurow, *The Zero Sum Society, op. cit.* p. 9.

Thus, according to Thurow, if the price of *domestic* energy rises even astronomically, on the average Americans are not made poorer on that account. It is simply that funds have been transfered from one set of Americans to another set of Americans.

I think Thurow is wrong, that we are not engaged here in a zero sum game. If and while energy prices are lower, more energy will be used than otherwise (and the resource will be more rapidly depleted than otherwise). The availability and use of cheap energy is the basis of a boundless range of technological initiatives and transformations, determining the potentialities for growth.

One is reminded of the critical turning point of British economic policy in the early Nineteenth Century, the Ricardian triumph *vis a vis* the corn laws. The issue then was whether to remove or not the tariff on the importation of cheap grain from the United States, thence ceasing to protect British agriculture. In the frame of Thurow's reasoning, this decision is to be understood simply as a matter of income transfer from one set of Englishmen to another set of Englishmen. Ricardo saw it differently. The wage of the laboring class in Britain was determined by the price of bread. Wages in that era could be equated to the cost of sheer subsistence. With the importation of American grain the cost of subsisting an English workman would be less, and therefore the British economy could subsist more, and would have more labor available to it at the same cost. Labor in that era could be regarded, and was regarded simply as an energy source. In opting to end protection for agriculture, Great Britain was opting for cheap energy; and that cheap energy was to be the basis for a period of extraordinary economic growth and the attainment of industrial preeminence.

But if there is an analogous value for us in low priced energy in petroleum and natural gas, there is also the cost of its accelerated depletion. How fast then should we allow this critical resource to be depleted?

How Fast Should the Petroleum Resource Be Depleted?

The whole of our economic superstructure has been erected upon the use of petroleum. Every element and phase of production in some way depends upon the availability of that resource, which has become suddenly scarce, to a degree that earlier was outside the scope of individual plan or entrepreneurial calculus. Scarce now, it will be scarcer still. The physical quantity grows small and smaller while demand leaps ahead as the world industrializes.

Surely the end is not far across the near horizon. We must at least assume it to be close at hand. Hence the critical social objective must be to find another energy base upon which to reconstruct the techno-industrial-agricultural superstructures evaluated and chosen in terms of environmental impact and stability. The rate of petroleum and natural gas depletion should be geared to the installation of the technologies slated to replace them; thus to assure that there is sufficient petroleum and natural gas to supply priority needs until the alternative is available.

We are not without options for an alternative energy base. Currently attention is focused on atomic energy and coal. Atomic energy, with present technology, contains the immanent threat of catastrophe. With the measures required to contain its dangers, it becomes very costly. Supplies of uranium are limited, and rapidly depleting. It does not serve as a substitute for gasoline in automotive transport.

Coal, besides producing heat directly can be used to produce electricity, to produce a substitute for natural gas, and to produce a substitute for gasoline. But with existing technologies, the production and use of coal is dirty and dangerous (indeed murderous). And, again with existing technologies, its production is costly. "From 1962 to 1978 coal costs in constant dollars have increased faster than that of oil costs."[60] Coal moreover is a depleting resource and its practical availability is far more limited (because, for example, in making synfuel it must be used in conjunction with large quantities of water, or in gasification where spaces are needed for the dumping of vast quantities of toxic wastes) than the data on estimated reserves would lead one to expect. Coal-based synthetic gas and synfuel using the selfsame technologies that were hastily put in place by the Nazis nearly half a century ago (Lurgi for gasification, Fischer-Tropsch for synfuel) are very costly.

Of course we may be obliged to install these alternative technologies and accept the poverty, the dangers, and the environmental blight implicit in their operation. What the existence of a petroleum and natural gas reserve affords us, is time to develop lower cost, more benign, more stable energy sources than now are available, before the tremendous, largely irreversible commitment is made to a new energy base and upon it to the creation of the different institutional *cum* technological superstructure.

When and whether more desirable energy options will be forthcoming, when and whether the commitment to an alternative energy base will be made, are questions whose answers alas are cloaked in the deepest uncertainty. On this score there is nothing else for it than intuitive judgment as a basis for any policy of pacing the rate of depletion. Let us suppose that on the basis of such judgment, we would slow down the rate of depletion of domestic reserves for the sake of greater safety and to give ourselves more elbow room in this time of choice and transition.

How to Ration Oil

The market is a system for allocating what is available and rationing what is scarce. It is however not the only possible system of rationing, nor necessarily the most desirable. Its vaunted virtue is that it gives the consumer "freedom to choose." And yet if the consumer was free to choose between a system where he received a fixed allocation of gasoline at 50 cents a gallon or one where he was free to buy as much as he chose at $2 a gallon, it is not unlikely that in his freedom he would chose the former. Certainly a system of per capita entitlement would be the effective means of controlling precisely the rate at which domestic supplies of petroleum were allowed to be depleted.

A practical scheme combining the control over the depletion rate and over price of domestic oil with the "freedom of choice" virtues of the market, would allocate,

---

[60]TRW, Inc., *Environmental Issues,* op. cit. p. 20.

but only domestic supplies of petroleum at a low price (thus allowing the consumer rather than the producer or the taxpayer to preempt the rent) on some per capita entitlement basis. Additional purchases of imported oil would be freely available at the uncontrolled price of imports.

For the consumer this would mean a basic ration of low priced gasoline, and the unconstrained opportunity to buy more at a higher price. The depletion of domestic supplies would be precisely controlled. Since individuals would purchase marginal supplies at the world price of imported oil, its use and value, reflecting that price as the index of scarcity, would approximate market "efficiency." The burden of accelerated depletion would be shifted to less secure sources of petroleum overseas.

How to Conserve Petroleum

We promote conservation. And the rationale of a policy of conservation, presumably, is to reduce the rate at which domestic, and also world reserves are depleted, and to facilitate institutional *cum* technological adaptation to the long-range prospects of higher energy costs. The economist's panacea is to let prices rise and leave conservation to the responses of the market. Higher prices are touted as the most "efficient" avenue to conservation. This is, in a word, an approach that would force poverty upon us so that we can learn to live with poverty.

It is hardly to be denied that higher energy prices and the income squeeze forces individuals to search for the means of economizing. Pressed by sky-high prices, individuals acting individually within the range of their competence and concern, do seal up cracks, insulate attics, buy Hondas instead of Chevrolets, even in the extreme instance, take a bus instead of the family car. But when the transformation of the established complex of institutions and organizations and practices that were formed over generations on the very cheap energy base, requires many simultaneous changes in a time extended series, it is beyond the reach of any multitude of individuals deciding individually in the fragmented, piecemeal response of markets.

The process of significant structural change in the market economy is not efficient. It is slow, uncertain, and terribly painful. It operates through periodic catastrophes. It is deaf and blind to the signals of future danger. For those caught in the instant, urgent stress and pressure of the competitive game, all questions, issues, imageries of the future become peculiarly unreal. And the more competitive the market game, the more that such foresight is precluded. In the economist's ideal condition of "pure competition," foresight is absolutely impossible. Industry in the market economy waits for the axe to fall; and in its windfall blows that axe shatters structures, crushes lives, leaving a bloodied and traumatized host in a field of pain and destruction. We will contend that there may be more efficient processes and less painful paths of structural and systemic change than skyrocketing price on the free market where energy conservation is the objective. For that purpose, we will consider two instances of market response and the alternative, in home construction and in automobiles.

Solar Heating/Cooling in Home Construction

We are told that the solar technology in home construction even in its present crude and underdeveloped state and without the benefit of low cost production for any mass market, is fully economic for substantial regions of the country. And yet, withall the skyrocketing cost of fuel and the demonstrations sponsored by the Department of Energy and the tax deductions offered,[61] for the country as a whole or in those regions, there has been no significant transformation in home construction in this regard. This innovation as other innovations confronts and is stymied by the same formidable barriers, the same hedgehog resistances to any significant transformation of that cluster of technologies in an industry of fragmented home-grown contractors and builders, of unsophisticated, risk-fearful home buyers, of traditional handed-down skills institutionalized in work rules and perpetuated through craft unionism, of architects who are quasi-artists trained in design not technology, and of building codes that break the industry into localized protectorates.

At a symposium on competition in the solar energy industry, sponsored by the Bureau of Competition of the Federal Trade Commission on December 15–16, 1977, I gave a paper[62] which argued that if the existing potentials for conservation and solar-based building are ever to be achieved, if the cycle of solar technologies being "not economic until mass-produced, and not mass-produced until economic," is ever to be broken, it would have to be through establishing a locus of responsibility and motivation, coupled with competence and power, which did not then and does not now exist. And that in fact such a locus of public responsibility, competence, and power could be brought quickly into existence (the institutional apparatus is already in place), in this way. Building codes should, at long last, be made a national responsibility under federal enforcement and control. The appropriate locus of responsibility for the design and enforcement of these codes, and for the development and testing of relevant technologies, would be the Bureau of Standards, an agency with a long tradition of service and a high level of R&D competence.

Given a powerful R&D backup and regional laboratories, regional codes should be formulated in rational relation to climatic and other significant, regional variables. There could then, and for the first time, be a systematic evaluation and a rapid incorporation of change in building specification, from the vast variety of (consen-

---

[61]A favorite dodge of a public authority without technological competence and without the power or capacity to manage complex change, is the gadgetry of tax breaks. A most amazing, a seemingly endless variety of these have been invented. In the present instance, intended to induce conservation measures in home construction, they are inherently regressive (richer fellow, bigger home, more costly installation, bigger tax break). Such tax exemptions, once incorporated into the tax code, inevitably become loopholes used for purposes the Congress never intended, and remain tenaciously fixed, seemingly impossible to eliminate even after their rationale has vanished. No better illustration of this exists than the vast tax revenue subsidy (estimated at $11 billion in 1978) in the form of tax deductions allowed on mortgage interest payments and property taxes for owner-occupied homes. Aside from its regressive character, this subsidizes the most energy-wasteful form of living accommodation.

[62]Bureau of Competition, Federal Trade Commission, *The Solar Market: Proceedings of the Symposium on Competition in the Solar Energy Industry* (Washington: U.S. Government Printing Office, 1978), pp. 146–156.

sual) trade standards, and, more significantly, an evaluation and accommodation of codes to emerging new technologies. The building codes then need no longer be merely protective but should become the spearhead of innovation. Then, solar installations and solar building in appropriate regions, could be required within a range of standard specifications. Industry would be simultaneously offered a set of developed and tested technologies and the mass market for their low cost disposition.

What I suggested was no replacement of liberty with coercion. The coercion exists. Codes exist, and no one denies their necessity. Houses are built under one code or another. What was suggested was a rationalization of that system of coercion, so that it would for the first time have an R&D back-up, so that there might exist the possibility of systematic evolution and rapid accommodation to new technological potentials, and so that the codes, rather than a barrier to innovation and development as they have been hitherto, could become a spearhead of innovation and, in this instance, an instrument for an organized and effective response to a national need for a rational and painless transformation to a more energy-conserving technology.

The suggestion I made at this symposium provoked no visible response on the part of the federal agencies or Congress. It appears now to have been experimentally validated, so to speak, by ordinances of San Diego County in California requiring building contractors to install solar water heating devices in dwellings built after October 1, 1979, in areas served only by electricity, extended on October 1, 1980, to areas served by natural gas, and requiring developers to show that each lot within a subdivision had adequate access to the sun. The results have been extraordinary. From *The New York Times* story:

> In the two years since San Diego County adopted the nation's first law requiring more use of solar energy, this sun drenched city has become a national leader in its use and development, according to industry and government officials.
> 'San Diego is the biggest market nationally.' . . . More than 3,000 new residential units have been equipped with sun-activated heating devices; and 8,000 more are scheduled to have them within the next several months; . . . 29,000 city utility customers are to replace electric or gas water heaters with solar devices over a three-year period; . . . estimated that 20 percent of all purchases of solar equipment were currently made here; . . . estimated that solar energy installations were saving local homeowners a little more than $800,000 annually on the costs of heating water. . . .[63]

Automobiles

In 1981 the mighty American automobile industry is in shambles. The annual losses suffered by each one of its giants are staggering, and unprecedented. Chrysler on the edge of the precipice, exists month by month only on the basis of massive government handouts. General Motors and Ford are next in line. American Motors lives by assembling French automobiles as a virtual subsidiary of Renault. Sustained unemployment in Michigan's cities reaches depression levels, and only public pay-

---

[63] *The New York Times,* February 10, 1981, p. A-14.

ments to the workers have forestalled waves of collapse from spreading throughout the land. Families pull up roots and flee the state. The UAW is traumatized. The reality or the threat of depletion, deterioration, or disaster infiltrates the prospects or crosses the vision of every Michigander.

Such is the uninviting spectacle, scenario of a blind and painful process come to life, of the market economy adjusting, adapting to clear, long standing imperatives to conservation, in the face of increasing scarcity at the essential energy base. It gives tragic witness to the incapacity of firms caught in the strategies of a going competitive game to detach themselves from its dynamic, even as the industry is carried to its destruction.

Bad as it is, it would have been worse if a timid and incompetent state in the administrations of Nixon and Ford, had not pressured and at last insisted in the face of industry scorn and resistance, that some mild steps be taken to shift production from the big gas guzzler to smaller more fuel efficient cars. These years of disaster could have been avoided if the state had acted forcefully to require a major transformation of the industry in response to imperatives writ clear in emerging circumstances and events.

The fate and future of the industry, indeed of automotive transportation, depends on the development of a low cost replacement for the dwindling stocks of petroleum. General Motors' existence depends on that development. A week before this writing, I visited with the director of the General Motors Division of Energy, who treated me with great courtesy and, I think, with openness and honesty.

What I found to be more interesting than what he and his division were doing, was what was being left undone. A lawyer with an engineering background, he and his colleagues are heavily (and usefully) engaged in representing industry and GM interests in those regulatory rules and processes that affect the rates paid and the provisions made for a steady supply of electricity and gas. But there was no evidence that any expertise and competence had been sought for or developed that would enable the promotion and development, or permit the systematic evaluation of the potentialities and consequences of synfuel alternatives, although it was upon these that the fate of General Motors must ultimately depend; nor of any serious concern with or systematic attempt to foresee and anticipate the future in these terms. If not in General Motors, where then in industry could such a concern exist? In this market milieu, with executives dancing on the griddle of competitive heat and pressure, skipping from urgency to urgency, futurism reaches only the peripheral vision. Foresightful planning cannot function there.

Certainly there needs to be a locus of public management for the auto industry: a locus of public management rooted in, and deriving its capabilities from, and acquiring its experience through a powerful public R&D operation designed to promote the development and to contribute to the solution of the problems of this industry. That operation should be autonomous, bound to the purposes and plans of public management, with a continuum of R&D oriented to the development and design of pollution-minimizing, energy-conserving, lower-cost vehicular technologies, these to be introduced through the agency of public management by at once imposing progressively higher performance (mileage per gallon, safety, pollution) standards while at the same time making available technologies to satisfy those standards, and by systematically depleting the existing stock of old vehicles at the lower end of the performance scale by buying and junking them.[64]

This R&D operation should not be thought of or organized as a cooperative endeavor of automobile producers, nor should it be thought of as servicing, nor should it be organized to service or serve those companies. It could, nevertheless, and it should be enormously useful to the industry and to particular automakers. American (this defined by the proportion of total output manufactured in the United States) automakers would be privileged to have a participating role, and would be obliged to pay for that privilege with an annual contribution to help cover operating costs, so that they might make scheduled use of its general R&D facilities, for example, wind tunnels; have their R&D staffs coparticipate in experimental and developmental activities, license inventions created at or purchased by the Center for use in manufacturing activity in the United States, and have immediate access to all R&D information produced at the Center. Thus the Center would perform something of the function of a patent and information pooling arrangement to assure a balanced advance in the automotive technology, so that no firm need fall inextricably, irretrievably behind and be lost to the competitive race. It would not, however, prevent an individual automaker from pursuing its own lines of R&D in pursuit of competitive advantage.

Its most important advantage for the individual automaker would be in being privy to and in having the opportunity to act upon and within the planning function of public management, in this case combined with the technological planning of its R&D center; for rational planning would at once take multifacted transformations of the transportation infrastructure as its target while simultaneously preparing and creating the institutional context needed for that transformation, and developing the required technologies. This, from the point of view of the automaker, would mean a foreknowledge of solidly established new product markets combined with possession of the technology needed to satisfy those future demands.

Consider for example the decline of our great cities. They have been literally choked to death by the automobile; through the congestion it produces, through its omnivorous demand for space, a space that pays no tax and can be used neither as a place for dwelling or for selling or for production; through its pollution of the city's air; through at once forcing and making possible the flight from the city, generating the mass of commuters as free rider on city services, with service industries and manufacturing facilities, leaving city centers and dispersing to out where money is and the automobiles are. Now the changing character of the energy infrastructure presses us towards a reconcentration of population and industry in arrangements less dependent on the private automobile.

The degradation of our cities has been in process for four decades; a disordered dispersal of the population, a deterioration that eats outwards from the center, leaving behind wider and wider belts of desolation, as in the path of locusts. And nowhere has there been a turnaround. There are nevertheless options for resolving

---

[64]My colleague, Harold Wein, explored and made clear to me the importance of a program to accelerate systematically the depletion of existing stock.

the crisis, recreating a satisfying and efficient urban life. None are achievable without a high degree of public management.

It is possible for example that the high density business areas of major American cities (call such areas "the zone") be closed to all private vehicles save trucks, and those allowed in only in the very early morning hours. A given city might have a series of such zones, or the whole city might be so zoned. At entrance and exit points on the periphery of the zone, parking facilities would be established for those driving to the zone. Those within or entering the zone would rely on public transit and on a fleet of very light (plastic bubbles in effect) low-speed, electric-powered, passenger driven autos. To start the car would require that a special credit card be inserted into a slot; from that card, mileage and charges would be automatically computed. After its use, the car could be left on any street, and a car could be picked up for use on any street. This follows a prototype system already in commercial operation in Europe.

At night, carrier trucks cruising the streets would hoist aboard these plastic bubbles and haul them to stations at entrance/exit points and elsewhere. There batteries would be recharged, data extracted from the computing mechanism for billing drivers, with the cars themselves stored on overhanging cables, available for the next day's custom.

Thus the zones and even the cities would be made into places where the air was clean, streets accident free, with walking space and bicycling space, and space for trees and for the forgotten green stuff called (another kind of) grass, space reclaimable from the automobile to be used for living, for work, and for recreation. And with that a very considerable reduction in the use of gasoline. For the automakers this would mean a massive production outlet, in building up and maintaining those fleets for the city zones. They would have in production besides the basic model of a low-cost, electric-powered vehicle easily adapted for sale to the general public and geared to family needs for safe and inexpensive driving.

In its essentials the scheme is very simple, but complex in its details and execution: in the means of controlling access and exit, in the creation of parking facilities on the periphery, in the development of full-coverage public transit, in building and maintaining recharging stations and storage facilities, in the design and installation of a viable system of credit and control for the passenger-driven vehicles, in dealing with the vested interests (motels, taxis, gas stations, parking ramps,) established to service a different system and, of course, in developing the vehicle itself. It is an option certainly that could not be achieved through increments of decentralized, market directed choices. It would only be possible through public management.

Managing Innovation

It is surely not only those critical changes relating to the conservation of energy that are at issue. Whenever innovation demands multifaceted change and a transformation of the infrastructure, it is likely to require a combination of public and private initiatives and management.

Consider the case of Melvin Calvin, a famous biochemist, Nobel Prize Laureate, world authority on photosynthesis, who has undertaken an interesting and important project intended to create an alternative source of synthetic fuel. For that purpose he has engaged in the selective breeding of a species of milkweed that can be grown and harvested in the semiarid wastelands of the United States and of other countries, which, when pressed, yields a high quality of oil.[65]

Suppose that Professor Calvin achieves all of his R&D objectives. Suppose that he demonstrates the technical feasibility and the conditional economic worth of his scheme. Then what must be done? Implementing this project would require the repossession of barren lands with titles of ownership obscured and forgotten in the passage of centuries; the construction of roads; the piping in of water; the development of a utility complex as the infrastructure for agricultural cum industrial operations and for living; the recruitment and training of workers and operators; the provision of housing and all the facilities for living and recreation; the development, installation, and operation of new technologies for harvesting the plant and for its conversion, distribution, and use, with whatever adaptations in habits and technologies of consumption this might require.

Can anyone suppose that all of this will spring into being spontaneously upon Professor Calvin's successful demonstration? Perhaps in half a century, given very favorable winds of chance, but not in a decade. For that there must be a locus of responsibility, competence, and power of which there is now no evidence.

Or consider this. Current energy planning calls for the massive near term use of coal. Aside from the carcinogenic agents which may then pollute the air, this will greatly accelerate the thickening of the carbon dioxide layer enclosing our globe, whose grave and dangerous consequences are still unknown. This overloading of the atmosphere with carbon dioxide can, indeed must, be offset by a vast increase in the biomass, in the greenstuff on the surface of land and sea, which is, of course, also a potential energy source. But where is the locus of responsibility, competence, and power needed for that level of planning and programming for an energy-environmental balance?

New Technology

No escape from energy scarcity and closure, nor from the consequent down drag of poverty, is possible except through the creation and development of new technology. We have already said what we have to say here about public policy for the organization of science and R&D in the system of technological advance. In the light of the particular circumstances, however, we shall conclude this chapter with some precautionary notes on a policy for the development of energy technologies.

This is not a task that can be left to the market. At least during the last half

---

[65]*See* Melvin Calvin, "The Petroleum Plant: Perhaps We Can Grow Gasoline" *Science* (October, 1976), p. 194. Just so the latex of the rubber tree (hevea brasiliensis) is in fact a high grade fuel oil. One wonders whether guayule, which has been cultivated in Mexico and in the American southwest as a rubber source, and which would be easily subject for modern techniques of mechanical harvesting might not be alternative avenue for study in line with Professor Calvin's approach.

century, no major new technology—chemicals, synthetics, electronics, catalytic engineering, atomic energy, aviation, space orbiting, computers, microengineering—has come into being without state and/or institutional support and involvement in the zone of its origin, with the single exception of the transitor developed by Bell Labs. But Bell Labs and the telephone system, safe and secure from market forces in its monopoly enclave, controlled by a self-perpetuating, technologically competent bureaucracy, sensitized to social purposes and answerable to the political authority is (or was) the very model of the public management of a multifaceted, technologically-complex activity.

The experience with synthetic rubber has been used (misinterpreted and misunderstood) to rationalize recent policies for the development of energy technology. Hardly an appropriate model, the synthetic rubber program was a scandalous, nearly catastrophic failure of wartime planning and a complete failure in the peacetime planning of technological advance. If we need an American model for the technological development task under public aegis, take NASA, or the Manhattan Project, or Admiral Rickover's nuclear submarine. All are flawed, no doubt; but they are perhaps the best we have.

There are nevertheless lessons to be learned from the synthetic rubber experience. We should learn not to rely on U.S. corporate enterprise to develop and sustain new from-the-ground-up technologies, or assume, even by the measure of profits, that what they do not develop is not worth developing. Synthetic rubber has been highly profitable: as an operation in itself, as an outlet for petroleum derivatives, and as a low-cost source for a raw material that tire manufacturers can tailor to their specifications. But American corporations did not invent and develop the technology. When it was developed, they would not invest in establishing a synthetic rubber industry, even when faced with the possibility of a total cutoff of natural rubber supplies; and at the close of World War II, they would not sustain it during the transitional period of technological shakedown and development.

If by selling better deep drilling equipment to the Soviets, they are able to find new sources of oil, we will benefit, because the pressure on dwindling world supplies will thereby be lessened. If the Indians develop new and better techniques of solar heating and cooling, we will benefit, not only because inevitably we will use those techniques but also because the Indians in using them will lessen the pressure on dwindling supplies of oil. If French scientists should develop a technology that could produce synoil from coal at $20 a barrel, but in response to the availability of that technology OPEC reduced the price of oil from $30 to $19.50 a barrel so that the operation was unprofitable, France would nevertheless benefit and so would we. In this world where all drink from the same depleting well, and we all face the same threat of closure upon our economic life, a sensible R&D program to develop energy technologies would be transnational, drawing on the scientific and technological process of all the oil consuming societies, regardless of their political complexion. Alas for Americans there is more at stake today than the advantages of collaborating in a transnational program. For the American State at this time (for only an interim, hopefully) is without the competence and without the inclination to engage in or to support any program for the development of new energy technologies. Given our government cop out, it becomes the more important to seek foundation support for a strong and continuing liaison with ongoing R&D programs for the development of energy technologies in Germany,[66] in France, in Brazil, in Great Britain, and in Japan.

The appropriate aim and objective of such a development program far transcends the development of synfuel or any other specific energy source. It should as well probe and explore avenues for the development of technologies for the conservation storage, transportation or transmission, and for the more efficient utilization of energies across the board. The development of cleaner, safer, lower cost coal mining technologies may be more important for the development of a viable synfuel than the development of technologies for the conversion of coal into synthetic fuel. By-product development and the development of by-product outlets can be of the greatest significance; natural gas after all, and for generations, was a waste product of petroleum outputs. Technologies for the low cost and safe disposition of waste can be of enormous importance; they are critical in the case of atomic energy and perhaps in coal gasification. Nor should all this be left to any R&D establishment. The R&D establishment does not weigh the costs and benefits, the risk and payoff, in the choice of avenues of inquiry. It will of itself follow the grooved-in path and the habituated practice. It must be managed, directed; for which there must be the competence.

Beyond the organization and direction of public sector R&D, public management would have the task of exercising surveillance on research and exploration wherever it was conducted in order to evaluate and select out potentials for the development/innovation pipeline: this in turn geared into the dynamic plan to maintain or upgrade the energy infrastructure inasmuch as this was not occurring spontaneously through corporate initiatives. It would besides, assess environmental and social impacts of planned or anticipated transformations and undertake to offset detrimental impacts and to provide infrastructural supports.

---

[66]For some facts on the ongoing, 13 billion DM West German R&D program on coal-based synfuel, see "Coal Synfuel Facility Survey," *National Coal Association* (August, 1980), pp. 65–76

A POLICY FOR THE COMMUNICATIONS INFRASTRUCTURE

The venerable post office once the keystone of the communication infrastructure, with ancient roots and an almost forgotten tradition of indomitable service, victim of current fashion, has donned the robes of conversion and been baptized with the waters of free enterprise. Subordinated to the control of borrowed businessmen, it masquerades (not to much effect) as a private business corporation. Neither fish nor foul, it has abandoned the motivating forces of pride, tradition, duty that can be invoked in service to the state, but it cannot attain the discipline of the competitive market nor enjoy the opportunities of the competitive game.

Eminently efficient, technologically progressive, commanding the loyal service of a vast working host, unfailing in the fulfillment of its commitment to investors, providing an integral and a universally accessible service at stable rates and yet operating outside the domain of market competition, the telephone company would seem to demonstrate the possibility, indeed to provide a model for the development of viable, efficient, progressive agencies of the positive state. Yet the telephone company is currently under antitrust attack. And it may well be that whatever its achievements in the past, things are now going wrong. It well may be that structural corrections would lead to an increase in efficiency, in productivity, in an acceleration of technological advance. Whether or not this is so, neither lawyers nor the Department of Justice are equipped or able to act as social engineers with standards of performance (cost, price, equity, productivity, employment opportunity, technological creativity) in mind; nor have they any notion of the consequences of structural change for efficiency, productivity, innovation, technological progress, or equity in the distribution of income. They operate only by reference to a grotesquely irrelevant

model of pure competition. They come into the fray as giant killers with no objective
other than to carve a notch in the handle of the antitrust gun, little Saint Georges
out to kill the dragon.

Finally, along with the other agencies of federal regulation, the FCC is in the
process of dismemberment and dismantlement. But it will not be problems and issues
related to these established components of the communication infrastructure that
will detain us here. For the energy infrastructure, our concern was with surmounting
a crisis. Here it will be with grasping and exploiting a not-to-be-repeated opportunity
before that opportunity vanishes.

A Conjunction of Technologies

The past several decades have witnessed the extraordinary development of two
distinct sets or arrays of technologies; first, of computers with the capacity for the
storage in memory banks, of unbounded quantities of information, and for the
programmed manipulation of that information at an incredible speed and, beyond
a quantity threshold, at a very low cost; and second, in technologies for the electronic
transmission of sound, image, and notation, by laser or cable or microwave or
telecast or satellite. The two sets of technologies are moving into a conjunction
possibly to become component parts of an integral functional system, tying the
massive, low cost, global transmission of image, sound, and recorded observation
into the massive, low cost capability to store, organize, automatically interpret, or
otherwise program the use of that which has been transmitted.

Thus emerges the prospect of an integral system with an immense transmission
webwork to carry encoded image, sound, and symbol from anywhere to anywhere,
serving (1) for person to person communication, (2) for the ingathering of information inputs and recorded observations from numerous points of origin and their
sorting and storing, storing for selective release in functional control and problem
solving, and (3) for mass and selective broadcasts and telecasts. These multipurpose
technologies are complimentary and competitive, overlapping and integrable with
respect to particular functions and purposes. In quite the same way, roads, railroads,
canals, rivers, river barges, container ships, freighters, tankers, pipelines, automobiles, trucks, trailers and piggy back trailers, busses, airplanes and airfields are
complimentary and competitive technologies, integrable with respect to particular
function and purpose, alike components of the national transportation system.

Call this functional system for the Electronic Transmission and Processing of
Information (ETPI). In what we do or fail to do, in its actuality or in its potentiality,
in its positive and in its negative values, ETPI must become a critical component
of the communications infrastructure.

Nor is this the first time that technologies have been arrayed on the threshold
of revolutionary transformations. It was so with the railroad, the airplane, the
pipeline, long distance transmission of electric power, the telegraph, the telephone,
wireless broadcasting, telecasting. Invariably the state has become involved and
deeply involved in subsidizing, in activating, in regulating such transformations. But
never has there been an attempt to conceptualize and organize and provide for the
rational development through time of an integrated system to perform a basic

function of the infrastructure, except in the case of the telephone where a great corporate monopoly has planned and acted in proxy for the state to develop the national and transnational organization of that integral function. Rather our infrastructural systems have evolved, irreversible bit upon irreversible bit, each a piecemeal event that constrains and fixes the direction of the next piecemeal event, following the initiatives of numerous public and private agencies with narrowly vectored interests, until our future is locked into what has been haphazardly formed. For all that we are now paying a heavy price.

The challenge to which this essay would respond is to prevision and to explore the potentialities inherent in this conjunction of technologies, and to propose a program for achieving the values of a rationally organized, national, and transnational system for the electronic transmission and processing of information.

The Grid

The rational development of ETPI must take the form of a national grid. We think of such usually in terms of the electrical power grids established and invaluable in every advanced industrialized country of the world, except (alas) the United States. Those grids have power generating centers linked by transmission lines to networks that control the availability and distribute electric power to factories and farms and private homes and public places. Transmission lines also link together distribution networks and link together also the power generating centers, with controls on the cross-flow of electric power designed to provide a back up of power reserves in the case of emergency or maintenance shutdowns, and also to enable a fuller, lower-cost utilization of the efficient power generating units.

The ETPI grid would not be the same, it would operate through input points (ranging for the nonterrestrial observation by earth-orbiting satellites to recorded bank deposits, or the payment of tax dollars, or hospital-recorded footprints of the new born infant) with information carried as image, sound, or symbol by the diverse technologies of transmission, to computing centers. These would process the incoming streams of information and, as programmed, transmit that information in raw or processed form to the memory banks at storage centers, in order to compare, share, accumulate, and restructure data. From the storage centers via the computing centers, processed data programmed according to demand would be transmitted to clients (businesses, libraries, public agencies, individuals) via a distribution network. In-and-out transmissions would be by telephone, cable, satellite, laser, microwave, as is appropriate for the input source and the receptivity point. Transmission facilities would operate as a common carrier and the computer/storage centers would operate as a public service, universally available at a standard price. Nothing would preclude the coexistence of individually owned and operated transmission/computer/storage facilities and services anymore than the existence of a public electrical power system precludes the ownership and operation of an electrical generator, or a public telephone system precludes the ownership and operation of a private intercom.

NASA, already involved via its observational and communications satellites, is obviously the agency to plan, develop, and control ETPI as an integral component of the communications infrastructure. In contrast to what must occur under a no-policy of chance and drift, the selfsame facilities for ETPI could serve virtually unlimited sets of objectives, responding to highly variable and unfolding circumstances, needs, values, interests, purposes, and cognitive capabilities; but only if ETPI is rationally conceived and designed as an integral national and transnational system, open to the multifaceted demands and purposes of a society swept by rapid currents of change. Indeed it is the design of the system that will determine the spectrum of its possible use and potential values and, as an element of the infrastructure, that will be instrumental in determining character of society.

Surveillance and Control

A national and transnational system of ETPI would provide an entirely unprecedented capacity for low cost, universal surveillance of natural phenomena and social event, and in so doing provide the information base for policy implementation and control. That ETPI network observing through automated means (sensors, cameras, measurement devices) or otherwise, from points throughout the world and in space, recording, transmitting, storing observations, and through computer programs that operate continuously and autonomously or that are tailored to special problems and transitory phenomena, interpreting and generalizing upon the universe from which the data was drawn, could be geared to a diversity of purposes. The enormous power of the instrument could be harnessed to universalize and vastly extend what is now being done in fragments and bits by laborious means and without the possibility of aggregating, generalizing, or drawing upon the common information store to be examined from many perspectives and brought to bear in the solution of a variety of problems.

Such a system could be used to monitor the biosphere with space sensors to observe, record and transmit information concerning the condition of the atmospheric layers that enfold the earth; this linked with the observation and recording of those exudations (wastes, pollutants) from natural catastrophe, industrial chemistry, atomic radiation, with programs to calculate and chart the relationships between these inputs into the atmosphere and the conditions of the biosphere; that linked to a worldwide recording, reporting, analysis, and forecasting of temperature and weather, and in relation to the formation and movement of storm, hurricane, typhoon, tornado, tidal wave, fog, and flood, with programs continuously exploring climatic and biospheric relationships; that linked to the continuous, worldwide recording of movement in the earth's crusts and of its internal geophysical turmoil, and of soil structures and of soil conditions, and of the nutritional deficiencies of flora as a basis for conservation-planning and the maintenance or upgrading of soil fertility and of the location, movement, and condition of fish and wildlife populations, and of the location and migration pattern of locusts and other insects and their predators, and the continuous, automated observation and computer-programmed analysis of the chemical composition, levels of pollution, and toxic elements in rivers, lakes, oceans, air currents, and in the soil, and in the food chains; all geared to and programmed to produce information relevant in understanding and controlling the basic ecological systems.

The ETPI system could be used as well to provide a continuous stream of information (a) on employment, disemployment, unemployment, quasiemployment by all occupational, regional, sex, race, age categories, and on the composition, expectations, aspirations of the unemployed or quasiemployed; (b) on production in relation to plant capacity, by industry, by region, by firm, by plant; (c) on invention and innovation in product and process; (d) on output planning and output mix; (e) on inventories; (f) on investment intention, and investment actualized in the procurement of categories of industrial equipment, and of investment in R&D, and in other quantifiable elements of the process of technological transformation; (g) on productivities; (h) on mergers and the changing topographies of corporate control; (i) on accident, injury, and work-related illness; (j) on wages and net incomes by work-related categories and by region, race, age, sex; (k) on the distribution of wealth and income, and on the degrees of inequality, overall and in relation to work, regional, age, education, race; (l) on locational shifts in economic activities and populations; (m) on intercity, interregional, international trade flows; (n) on changes in price and in product quality; (o) on the matrix of input and output coefficients; with the analysis of all this programmed to satisfy the variety of research interests, to provide information useful for client groups, and to provide an information base relevant in the formation or monitoring of public policies. Linked to all this, ETPI could monitor the social condition via the ingathering of indicators such as suicides, stress-syndromes, categories of crime, varieties of drug use and alcoholism, marriage and divorce, programmed to determine and explore the relationships between the social condition and economic, demographic, environmental variables, all simultaneously inputs into the system. Linked with all of this, the system of ETPI would organize a continuous, worldwide reporting of the varieties of illnesses and disease and of psychosomatic syndromes, correlating the change in their magnitude and character, and their movement territorially in time and as between age, sex, race, and income categories with the data on physical environment, economic change, and the social condition, as might conceivably be related to physical health and mental stability; thereby to introduce new dimensions of medical research and disease control.

These are, of course, only potentials for surveillance. What would in fact be practiced given the existence of an integral system of ETPI would depend on scientific and political interests as they come to exist and develop over time. But certainly it is clear; the potentials for surveillance would be very great, and that such surveillance could be for purposes, and could have consequences that are malevolent as well as benevolent.

Given ETPI, it becomes feasible and "economic" to have immediately available the health record, the record of criminal offenses and misdemeanors, the record of earnings and other income receipts, of savings and expenditures, a work record, a record of residences, of education and training, of publication, of political associations, of participation in organizations, in demonstrations, in meetings, a record of the opinions of neighbors, friends, and enemies concerning the moral character, political sympathies, associations, activities of every American from birth until death.

Every category of event subject to surveillance will have its proponents and its social values. Health records are valuable for medical treatment and in preventive medicine. The record of the individual's financial transactions, his spatial movements, and his encounters with the law are all relevant to and useful in crime control. The complete income and expenditure record can provide the basis for a more equitable and efficient tax system, and so on.

We are confronted with an old issue, in a radically more volatile form. If surveillance extends the powers of control, how far should the powers of control be extended? And who is to exercise those controls, under what constraints, and with what individual safeguards?

ETPI as a national system would enable a universal income-expenditures balancing and credit clearing mechanism, with debits offset against credit continuously, permitting an immediate check on the liquidity and credit line of any individual, business firm, or institutional entity. It could eliminate the need for cash and checks and, in large part, replace the function of the commercial bank. The credit card has carried us a considerable distance in this direction already.

As the universal mechanism for credit and exchange, monitoring every receipt and expenditure, ETPI would provide a very powerful instrument for precise tax assessment and collection on an income or on an expenditure basis. Moreover, the continuum of recorded financial transactions, specifying sources of income, objects of expenditure, the recipients of expenditures, gifts and transfers, the place and the time of each transaction would constitute a means of monitoring, policing, and controlling the behavior of firms and individuals.

How are the values of control to be balanced against the intrinsic worth of privacy? What will be the psychological effect of coexistence with the machine that records so much and never forgets?

ETPI as a national system could enormously magnify the powers of surveillance and control, and that control could be exercised by those (whom you and I might consider) the wrong people for the wrong purposes. It could assist in tracking down of ideological heresy, and cracking down on political dissent. Anyhow, surveillance itself is unpleasant. We don't like to be watched. We don't like to be policed. We treasure our "air of freedom." At least it is incumbent upon us to foresee, forewarn, and prepare institutional protections against dangers to privacy and freedom.

The Dangers of Surveillance?

In the Orwellian fantasy, Big Brother speaks from the television screen, the moving cameras are watching, the electronic ear is listening, there is no escape. Electronic surveillance is the devil's instrument. The powers of electronic surveillance are a libertarian nightmare. It is a nightmare that has its source in a deep psychic confusion, intermingling the experience of the ideological absolutism of totalitarian states with an awakening from the old imageries of individualized choice into the reality of the universe of systems.

In fact the ferocious force of ideological absolutism is as old as human society. Throughout history it has had, and has exercised the power to strip the individual naked of all protection, to drive him to his knees, and to purge his mind of heresy and doubt. The Catholic inquisition with its flaming fields of heretics burning alive needed no ETPI, nor did the Okhrana of the Russian czar, nor did those terrible waves of Stalinist purgings, nor did the Nazis in their upsurge from the gutters, nor did the Cultural Revolution in China, nor did our own McCarthyites. ETPI had no role on the Gulag Archipelago. Those are terrors, not particular to futureworld, but of an ancient ignorance and a recurrent madness. Here the threat is not ETPI and its powers of surveillance, but is of any genre of ideological absolutism.

Mingled with that menace is the other specter that haunts the liberal's vision of futureworld: the end of property-based autonomy, of individualized choice, and one-to-one relationships in a society of exchange, where instead the individual occupies but a tiny niche in systems vast and complex beyond his comprehending, and where he is confronted with invisible mechanisms of control and distant and disembodied signals of command, his existence bound into the intermeshed and moving matrices of a plan. Orwell reduced that complexity to the familiar form of synthetic man, and gave to it the face, the voice, the purpose of Big Brother. Such, he prophesied, would be the human condition in 1984.

We live now in his dreaded decade of the 1980s. And the universe of systems prevails. And the powers of electronic technology have gone beyond the Orwellian fantasy. But no Big Brother! No futureworld! Instead of stultifying constraint and of total control, with difference and idiosyncrasy stripped away, ours is a time of unprecedented "liberations" and unconstraint. The danger of our time is exactly the converse of the prophecy. It is of the disintegration of control, the end of constraint. The price and the consequence of that is a rage of crime, the crime of the streets, assault, rape, robbery, murder on a scale not before imagined, and bribery and corruption in the high offices of power, and the worldwide terrorism and casual assassination by urban guerrillas. This very disintegration of control and constraint, with its liberations on the one side and its criminality on the other, is a consequence of the transformation of societies from the world of man to the universe of system. In the older style community there were indeed constraints of iron. In rural, in village, in small town life there was and is a surveillance, life-to-death, more total and compelling than any ever devised through television monitor, phone tap, and electronic bugging, where the eye of thy neighbor watches from every window, where the sign and mark of ancestry, and of childhood, of follies and of crimes, of works, and of wanderings, of illness, and of breakdown are all embodied irretrievably in the circle of surrounding memories.

But in the city, the community of passerbys, where each is to each a stranger; and, slotted in roles that have been stamped out with the same stamp, in-out of the anonymity of niches in the overreaching facades and in the innards of systems, the stranger is lost even to the eye of the stranger. The old spontaneous neighbor upon neighbor mode of surveillance can be no more. And yet there cannot be a constraint upon or containment of the explosion of crime and terror without surveillance, without keeping tabs, without marking Cain with the mark of Cain as a warning to his brothers. In the universe of systems, the old way gone and irretrievable, it is only through the rational use of ETPI, that effective surveillance is possible.

The old is no longer workable, and the new has its dangers. Nor will the traditional formula of freedoms and liberties and inalienable rights suffice to guide us in developing an alternative way. Rather, in staking out areas of action and those of protection, we had best begin at the beginning, to ask "What's important?" "What kind of living are we after?" "How to organize the organization and get from it what we value?"

What is it, for example, beneath the slogans, beyond the "sacred principles" of freedom of speech, and freedom of the press, that we really want? What are the opportunities we would insure; and on what processes would we rely, and from these, what values do we look for?

Is it the right of pornographers to peddle smut and titillation? Is it the press baron's freedom to unload the slime of private foibles for the sake of a quick and easy buck? Is it the right of provocateurs to march down city streets in the bedsheets of the KKK or wearing the uniforms of Nazis? If that is what we value and would protect, then we have good reason to congratulate ourselves, for we have pretty well protected those rights and values. But I don't think it is. Our objectives I suggest are or ought to be of another order. What is to be sought for, I would hold, and what ought to be the purpose in terms of which we shape law and policy are (1) to enable the individual to enter into and meaningfully to participate as an independent and thinking being, that is, to express his needs and to have his say in the processes of group and collective choice; and (2) to have and to maintain a public discourse where the whole spectrum of outlooks and potentials for choice are fully and deeply explored and openly debated; and (3) where what is relevant to individual and to public choice is examined, studied, reported, and interpreted diligently and in depth and from diverse perspectives. If these are the values to be sought for, and by which the media and the opportunities to publish and to speak are to be judged and evaluated, then we have no reason to congratulate ourselves. The information laid upon us by the instruments of public communication is shallow, filtered through stereotypical preconception, without depth of analysis or significant variety in perspective. And in no Western society is the spectrum of (political, philosophical) discourse so narrow and bland as in ours. But let it be noted, that to change any of this requires a recreation of social organization and no mere holding the line on the "freedom" and "liberty" of individualized choice.

The public and the public press have no right to that which is not of legitimate public concern and can have no bearing on public choice. The individual has no right to withhold information that is of public concern and bears on public choice. Financial records are not the same as bed sheets, and I can conceive of no loss of human values or social opportunity or in the capacity for individual self-fulfillment in opening all financial records for full public surveillance. Nor is it conceivable to me that the capacity of some to evade taxation through foreign accounts and hidden manipulation, shifting the burden of public costs upon all the rest, serves to preserve or protect any human value or social good.

The use of ETPI to maintain for every individual from birth to death, a continuing and current record of the physical condition, of symptomologies, of diagnoses, of sicknesses, of breakdowns, of medicines, of therapies, of treatments, of hospitalization, of confinements, of responses and of cures, of the environmental conditions of living, could be extremely useful as a basis for medical research and of great value in dealing with the problems of the individual as well. But the existence of such a record of illness or mental breakdown might be a burden and an embarrassment in applying for a job, in running for an elective office, in seeking admission to a professional school. A complete and current record of criminality linked to a continuous surveillance of the movements and activity of those possessing such a record would protect those who might be victimized by crime. But it would not be agreeable for the criminal. And it could be protested that some early mistake, some juvenile delinquency should not foreclose future opportunities or burden a whole career. There is another side to it as well, for there is protection to the individual in universal revelation. When the full record is open, a particular failing falls into its proper perspective. When the closets are emptied of all the skeletons, then a few bones are the sign no more of a freak and a monster but only of the fallibilities of everyman and anyman.

The danger is not in universal surveillance but in selective surveillance, vengeful and at the direction of an ideological absolute, that drives truth into hiding. With ETPI or without it, ideological absolutism is the menace to be guarded against.

The Automated Library

A national or transnational system of ETPI would constitute a powerful research tool in its capacity for the accumulation and storage, for the programmed manipulation, and for the search for and retrieval of stored information. Consider this capacity for the enormously rapid search and retrieval of an unbounded body of information, to be made universally available through the "automated library."

The technique of search could be in the familiar mode, following user's specification of subject/author of any other established system of clueing, for example, by reference to key words in predetermined sets which, in a separate operation had been noted in the texts. Thus specifying "blessed virgin," I would receive a reference list of theological tracts in which that term appears. Or the search could take another form, matching the encoded character of an existing body or of an incoming stream of information, against "profiles" of the user's objectives, interests, or queries. I might profile, for example, the subject areas covered in my course on "public expenditure," which would then be matched automatically with, and I would receive reference lists covering, the stream of newly available reports, documents, articles, books, relevant to the subject matter of the course. Thus NASA has installed in several universities a system for profiling and coding the technological interests of client firms and, by using encoded keys that signal the particular relevancies and characteristics of its research reports, matching firm profiles against the large incoming stream of encoded space-related R&D materials, with such research outputs as might be of interest to each client firm, continuously searched for and selected out. Similarly, by encoding the results of a series of medical tests made upon an individual ("profiling" the individual's physical condition) and matching these against syndrome patterns prespecified in medical analytics or abstracted from medical case histories, the automated library could immediately pull information useful in diagnosis and treatment. So also it could search law cases for precedents and relevant decisions as part of the lawyer's task in developing a brief. So it could be organized for the spot or continuous searching for information to specification of interest or in response to inquiry.

Beyond reference lists it could transmit abstracts, or the textual information to be read or replicated in schools, offices, laboratories, hospitals, production sites, factories, and homes. Given an integrated national system for the electronic transmission and processing of information, it would be technically feasible (and far more economic than the present system of procurement and storage by many separate libraries and through the printing and distribution of printed matter) that I sit at my desk and you at yours, and that we each have immediately available to us for reading or replication, every text of every book, article, document, report available, say, in the Library of Congress.

But what of the problem of arranging for permission and negotiating suitable royalty payments of copyright holders for every such work in that great library? What is technologically achievable and economically feasible may be institutionally impossible.

NASA has reproduced the whole gamut of Soviet and East European scientific publications on $3'' \times 5''$ microfiche so that the entire journal library can be stored in a few square feet, and every page can be read or cheaply replicated for the researcher's use. These libraries have been made available to the agency's scientific personnel in laboratories and offices throughout the country. But nothing similar could be done for American or West European journals and papers because of copyright constraints.

We have seen that information is distinguished from every other form of economic resource in this very important respect, that the real cost of its incremental use is zero. Granted that society is best served when information is made freely available to all, such is the rule of the public good. Still, while the incremental use of existing information is costless, it certainly costs something to produce it in the first place, and those costs must be covered. As a means of motivating the costly production of important categories of information, copyrights and patents have been used to convert information into property. Hence the institutions that promote the production of information serve also to constrain its use to below the social optimum. That paradox is not new. But new technology, by greatly increasing the technological potential for free access and widespread use, correspondingly magnifies the cost, measured by opportunities lost, of these traditional constraints. When information is conveyed by a book or a journal, the copyright holder's monopoly is normally a minor barrier to dissemination. Far more significant are the costs of publication and of distribution. But inasmuch as ETPI makes possible the rapid, massive, and universal transmission or replication of information at something approaching zero marginal costs, the property format creates a formidable, perhaps eventually an intolerable gap between what is technologically feasible and what institutionally permissible.

Our existing system for the conveyance of property rights in information, developed in centuries past, is certainly not the only way to motivate its production and dissemination. The advent of ETPI demands a search for alternative institutional means of fulfilling this very vital function in ways compatible with the potentialities of the new technology.

Market Power

Inasmuch as facilities for the electronic transmission and for the high-powered computer processing of information are costly, and economical in use only when very large volumes of data are processed and communicated, and inasmuch as such facilities are items of private property available only through purchase or rent, their use will be more or less confined to big public and private organizations. Hence and to that degree the benefits of the advancing ETPI technology will accrue only to large enterprise. The small firm will be less able to survive in competition with the large; and the economies of scale will become a more formidable barrier to new entry.

But if ETPI is developed as an integral national (utility) system organized to service the public at large with transmission facilities organized as common carriers, with computers and data banks built into the grid, and with information and programs in memory cores to be selected out for the client's purposes, available to all on a shared time basis, then ETPI technology would be neutral as between big and small enterprise; and indeed by providing access to programs designed by specialists and to large bodies of data relevant for market forecasting, production planning, and product design (now available only to the large), ETPI could much improve the relative position of the small independent.

The Cable

The advent of an intergral, national, or transnational system of ETPI, rationally organized and deliberately developed, may seem distant and improbable. There is, however, another transformation of the system of electronic transmission, technologically simple but of great social consequence, directly and immediately upon us —that of cable television. There is nothing technologically new in this mode of transmission developed by small operators in communities off the beaten track as a means of receiving telecasts beyond the range on antenae set up on private homes. But once the cable is laid in the city, with virtually everyone owning a TV receiver and where every TV receiver can readily be wired for cable telecasting, there then ensues a basic change in the potentialities for communications.

These are some of the salient facts:

1. The cable is rapidly becoming a general element in the system of television broadcasting.

2. The costs of laying the cable, and of tying it into home receivers, and of merchandising the service may be considerable. But, given all that, the incremental cost of wiring in a virtually unlimited number of channels with the initial installation, in addition to those linked into regularly available broadcasts, is very small. This is a fact of greatest importance to public planning and control. Thus it would make very little difference in costs, whether the initial cable is wired to deliver 20 channels or 400. Once the

cable is installed, however, it then does become costly, and correspondingly more difficult to require that more channels be made available.

Consider the character and history of broadcasting in the United States. Of all the great nations of the world, only in the United States has radio and television been left more or less entirely to the market, its development dictated by considerations of profits. The primary role of the Federal Communications Commission and of its predecessor agency has been to allocate an absolutely limited, very scarce, and enormously valuable commodity—the airwaves. The allocation of a space on the airwaves became in effect an inalienable license, the private property of rich men and big corporations, acquired by them from the public without charge, without fee, without the auctioning of rights, exercised without conditions except certain easy rules in the interests of public acceptability. The very lack of Congressional protest or of Presidential resistance to this big and blatant giveaway to the rich, tells something surely about the competence and character of the American political system. Inequity, however, is not the real issue; what matters is performance. And it must be conceded that left to the market, following the dictates of profit, mainline broadcasting in the United States developed into a highly effective instrument of mass entertainment, with a news "coverage" that, if shallow, at least has been pleasingly packaged. The increasing hunger for quality has generated institutional and university broadcasting, and more recently a public radio and television/network relying on voluntary contributions and foundation support and importing a good part of its fare from the British Broadcasting Corporation.

Mainline broadcasting in the United States, as an effective instrument of mass entertainment, has added an important dimension to American life; and, our tastes being what they are, our culture being what it is, it is highly improbable that the very scarce space of the airwaves could have been used for any other purpose. It is here that cable makes the difference. With not 13 or 30 television channels available, but 400, where each gives the same high quality image and offers the same ease of access, then aside from and in addition to satisfying the public's need for, and the merchandiser's interest in mass entertainment, it becomes possible to plan and to install a broadcasting system of another genra that has as its objective to develop the range of social discourse, to vitalize the political system, and to serve the interests of education and art.

While the installation of the cable can bring to an end the old scarcity of the airwaves, and hence eliminate the monopoly powers of telecasting companies and national television networks, correspondingly reducing the value of their licenses, the cable itself represents a new and powerful monopoly controlling access home by home, street by street, city by city to all of the potentially boundless fare that could become available through the new medium. Reflecting a mood of radical libertarianism in the face of the rapid installation of the cable, and the hard-to-change formation of its basic technology, the Federal Communications Commission is detaching itself from responsibility and denuding itself of function. And neither Congress nor the Executive display any concern at all for a technological formation that may be irreversible, and potential social benefits that may be lost irretrievably. Instead, franchising arrangements are left to local governments, with the resurgence, inevitable, given the character of local governments, of giveaways and payoffs, overt and covert, reminiscent of the episodes that Lincoln Steffens and the muckrackers described. But that too is of small importance. The great threat is of opportunities lost forever. If they are not to be lost, the state must act; with the federal imposition of the standards required for the interconnection of networks and the development of an integral national system of cable telecasting, with something approaching universal access. With each cable franchise, a private company, receiving from the public a valuable, possibly an enormously valuable property right, should be expected to give something in return for that right; not in cash or rents, but in so selecting, organizing, installing, and operating its cable technology that the basis is laid for a national system to serve the public interest. To that end the following should be required.

1. That all installations make available 400 channels, to be reserved for public purposes; those channels being subject to allocation by a designated federal authority.

2. That cable services be made available at a standard rate to all private and public entities within the block of territory covered by the franchise, with that to include all adjoining suburban areas except when nonfeasibility of so doing can be clearly established. The purpose here is simply to assure the availability of service not only for high income, high density areas where the profit-to-cost ratio is likely to be high, but throughout the populated areas. For the purposes of a national system, universality of access is of prime importance.

3. That all cable companies shall be subject, at the discretion of a designated federal agency, to rate regulation on the criterion that rates should not exceed operating costs plus a fair return on *original* investment, that is, the sum of funds actually spent for legitimate purposes of investment; hence that authenticated records of such expenditures be filed with a designated federal agency (in the first instance with the Securities and Exchange Commission). This in order to safeguard against an exercise of the gatekeeper's monopoly power to limit at will and for purpose of private gain, public access to the cable offerings made through a national network. Requiring original investment as the basis of possible regulation, would prevent companies from capitalizing their worth on the basis of unwarranted profits, and then justifying high rates as no more than allowing a fair return on capitalized worth.

Given compatible distribution networks, the designated federal agency should undertake to establish interconnections for the transmission of public programs between those networks. Through a subsidiary agency, it would also lay cable and make cable services available where private companies have failed to do so, at least to the extent that there is a reasonable expectation that revenues from rental fees might eventually cover costs; this again in the interest of making access to the national system universally available.

Thus could be brought into existence an integral, national system able to offer 400 or more channels of publicly sponsored telecasts to each of the great majority of American households. But all this is only to establish a technological potential. It says nothing about the purposes and substantive character of the system, as it might emerge through time.

The Spectrum of Discourse

There are consequences, boundaries of and constraints imposed upon any system that transmits sound and image to a vast and heterogeneous body of recipients, from but a few broadcasting centers; when, in a word, the airwaves are scarce and the audience is huge. Call these consequences the laws of the mass audience:

1. That the messages must be directed to the lowest common denominator and confined to the boundaries thereof, so that what is said is understandable if not to all, then at least to very large numbers; so that broadcasts focus on that which is of interest, if not to all, then at least to very large numbers; so that any interlinked sequence of thought and argument cannot overtax by its length and complexity the concentration span if not of all, then at least of the very large numbers. Hence, that there can be no dealing in depth, no transcendence of the conventional, no climbing steps, step by step, of an edifice of thought.

2. That the words are mouthed, the message is given not by persons but personages, with the enormous, paper-thin reality of figures painted on billboards; synthetic words spoken by synthetic beings.

3. That there can be no discourse. The performer on the podium performs. The passive audience watches from its invisible distance.

But with the cable, transmission escapes the necessity of these laws of the mass audience. An unlimited number of channels can be made available at a low incremental cost. It becomes feasible economically for the medium to serve the interests of relatively small and homogeneous audiences, of physicists or even high energy physicists or biophysicists, medical practicioners, and even gynecologists, or orthopedists, or cardiologists, or neurologists, or psychiatrists, or psychoanalysts, civil engineers, and electrical engineers, and chemical engineers, and engineers who work on synfuel, or those who are concerned with air conditioning, balletomaniacs, stamp collectors, and art collectors, and those passionately devoted to the art of German expressionism, Marxists, Buddhists, devotees of Zen, poets or devotees of Russian poetry, soccer fans, preschool children, connoisseurs of the new theatre, and so on and on and on.

Then the medium can become an instrument of discourse. Discourse becomes possible. Controversy, debate, passionate involvement become possible. In the diverse corners of the world, or rather through communication linkages that bring together from all the corners of the world those who share a knowledge of, and an interest in subjects that then can be dealt with at length, in depth, and in detail, climbing, step by step, an edifice of thought; and, through such discourse, raising higher that edifice. The audience could merge into the mass for that which was of general and overriding interest and of mass concern, and still divide itself into workable communities of discourse. In that way the medium of communication would serve to associate, to integrate, to stimulate, passionately to involve, to disalienate the individual and to enrich the social life. Particularly would this apply to the development of meaningful political discourse.

Politics

There are at least these three regions of failure in our political system, where ETPI has been of consequence and where the cable could make a difference: (1) in the continuous formation of a basis, a blueprint, for public choice that is acceptable and works in equating purpose to policy, policy to its implementation, and implementation to the sought for objectives; (2) in the recruitment and selection of political "leadership"; and (3) in enabling an effective participation of the governed in the processes of government.

Even with the most inept of political systems, there is the illusion of participation and democracy seems viable in times when beliefs are strongly held and are generally shared and a common ideology prevails and when the accepted operating blueprint for public choice is working well. For in such times, the political organization closed and self-serving though it may be, and even a "leadership" of creeping morons has no problem in echoing the credos of its partisans, in "representing" the will of the people, in satisfying the expectations of the electorate without disappointing client groups, or disturbing the play of the players in the political game. But when the built-in blueprint of public choice is no longer workable, when there ceases to be a depth of consensus or any strongly held and generally shared beliefs, when the charts of navigation are gone and the sightings of the helmsman becomes of paramount importance, when in the gathering of clouds and on the dark horizon, there are only questions demanding answers; in a word in times like ours of ideological bankruptcy and of alienation and frustration, the illusion of representatives who represent, of a leadership that leads, and of a general participation in the process of governance are tested and vanquished.

It all hinges on finding our way to an ideology that unifies and a blueprint that works; and if this is something that must come out of society, and must be understood and accepted by society, then at least or at most one can attempt to conceive of and to develop the conditions favorable for social creativity and social learning. For that a viable system of discourse, where thought can enter from many sides and be viewed and judged from a diversity of perspectives, is surely prerequisite. Thus the importance of the indicated development in the system of electronic transmission as a precondition for the continuous formation of a workable, acceptable basis for public choice.

What of the quality of our political leadership, even at the level of the presidency itself, a place of the most critical responsibility, of enormous opportunity and the richest rewards? At the time of this writing in 1981, with the vast human resources of this great nation from which to draw, the Presidency belongs to Ronald Reagan, and before Reagan to Jimmy Carter, before Carter to Jerry Ford, and before Ford, to Richard Nixon! How is it that our political system manages to recruit and select out and send such as these to the top? Surely that feat is accounted for in part at least as a consequence of the laws of the mass audience, and by the character of communication, in press, radio, and television shaped by those laws.

How was Abe Lincoln recruited for the tasks of government? He was selected out and elected by the people of his community because they knew him, and well. Living, working, talking, they knew his character and ideas; he was a teacher from whom they learned. As their champion and representative, he was selected out and supported by a larger audience after they listened to and tested the metal of his thought in long debate where no hold was barred. Through the judgment of the people themselves of Abe Lincoln as one amongst themselves, he entered and rose to the crest of the political system.

It doesn't happen that way now. It cannot because we are no longer a country of small towns and of families rooted in the land. For most of us, isolated in our specialized niches, atomized by the vastness, complexity and movement of this urbanized society, that capacity for a wide and intimate knowing of each other and for the spontaneous choice by the community of its leadership, is gone. Our recruitment is handled instead by political professionals through the machinery of party organization.

The path to political "leadership," with us has been either through selection by, or through trading with and working through the pros of a political organization that encompasses the parties, vast and loose conglomerates of professionals, amateurs and hangers-on, runners and stamp-lickers, politicians in and out of office, operating in wards and districts, in legislatures and as commissioners, chiefs, mayors, bosses, councilmen, congressmen, senators, governors, each with a bit to bring to the pot, and ready to scoop out from the pot with a ladle, ranged in echelons of officialdom, up and down the hierarchies of power; concerned above all like all organizations, to self-preserve and self-perpetuate; like all organizations organized to serve the interests and to further the prerogatives of those on the inside. It is this organization that controls access, opens the door and ushers "leadership" on to the spotlighted podium to perform its antics, to do its act before a public that watches passive and as from a great distance. Our "leadership" is seen in snippets of smiles, grins, handshakes, and wavings, heard in snippets, questioned in snippets, with quick lifts of the curtain by television maestros themselves performing their act. It is all pitched to, and held at the newspaper level, at the television level, at the Cronkite level, the lowest common denominator of the mass audience, bound to the conventional, without any possibility of sounding the depths of mind, without any possibility of climbing, step by step, any edifice of thought.

Could the cable change all that? Given the proposed system of transmission, with its opportunities for discourse, and supposing a continuum of debate operating at many levels, with problem and regional foci, it is possible that other doors would open, providing an entry onto the arena of public choice, outside and independent of political organization; and that through those doors would enter others, into the contest for leadership, having acquired a nucleus of supporters through the long process of discourse and debate where the quality of thought could be tested closely and in depth. The cable then would serve in proxy for the old cracker barrel as a site for the testing and selection of those who might represent and lead.

The montonous sterility of Congressional decades was broken by one extraordinary achievement, a seeming triumph of democratic answerability, where for once the political organization did not close ranks to preserve itself; Watergate, that led to the resignation of a President and the jailing of his cohorts. That single triumph of the political system was due to national involvement in the process itself, via television. Thereby an electorate listened, observed, and rendered its verdict, not only on those who stood before the bar, but on the Congress behind it. There is a lesson in this surely, that through this medium, society could be involved in political inquiry, public answerability, and in policy formation to a degree not thought possible before. The cable could enable a wide ranging and continuous focusing on the processes of political choice in Congress and in the Court.

The development of the cable as an instrument of participatory democracy should be the task of an autonomous entity with that as its prime responsibility. The same agency might also organize the continuum of political debate allocating cable channels for that purpose, bringing into play the whole range of public associations and institutions including progressional and trade associations, labor unions, state and local political parties, university and college faculties, and student organizations with each entity independently proposing panels of those who would participate in the multilevel debates. The Corporation for Public Broadcasting is an obvious candidate for the organizing task, though its functions might be shared with, and integrated into the operation of a University of the Air that will be argued for in an instant.

Education

To educate? Communication is essential. But the extraordinary communications potential of the airways has not in this country at least, been significantly integrated into the system of education, in part because telecasting and radio space has been preempted for entertainment, with even educational programs understood as a species of entertainment. And the laws of the mass audience have limited the scope and constrained the force such programs. The cable could change that. Fifty telecable channels allocated for university programs would enable an offering to each listener of more than 4,000 different courses each year, assuming a three-term year and three-hour per week lecture courses. We speak, and think here in terms of "courses," for beyond the communicated word, systematic education requires guidance, criticism, discipline, to be obtained through examinations and graded assignments, with incentive of degrees, certifications, and diplomas that are likely to be of value in the pursuit of careers.

What might the use of the cable add to or subtract from the educational system? It has economic value. Relative to traditional modes, it is extraordinarily "productive" as a way of bringing together the professor giving a lecture and the student listening to it, enabling a revolutionary increase in the student to teacher ratio. Its economic values would be enhanced through the use of simple, automatic televising without intercession of producer or cameraman, simply transmitting proceedings in the lecture hall or classroom from a student's eyeview. Closed circuit television has been used in this way, with some success.

The gain in productivity is offset by a decline in teaching quality, for these reasons. As there is an increase in the number of students whom the teacher addresses, there is likely to be an increase in the audience's heterogeneity of background and training, which narrows the common reference base needed for effective communication, and makes it more difficult to achieve a fusion of minds in common pursuit. The larger the audience becomes and whatever else separates the student from the eye of the teacher, reduces the teacher's capacity to sense and to respond to the puzzlement, the interest, the limitations of those to whom his words are spoken, or to gauge in subtle human ways the boundaries of comprehension and the breakthroughs of understanding. These are the real losses, even great losses with each increase in the numbers taught, up to that threshold where the teacher becomes a lecturer and the faces of students are lost in the audience. Beyond that threshold it matters little whether the audience is of 200 in a lecture hall, or 2,000 through closed circuit television, or 200,000 via a regional or national cable system. Nor should it not be forgotten, that the students in the modern university spend most of their time lost in a faceless audience, taking notes on the words of a lecturer who is to them a personage not a person, a performer not a teacher.

Whether the use of the cable would, in increasing the productivity of the lecturing function, lower the quality of education depends entirely on how the released faculty resources are used. If one lecturer does what 100 did before, what will happen to the other 99? If they are disemployed, or even if they are drawn with the current drift, into academic research and graduate training, accentuating a stratification of higher education that leaves on the one hand a vast undergraduate mass subject to a depersonalized, synthetic processing, and on the other hand, selected elites, intensively trained and geared into academic research, the quality of education indeed would suffer. But if those resources were used to increase the opportunities for small group discussion and to provide the individualized attention now so rare, then there must be a net gain in the quality of education.

In addition to greatly increasing the productivity of the lecturing function, the cable could raise the quality of that function as well, by more fully exploiting unique talents and great minds. Creative thinkers are rare. Men of genius are very few. Normally they interact only with a handful. With selective telecasting through a national educational network, the excitement and light of their minds, though somewhat dimmed by the screen's intercession, could nevertheless be carried to those able to respond to their message though these are separated in space and even in time. Albert Einstein or Neils Bohr could hardly have given their scientific best in lecturing to a mass audience in the usual sense, but it would have been quite another matter if their lecture series were oriented to physics faculties and advanced students and to research physicists throughout the land. With a few exceptions, such as Bronowski's *Ascent of Man,* that extraordinary achievement of the British Broadcasting Company carried here on public television, the airwaves have not been used to augment the impact of the rare spirit or to carry the light of the first class mind. This is so even in the university's closed circuit TV; perhaps because academics not yet familiar or comfortable with the media, disdain the actor's makeup, the klieg lights, the producer's intercession. Perhaps because the entreprenurs of such enterprise with their show biz mentality, have looked for and solicited showmen, performers, clowns.

In addition to increasing the productivity and raising the quality of the lecturing function, the cable offers another advantage. It is highly mobile in space and flexible in time, so that it can be fitted into activities in the office, the factory, the laboratory, the home, and could therefore provide the most viable basis for the development of multileveled, continuous education as a regular part of professional and working lives. It could give new force and meaning to continuous lifelong education, not only in bringing distillations from the university nexus to the working engineer, research scientist, doctor, business executive. It also could capitalize on the experience and "learning" of the working engineer, the practicing doctor, the R&D scientist, and the business executive, feeding these back into the educational process. Courses currently organized at the Cleveland Flight Center or at Bell Laboratories and elsewhere to train engineers and scientists to skills and operating capabilities beyond those learnable in the university would, hopefully, also be fed into the cable network.

Finally it would be possible through the educational network, geared as well to the high school, primary school, preschool levels, to reach as never before, into the home to upgrade the cultural environment, particularly of the disadvantaged child and its mother, not only teaching but inculcating a sense of the value of learning, stimulating the curiosity, raising the level of awareness.

In the first instance, the educational network should be developed regionally, linking together the universities, colleges, junior colleges in geographical proximity or within an integral (state) system, or having other institutional ties. This would permit the sharing of course offerings, hence the conservation of faculty resources and the fuller use of academic stars. Courses shared or otherwise programmed on regional networks would be available on public channels to all cable users in the region, hence would be fed into households, factories, laboratories, and so forth; and on that basis, courses could be offered for credit as part of degree programs by and at the initiative of the universities, colleges, junior college of the regional network, with study guidance, reading assignments, examinations, and critiques arranged through correspondence, and with centers organized for counseling and for course discussions.

The regional educational networks would in turn be linked together into a national system, further widening the opportunities for course sharing, for the conservation of faculty resources, for an expansion in course variety, and for an increased availability of rare talents in the lecturing function.

A University of the Air, in charge of this national educational network would facilitate and coordinate the intercollegiate sharing of courses. It would use its control over cable access to assure that there would be no reduction in the faculty to student ratio as a consequence of the use of the cable, requiring rather that displaced resources be used to intensify individualized instruction and to increase the opportunity for small group discussion. It would sponsor, and organize its own lecture servies by scholars, scientists, artists, and creative writers of a world renown, preparing supplementary materials and otherwise supporting the integration of such series into collegiate course offerings. It would itself offer a degree program, drawing upon courses offered through all the regional networks and assuring a balance in those available to the public, with national examinations, with supporting materials through correspondence, and regional centers operating for counseling and course discussion.

13

TO SURVIVE THE NUCLEAR TRAP
OF NATIONS

We cannot leave off without considering, even if very briefly and inadequately, the most pressing and critical policy problem of all. We live in a world of nation states, building, straining nerve and muscle to build, more rapidly, higher and higher, their funeral pyre. Xenophobia runs very deep. Demagogy thrives. The intelligence of "leadership" is at its nadir. How can we survive in this nuclear trap, or eventually escape from it?

Three agencies of the American state have the nationalist ideology at their institutional core, and are organized as the functional expression of that ideology. They are, of course, the Department of Defense (Army, Navy, Air Corp), the State Department, and the Central Intelligence Agency (CIA).

The American Department of Defense, like war agencies throughout the Western world, belongs to a cultural configuration that predates by centuries the outlook of liberalism and democracy; operating on the principles of obedience and fidelity, of the primal solidarity of the flesh and the loyalty of the embattled, of hierarchy and of functional class, following the model of an aristocratic society wherein the collective power is exercised by a closed elite trained and acculturated to rule as possessors of the higher, private knowledge and of the sacred purpose. Thus everywhere military organizations presuppose a closed warrior (officer) elite, sharing a caste honor, the values of *la gloire,* the habit and capacity to command, with the ranks below battered or exercised into total, automatic, and unquestioning obedience.

Everywhere, the military exists as a society apart. Of all the agencies of the modern state, they are the only ones able and ready to assume the sovereign power, operating, still as an enclave, at its command center.

The Department of State and its Foreign Office counterparts throughout the Western world have also ingrained a cultural configuration and an ideological outlook that predates the era of liberalism and democracy, presupposing an elite who, in proxy for the King, detached from and beyond individual interests, group interests, the expertise of specialists and the knowledge of functions, know and enunciate the *national* interest in the universe of nations. They are the priests and purveyors of the interests of the nation *vis a vis* all the nations. It is theirs to formulate that national interest as foreign policy and to interpret and express that policy through their embassies in the courts of foreign powers. There the ambassador, as plenipotentiary, speaks with the voice, expresses the will, and carries into the foreign court the power and pledge in honor of his king, that is, as proxy for the nation, the ambassador knows, expresses, and negotiates in the name of the national interest. Call this the plenipotentiary function.

And then there is the CIA. Though it is engaged in most ancient pursuits, this post-World War II arrival on the public scene, is a creature of our time, operating on the model of corporate enterprise, with its supertechnicians and supercomputers spewing reams of printout, with its high powered, superactive executives and behind them packs of well-clad, well-barbered go-getters, with its international representatives giving service on the spot. A dirty business maybe—but a business all the same.

Here we will consider the CIA and the Department of State in a society that would survive the nuclear trap of nations.

Trade Away the CIA

Under present circumstances the CIA helps in the performance of one important function, the surveillance and monitoring of nuclear weaponry, primarily through the reading and interpretating photographs made by earth orbiting satellites. Effective, reliable monitoring on this score is in the interest of both of the great antagonists since it is a prerequisite to orderly disarmament or negotiated arms limitations. Hopefully, therefore, it is a task that might be developed more or less cooperatively; but certainly it is not one that needs a CIA to perform, nor is it a task that the CIA should be entrusted with since that agency, given its orientation, cannot play the role of honest broker or objective observer.

That function aside, we should rid ourselves of the CIA. It should cease to exist as an organization. Above all, we should be rid of its covert activities.

The United States emerged in World War II as the mightiest military power, the dominant economic power, its productivity unmatched, and as the country most endowed with a good name among the nations, after more than a century and a half of history without a CIA or any equivalent.

The records of secret agencies are of course obscure, and certainly their powers of secrecy are used to hide their failings and failures. I have diligently examined the facts that I can find, and have come to this conclusion (I urge the reader also independently to examine the record as a test of this postulate) that these secret enclaves outside the surveillance of the political system and without public answerability or responsibility, legitimating, supporting, protecting, and promoting the lawless exercise of violence and deceit, intended by hidden means to hurt, subvert, weaken, destroy the Other, whether in the United States or in any other country, whether their power is applied only abroad or domestically as well, wherever they exist, they have always produced and by their existence made possible and led to misadventure, folly, betrayal, crisis, shame, and disaster for the nation that harbored them. Are we not still paying the price for the Bay of Pigs invasion and for the installation of the Shah? On the other hand, I cannot discover any significant benefit brought about by these agencies to the nations that harbored them. If another balance of accounts can be demonstrated, let them show it.

Of course an agency of lawless violence and systematic deceit, that must nurture the flames of hatred as its guiding light and as its reason for being will attract into its dark recesses, violent, sadistic, deceitful persons, scoundrels, fanatics, madmen who will exercise an autonomous power and will influence the agency's policy.

That the agency is linked to the Presidency and that its directors answer to the President does not reduce but increases the dangers of disaster, for its offers to the President and his cohorts a space where they can play out their fantasies at will, without surveillance, without constraint, outside the law. Those who achieve that office, almost of necessity, hunger after power. But when they have reached the pinnacle, they still bear the heavy yoke of surveillance and answerability, as does the vast organization into which their powers are embedded. To act upon, and significantly to affect the direction of this great ship of state is an enormous and laborous task of accommodation, coordination, persuasion. But the CIA, not because of its policies or its personnel but by the very fact of its existence, offers an outlet for the free exercise of power to do what cannot be done under the rule of law and the eye of society—opportunity for scheming and trickery (so dear to the childish heart) in the expectation of cheap victories. That one President knew of and approved the assassination of the popular head of the Iranian state and the installation of the exiled Shah upon the peacock throne, or that another President knew of and approved the invasion of the Bay of Pigs made these no less evil and unwise acts, or less disastrous for us immediately or in the long run.

There has never been, and there never can be public surveillance and control of such an agency as the CIA so long as it continues to be what it is, an enclave for the secret exercise of power. The "watchdog committees" simply co-opt a handful of Congressmen and Senators into the enclave. If these Congressmen and Senators are a bunch of decent fellows, so be it. There are other decent fellows in other niches of the system as well. But nothing is changed in what the organization is and what it does.

Such an agency as the CIA is inherently a corrupter and a spoiler. By infiltrating associations and organizations, by co-opting and using for its own purposes students, scholars, scientists, artists, ministers of any faith, engineers, business executives, it destroys the good name of associations and professions; the good name of professor and of scientist, of businessman and of church; that good name which is the soundest coin of social intercourse. Gaining little or nothing for themselves, they destroy the bridge of trust between peoples. Nor do they allow us anymore to believe our own government, our word is corrupted. Nor disbelieve the most outrageous accusations made against us.

It will be said with the hard-nosed naivete of the sophisticated fool, that since the Others do it, therefore we must do it too; since they are worse than we are therefore, we must be as bad as they are. Why do as the Other does, if in so doing we only harm ourselves?

Let us try another tack.

If anything is clear in Russian policy and in Russian history from its very earliest days, it is their obsessive fear of foreign subversion, a fear that in their eyes justifies Gulag and the very heavy burden upon themselves of a secret police. How much then would a guarantee of no covert, no subversive activity by any American agency be worth to them? Would it not be a positive step in detente and in disarmament for both sides by agreement to phase down and to phase out the covert and subversive, leading to a general renunciation by the Western Nations and their Eastern counter-parts of all such activities and of the agencies that carry them out? Consider. It would be the easiest of all disarmament agreements to monitor, for each country would be monitoring what does or does not happen within its own borders. It could be more important than specific limitations of weapons for it would permit the building of bridges of trust and the development of peaceful intercourse between the peoples. It could restore a degree of honesty in our dealings with each other and with ourselves. Surely it would serve the quest to survive this nuclear trap and perhaps eventually to find some way out of it.

Information from Abroad

The traditional model and still the organizational blueprint is of embassies gathering and sending back to their Foreign Office or State Department centers streams of information and interpretations of events relevant to the formation of foreign policy; with that information analyzed and integrated by specialists at the center; and on the basis of this accumulated knowledge, in collaboration with the experts, a foreign policy is formulated by those at the higher echelons of authority; with that policy in turn interpreted and expressed country by country under the particular circumstances of each, as the plenipotentiary function of the ambassador. This model was appropriate as a working instrument in another age, when policy-making was the prerogative of a select and autonomous elite, when the information that mattered for the formulation of foreign policy was confined to the inclinations and choices of a few at the inner circle of the governing power, for example, of the monarch and his court, and when communication between nations was slow and difficult. Consider how much time it would have taken for a single communication between the government in the United States and the government in Paris during the administration of Thomas Jefferson. Under those conditions the delegation of the plenipotentiary authority was necessary.

Whatever once was, the model is no longer workable. International communica-tion is instantaneous. The space-time barrier to meetings face to face, has shrunk to insignificance. Communication and negotiation, government to government, spe-cial agency to special agency, replaces the plenipotentiary who spoke of all for all. The ambassador becomes a master of ceremonies and the embassy a contact point. Diplomacy stands aside for the meeting of scientist with scientist, specialist with specialist, agency head with agency head. With the crisscrossing of transnational systems, and the complexity of issues and interests, there ceases to be a national interest to which only the diplomat and the State Department elite are privy. Foreign policy emerges out of variable sets of interests and as offshoots and projections of domestic policy.

Information is needed of course, information and a currently relevant analysis of the complex conditions and interests, and of underlying developments in every society to which our choices and interests relate; nor is the information-gathering network of the State Department equipped to satisfy that need, at least for two reasons.

With rare if important exceptions, the diplomat is an amateur without professional commitment to or skill in the task of information-gathering and analysis; his reporting is likely to be narrowly vectored on governmental encounters. And his information, even where it is significant, is fed back to the departmental elite and is treated as an agency monopoly, perhaps giving the State Department a leg up in the Washington scramble for influence, but in no sense shaping the outlook and deepening the understanding of the electorate, of the people and their representatives in the process of democratic choice.

If anything is clear, it is that our foreign policy has been a series of responses after the fact, surprised by and unprepared for every sharp turn of event, and reacting always with a shallow understanding of the deeper cause; whether to Mao's triumph in China, or the Sino-Soviet division, or to the cultural revolution, or to revolutions in Cuba, in Portugal, or in Iran, or to the Japanese rise to technological preeminence, or to terrorism in Germany and in Italy. But the greatest example of the failure and impotence of this information feedback into the processes of collective decision, was in the case of the rise of Nazi Germany as a prelude to World War II. None of the countries that would be victimized and attacked, foresaw and took into account the nature of the pre-Nazi and Nazi transformation of Germany or were ready for the onslaught that followed, or realized the industrial invulnerability to blockade that was quite overtly achieved there, or understood the character of the new enemy.

France did not, though it was the nearest and surest victim. And yet the Ambassador of France in Berlin was the rare exception, a trained professional in the business of information-gathering and analysis, an eminent scholar of German culture, a brilliant observer of the panaroma of event who organized his embassy to cover in depth every phase of the transformation of Germany. And information that explained the character and foresaw all the consequences of that transformation was fed faithfully back—back to where? To the elite of the Quai D'Orsay, with bits and pieces reaching a few of the political hierarchs in and out of the niches of power, but not into the political debate or the popular discourse. It did not shape the thought of the intellectual nor did it reach the outlook of the electorate. So in the end, that information mattered not a whit in influencing the course of events.[1]

Certainly information is needed. Informed politicians are needed. Presidents

---

[1]See Roselyn Solo, *Andre Francois Poncet, Ambassador of France* (unpublished Doctoral dissertation, Michigan State University, 1978).

need counsel, the counselors need advice. Those in the State Department who have acquired a knowledge of circumstances and relationships abroad, who have devoted a lifetime to the acquisition of such knowledge, are an important resource and one that should be used.

We need the information. We lack it. We need the knowledge. *We* are the electorate, those at the roots of public choice and policy formation. There is a great and critical gap between paper-thin coverage by newspaper and television and the occasional works of scholarship here and there assembling in authenticated detail configurations out of the past. What lacks is multilevel multiperspective continuum of studies and observations in depth and breadth of the here and now, of the current and emergent, integrating the cultural, political, the economic, the sociological, with no need for the daily story or a definitive volume. For that purpose, in lieu of State Department information-gathering, endowed and independent study centers should be established for every important nation or significant region, with resident and visiting researchers bringing different political and disciplinary perspectives to bear, prepared to offer advice and counsel to politicians or officials of any party, prepared and ready to participate in negotiation, prepared and organized to respond to the inquiries of journalists and to brief them and to guide them in acquiring some depth of understanding of the whole society into which they are usually but quick in-and-outers. The centers themselves would produce and encourage the production of books, reports, documentaries for radio and television, to convey to diverse audiences, the realities of the societies on which their studies focus.